Sharing the Good News With Children

Thomas W. Goodhue

SHARING THE GOOD NEWS WITH CHILDREN

Stories for the Common Lectionary

CINCINNATI, OHIO

To my wife,

whose encouragement

made me a teacher,

and whose critiques

made me a better preacher

Nihil Obstat: Rev. Hilarion Kistner, O.F.M., Rev. Edward J. Gratsch

Imprimi Potest: Rev. Alan Hirt, O.F.M., Vicar Provincial

Imprimatur: +James H. Garland, V.G., Archdiocese of Cincinnati, July 22, 1991

The *nihil obstat* and *imprimatur* are a declaration that a book is considered to be free from doctrinal or moral error. It is not implied that those who have granted the *nihil obstat* and *imprimatur* agree with the contents, opinions or statements expressed.

Cover design by Don Nesbitt
Cover photograph by Jim Whitmer
Book design by Julie Lonneman

ISBN 0-86716-136-1

Published by St. Anthony Messenger Press
Printed in the U.S.A.

Contents

Introduction

This book's purpose is to encourage the use of children's stories or children's sermons in parish worship. All these tales have been told in Sunday worship in my United Methodist parish or in the interdenominational weekday school where I taught for seven years. This book will, of course, also provide preachers with sermon illustrations, help teachers plan lessons and give parents a few stories to tell their children. (Parents might, for example, tell these stories to help the family prepare for Sunday worship, especially if there is no children's homily or Liturgy of the Word for children in their parish.)

Personally, I think there are few sights more joyful than kids bouncing toward the chancel (sanctuary, if you prefer) to hear a children's homily before I preach to their elders. Children need good preaching at least as much as adults do, but they seldom receive it. In too many parishes children are either excluded from worship or are forced to sit through a service which pays no attention to their unique needs, gifts and concerns. Or they are subjected to "children's sermons" which are saccharine "object lessons." We would not want to substitute object lessons for *adult* sermons, but we inflict them on the young week after week.

It takes more than a good story, of course, to make kids full participants in worship, but stories are a good place to begin. Stories often help us explore an obscure Scripture text or get around our resistance to applying the text to our lives. This is the reason preachers tell a lot of stories—parables, anecdotes, historical incidents, personal reminiscences—when talking to adults.

Those who attempt to tell stories to the young usually discover at once that it is not easy. When I first began telling children stories, I found it difficult to know what words or concepts a particular group of children would understand. Week after week it was a struggle to find a story appropriate to the Scripture text. This, I have come to see, is how it ought to be: We should wrestle as strenuously with Scripture's meaning for our youngest parishioners as we wrestle with its meaning for adults.

When I do my homework, my youthful audience is at least as attentive as adult worshipers. And when I have found meaning for children in a Scripture text, its importance for adults almost always becomes clearer to me.

How do you begin? Practice. Tell stories to nieces and nephews, Church school classes or the neighborhood kids. See what holds their attention and what doesn't. Ask a class to hear a story and then tell you what they liked or didn't like about it.

Finding the Right Story

These stories are matched to the Scripture lessons of the Common Lectionary, which was produced by the Consultation on Texts in 1983 and is an outgrowth of the 1969 Roman Catholic lectionary. This three-year calendar of Scripture readings is shared by an increasing number of Roman Catholic, Eastern Orthodox and Protestant congregations. Even if you use another lectionary, most of these stories will still fit. The chart on page 11 and the full listing of titles for each Sunday as story heads will help you match the Common Lectionary to yours.

Many of these stories can be used appropriately at other times, as well. "Let the Band Play 'Dixie' " might be used, for example, on the Sunday in February nearest Lincoln's birthday. You might tell about the lives of saints on their days, using the St. Anthony story on January 17, for example, rather than Trinity Sunday in Year B. The stories of Hannah Goodhue (Proper 22, Year C) or William Penn (Fifth Sunday After the Epiphany, Year A) might be used for the Fourth of July. The Witch of Endor (Transfiguration, Year A) is a good story for All Souls' Day or the Sunday before Halloween. And certainly you might tell about Squanto and the Pilgrims (Proper 16, Year A) at Thanksgiving.

The Topical Index (page 322) will help you locate such stories. In addition, a Themes Index (page 321) points toward Scripture passages you can draw on to make a particular point and a Scripture Index (page 319) will help you locate stories for a passage appearing in the Roman Catholic Weekday Cycle or chosen for a special occasion.

Stories are included for some days such as Annunciation (March 25) and Visitation (May 31), which are not widely celebrated among Protestants, because I want to encourage you to take a look at these Scripture lessons and to make use of them. Even if you do not have a worship service in your parish on these days, or have one which few children attend, you might use the story sometime during the preceding or following week. Many Christians, particularly we Protestants, know too little about Hannah, Mary, Elizabeth and other women of the Bible. These stories present opportunities to make amends.

Another benefit of using these readings is that they remind all of us how long Mary's pregnancy took. Protestants tend to read Isaiah 7:10-14, Luke 1:26-38 and Luke 1:39-45 only on the fourth Sunday in Advent, and our secular culture mentions the preparation for the Nativity (if at all) only in December TV specials just before Christmas. All this gives the impression that Mary went straight from the Annunciation to motherhood. By setting the stage for the Nativity in the spring, we can recall that Jesus was fully human as well as fully divine and that God often works slowly, as slowly as the growth of a mustard seed—or a baby.

Please treat this volume as a tool for sermon preparation, not as the last word on how you ought to embody the word in your preaching to the young. You will doubtless find ways to improve upon the material here, telling some stories yourself I have not yet heard.

Suggestions for Storytelling

1) *Make it your story.* Take each story and change both the content and the delivery until it is something that appeals to *you*. Don't like a minor character? Drop him! Do you wonder what Mary said as she reached for baby Jesus (Presentation, February 2, Years A, B and C)? Tell us! Move Lisa the Lighthouse Light (Second Sunday After the Epiphany, Year A) to a shoreline near your community. Explain words and concepts unknown to your audience. Alter story details to help your children identify with them.

You will note that some of these stories are told in the first person. If you wish to use them, change them to "There was once a man who...." As you may guess, in most of the stories which begin "There was a teacher who..." or "Once upon a time a pastor...," yours truly was the culprit.

I would encourage you to tell children about incidents in your own life where God has been at work. Children, who struggle so valiantly to be good, are fond of stories in which adults admit their weaknesses, their mistakes, their failures and their fears. If done well, this "confessional preaching" is a powerful way of embodying the Good News. (For more on this, see my article, "The (Wo)Manly Art of Preaching" in *Ministry*, January 1991.)

Integrate your own tradition, as well. The story of John Vianney (Fourth Sunday in Lent, Year A), for example, tells how many people came to "talk to him." Very young children of any Church are at ease with this, but Roman Catholics will want to mention confession to older children. Acknowledge the differences in traditions as well. Protestants may squirm, knowing that John Vianney was renowned as a confessor; Roman Catholics may talk about ordained women only with difficulty. But these differences do exist; children who are introduced to them matter-of-factly will accept them with an ease we adults might well envy.

Remember, please, that these are models for storytelling and not necessarily presented in the form that will work best for you. Included in this volume are examples of first-person tales which lose much of their power if transcribed into the third person. Those for the Second and Fifth Sundays in Lent in Year C are loved because I am talking about *my* cats. Try telling how *you* learned to talk to a cat or a dog. Try telling the children how *you* realized how hard it is to trust when hurting. Make my stories yours.

2) *Tell the story rather than read it.* Even if you are using a picture book, your delivery will be much better if you become familiar with the plot, ad lib where necessary and look at the children while telling the story. This also allows you to hear their questions more easily and to see their facial expressions—which provides valuable feedback as to whether or not they are following the story. Don't worry about memorizing the story word-for-word; all you need is its gist.

One year, just before Thanksgiving, I started reading my kindergarten class the story I had just written about my great-great-great-great-great-great-grandmother, Hannah Goodhue. The children were so inattentive and restless that I had to abandon the story after less than a minute. Was this really such a boring story? Then I realized that it was the *reading* of the story—without benefit of pictures—which was boring. I put down my manuscript and started the story again, telling it rather than reading it. I inadvertently omitted some details of the story, but I maintained much better eye contact and conveyed more feeling this time. This time the children heard, listened and remembered.

Storytelling in worship is powerful precisely because so many children these days have been deprived of it. While I was spinning a yarn to a kindergartner one day on the playground at Riverside Church, another child came up and stared incredulously at me. "What's wrong?" I asked her.

"How can you do that?" she wanted to know.

"How can I do what?" I asked.

"How can you read to her with no book?" she asked. She had been told stories so seldom that it seemed miraculous to her that anyone could know a tale without reading the words!

There is, indeed, something magical about storytelling. Sometimes I simply take a Scripture lesson for the day and retell the text, adding whatever explanation of detail the children (and adults) need to feel the drama of the story. An example of this is my retelling of Mark 2:1-12 (Seventh Sunday After the Epiphany, Year B). Or at other times, I translate a biblical parable as faithfully as possible into a modern setting, as my Vacation Bible School class helped me do with the Parable of the Good Samaritan (Proper 11, Year C). Simply proclaiming the word to a group of youngsters on the chancel steps can be a way of participating in divine magic.

3) *Use songs occasionally.* Either lead the children in song or sing by yourself. Young audiences are easily distracted, but the squirmiest of children will be all ears when the homilist bursts into song. And a song the kids already know or can quickly pick up will turn restless kids into a cooperative chorus.

Songs help children remember your message. You could, of course, *say* the words to "Amazing Grace" in telling the story of John Newton's dream (Fourth Sunday in Advent, Year A), but it will be much more powerful if you *sing* the words—and then have the entire congregation sing the whole hymn. On Epiphany (Three Kings Day) you might sing "We Three Kings," "The First Noel" or "As with Gladness Men of Old"—or the Puerto Rican song "Pastores á Belen."

Simple, repetitive songs are especially helpful to young children. Two- and three-year-olds often have difficulty following stories; catchy songs can help carry the story line. Before telling about Harriet Tubman (Fourth Sunday of Advent, Year B), I teach the choruses of "Go Down, Moses" and "Steal Away to Jesus" and then invite the children to sing these with me. The songs help carry young listeners through an important but complicated story.

Songs can help when you are explaining difficult theological metaphors, too. It is not easy for any kindergartner to grasp, for example, what the author of the Letter to the Hebrews means when he (or she, according to some scholars) describes Jesus as "the pioneer of our salvation" (Proper 22, Year B). If a five-year-old has any association at all with the word *pioneer* it may well be with something far from the author's intention, such as the cavalry chasing natives away from a burning cabin. The life of John Chapman, "Johnny Appleseed," is quite close to the image used in Hebrews. Chapman ventured forth ahead of settlers, enduring countless hardships to aid those who followed later. Befriending natives, planting apple trees in forest clearings and telling stories to the children he met in wilderness families, Chapman left those who came behind him a legacy of food, peace and hospitality.

Chapman's piety and generosity are expressed in a song which many children know as the "Johnny Appleseed Grace":

> Oh, the Lord is good to me,
> And so I thank the Lord for giving me the things I need:
>
> The sun, the rain, and the apple seed.
>
> The Lord is good to me!
> And every seed I sow
> Will grow into a tree,
> And someday there'll be apples there
> For you and me and the world to share.
>
> The Lord is good to me!

If you weave this song through your telling about Chapman's life, you can be certain that both young and old will have a better understanding of how Jesus was "the pioneer of our salvation."

Ah, but you can't sing worth beans, you say? Remember, children are usually quite forgiving of our meager musical talents—and most adults will be happy if the kids are happy. Unless you are blessed with a terrific voice or tremendous self-confidence, you will probably feel a little foolish the first time you lead the cherubs a cappella. But go ahead. Muster your courage. Practice in the shower a few times. Then try it. St. Paul reminds us in 1 Corinthians 4:10 that we have been called to be "fools for the sake of Christ." The least we can do is to risk appearing foolish for a few moments in order better to proclaim the Good News. The story for Holy Cross (September 14, Years A, B and C) tells how I learned to take this chance.

4) *Try moving and gesturing to music, too.* We learn best when our whole selves are engaged in an activity. Singing the "Johnny Appleseed Grace" is good, but it is even better to sing it and lead the children in finger movements representing sun, falling rain, a tiny seed, a growing tree, you, me and sharing around the world. The word of God is best understood and best remembered when dramatized and responded to with music and movement. Tell the story about the truce during World War I (Christmas, Year A) with gestures that make vivid the courage it took to step forward across No Man's Land and invite your youthful audience to sing the lines from "Silent Night" with you—and they just might recall this story every time they hear this carol. Likewise, you might teach—or invite someone else to teach—how to sign a line from an appropriate song in American Sign Language. Kids love it—and it helps plant in the minds of the whole congregation the possibility of sign-interpreting worship services.

5) *Ham it up!* Gesture. Act out the story through your voice. Add sound effects. Young children, particularly those under six, need concrete references in stories such as the "clip-clop" that reminds two-year-olds what the word donkey means, the "clang-clang" that helps them recall what blacksmiths do.

At times you may want to encourage them to ham it up with you. In addition to having the children sing "Go Down, Moses" with me as I tell about the Exodus (Propers 12 and 13, Year A), I try to convey the wonderful humor implicit in the call of Moses by encouraging them to sing the chorus a little more fiercely each time, shaking their fingers at Moses in exasperation as he throws up one objection after another. By gesturing passionately, both they and the adults come to a new appreciation of how funny the Bible can be, how human are its heroes and how persistently our God longs for our liberation.

Sometimes you can literally act out the story. Wash their feet on Palm Sunday or Maundy Thursday and they will never forget what Jesus did in the Upper Room. Invite them to "shout for joy" and they will *feel* what the Psalmist felt. Get out the nursery school's box of instruments and invite the children to use them to praise

Yahweh, and they—and the whole congregation—may experience the 150th Psalm (Easter Evening, Years A, B and C) at a deeper level than ever before. The more abstract the concept, the more it helps to dramatize it.

6) *Include a good balance of boys and girls, rich and poor, young and old, white characters and characters of every color.* If we want to speak to everyone in our congregation, we need to include everyone in our stories, for most of us are particularly likely to identify with a character who seems "like us."

After I retold the old tale from India of the Six Blind Men and the Elephant (Third Sunday After the Epiphany, Year C), changing the blind men to six blind boys and girls, one six-year-old girl assured me that she liked "the new story" much more than the original. What made it better? That the characters were young, like her? Probably. But it may also be that the inclusion of both male and female characters made the tale more intrinsically interesting. My 1982 study found that both boys and girls remembered stories in which male and female characters took part equally in the action of the story much better than they recalled all-male or all-female versions of the same stories. There is also reason to believe that inclusive material helps kids feel better about themselves. (See "Character Gender in Children's Stories and Listening Recall," ERIC Document Service #ED 215 755; "Let's Not Shame Our Poor Readers," *Momentum*, February, 1985; and "How Story-People and Language Capture Interest and Influence Students," *Share*, Fall, 1985.)

Moreover, if ninety percent of the heroes we present are men, we give girls little inspiration for Christian courage. If male characters are not permitted to cry, fear or hurt, we tell boys (and men) that their tears, fears and pain make them less masculine. If we teach only the experiences of Western Christians, we perpetuate the destructive myth that knowledge, civilization and enlightenment can come only from the West.

But if we wish to expand awareness of other races, classes and nations, stories are a good way to begin. The careful reader will note that this collection is not perfectly balanced. Some nations are not represented here, and too few children and teenagers, particularly girls, are the main protagonists. See if you can find a few stories of your own to make your material more inclusive.

Sometimes all you need do is change some characters from male to female, from adult to child, from rich to poor. The World War I truce (Christmas, Year A), for example, is an actual historical occurrence, but no one knows who first heard their enemies singing the carols they knew themselves. Many soldiers of this war and most others have been teenage boys, so why not make the protagonist a boy? Likewise, in the tradition that it was a servant who sent Ponce de Leon off on a vain search for the Fountain of Youth (Easter, Year A), the identity of this servant is unknown. Why not let it be a girl? Why not present her as clever enough to trick a tyrant and rid her island of him?

7) *Keep the distinctive needs and interests of children in mind as you plan your storytelling.* Familiarity may breed contempt among adults, but children love it as much as novelty. They enjoy the familiar "Three Little Pigs" as much as newer stories. Repetition may become tedious to adults, but children delight in being able to tell what is coming next. Watch them mouth the words "I'll huff and I'll puff" along with you. See how they start huffing before you even say the words!

In *Kindergarten: A Year of Learning*, Margaret Rudolph and Dorothy Cohen describe the concerns which kindergartners bring to stories as including the following: belonging to a family, one's status in the family, arrivals and departures in the family due to birth and death, illness, disputes, pets, coping with fears, the difficulty of waiting, the problem of being little. If your preaching touches upon these themes, five-year-olds are more likely to listen.

Some needs and interests, however, are far from universal. While four-year-olds love to repeat lines such as the Little Red Hen's "Not I!" (Sixth Sunday After the Epiphany, Year A), sevens and eights often prefer fanciful tales where justice triumphs and virtue is rewarded. Children older still may be ready for drama, danger and conflicts where the protagonist's ideals win out over great difficulty. Where you have a variety of ages, you need stories which hook kids at different levels.

"Hanasaka-jiji" (Proper 9, Year C) is one such story. The dog is a familiar, concrete point of reference for preschoolers. The magic and foreign locale intrigues kindergartners and younger elementary students. The struggle between kindness and greed appeals to the more mature. This is, by the way, the most loved story I ever told in Hawaii and the one that was the most asked for each year in New York's Riverside Church.

Remember, too, that you are preaching to children and not adults. Children often benefit greatly from material that adults may not like at all. A good example of this is the story of Sarah Winnemucca (Proper 7, Year A). Adult WASPs do not like this story very much and I have found it virtually impossible to sell it to magazine editors. Few adults—especially whites—like to be reminded of injustices done to Native Americans, particularly wrongs which were never righted. Least of all do white Christians want to hear about how white children and white parents rejected this young schoolgirl for being Native American. Moreover, her story does not have a conventionally happy ending: The United States government did not reward Sarah for her help and her extraordinary courage; what victories she won for her people came much later and only after years of continued struggle.

Children, though, *love* this story. Sarah is separated from her family but later reunited with them and she saves their lives. She is afraid—as they themselves are at times—but bravely takes enormous risks. She is both pious and spunky: She prays and rides a horse, wears a disguise and sneaks into an enemy camp. She is rejected by whites because of who she is, and later begged by them for her help. She endures war and works for peace. For children, this is an intensely exciting tale.

Children also *identify* with Sarah. They have experienced or feared separation and rejection. They would love to ride a horse. They want both to pray and to dress up in disguises. They have fears, yet dream of being brave. Three-year-olds probably identify primarily with Sarah's vulnerability and her separation from her family. Eight-year-olds exalt in her triumph over those who unjustly imprisoned her family. Eleven-year-olds may appreciate the danger and drama in the story. When material works this well for children at such different ages, preach it—no matter how much their parents may dislike it.

Remember, though, that the reverse is also true: I have wanted for some time to tell children about the black, Spanish-speaking, Roman Catholic pioneers who settled my hometown, Los Angeles, but every attempt has bored them silly. This bit of history turns out to be an excellent homily illustration for *adults* about the invisibility of blacks, Hispanics and Catholics in traditional presentations of American history, about the interracial harmony of these founding families and about their years of peace with their native neighbors. Most children, though, find tranquility a lot less interesting than cavalry raids. For the moment, at least, until I find a way to hook a youthful audience, this will remain a story for grown-ups.

8) *Make the kids comfortable.* If the chancel or sanctuary is carpeted, they will probably be most relaxed sitting on the floor. (In some parishes without carpeted chancels, a special rug is pulled out just for the occasion of the children's sermon. "Rolling out the carpet" for them is an excellent way of demonstrating that children are welcome in worship.)

You may also want to print in your order of worship words inviting all children to the sanctuary and inviting parents of shy or restless children to sit with them. Some people will appreciate permission to stay together as a family. Or include an announcement that the children will leave the church for a separate Liturgy of the Word. This is particularly helpful to visitors, who will not be familiar with how you present children's sermons.

You might want to haul a chair to the center of the chancel or to the meeting room so that you can have easy eye contact with all the children. You might ask two cherubs to sit on your knees for the sermon. Whether or not they hear a word you say, they will at least know that they are truly welcome in this house of worship.

Do the darlings fight over who will have the privilege of perching in your lap? Easy enough, just ask the recidivists, "Did you have a turn last week?" and tell them you need to let someone else have a chance today. Do too many flock to your knees at once? Just tell the third and fourth customers, "I'll try to let you have a turn next week." You may be surprised at how the youngest of children keep track of these promises and at how this increases their interest in attending worship—and that of their parents.

Once the children have made it to the proper place, how can you help them to become ready to listen? One good way to settle them down and to ensure eye contact is to ask each week, "Can you all see me where you're sitting? Why don't you move to where you can see me, OK?"

While you want your young flock to pay attention and not disrupt others, this is not the time to insist on proper posture and a great deal of decorum. Do they want to sprawl on the floor to hear your story? Fine. Do some want to sit in the lap of an older brother or sister? No problem. Do the youngest children come directly from child care for the story? Maybe you will want to let them know it is OK to run up the aisles to the chancel. Surely this is one way to "make a joyful noise unto God" and to "come into God's presence with praise."

And this, after all, is the point of using the stories in this volume: to remind us all that we are all welcome in the community of faith and that both young and old can come into God's presence with praise.

Names of Sundays and Special Days in the Lectionaries

	Date	Common	Roman	Lutheran
Advent Season	Sunday Between November 27 and December 3	First Sunday of Advent	First Sunday of Advent	First Sunday of Advent
	Sunday Between December 4 and 10	Second Sunday of Advent	Second Sunday of Advent	Second Sunday of Advent
	Sunday Between December 11 and 17	Third Sunday of Advent	Third Sunday of Advent	Third Sunday of Advent
	Sunday Between December 18 and 24	Fourth Sunday of Advent	Fourth Sunday of Advent	Fourth Sunday of Advent
Christmas Season	December 24/25	Christmas (First Proper)	Mass at Midnight	The Nativity of Our Lord, Midnight
	December 25	Christmas (Second Proper)	Mass at Dawn	
	December 25	Christmas (Third Proper)	Mass During the Day	The Nativity of Our Lord, Morning
	Sunday Between December 26 and January 1	First Sunday After Christmas	Holy Family	First Sunday After Christmas
	Sunday Between January 2 and 5	Second Sunday After Christmas	Second Sunday After Christmas	Second Sunday After Christmas
Epiphany Season[1]	January 6 or First Sunday in January	Epiphany	Epiphany	Epiphany
	Sunday Between January 7 and 13	Baptism of the Lord	Baptism of Our Lord	First Sunday After the Epiphany
	Sunday Between January 14 and 20	Second Sunday After the Epiphany	Second Sunday of the Year	Second Sunday After the Epiphany
	Sunday Between January 21 and 27	Third Sunday After the Epiphany	Third Sunday of the Year	Third Sunday After the Epiphany
	Sunday Between January 28 and February 3	Fourth Sunday After the Epiphany	Fourth Sunday of the Year	Fourth Sunday After the Epiphany
	Sunday Between February 4 and 10	Fifth Sunday After the Epiphany	Fifth Sunday of the Year	Fifth Sunday After the Epiphany
	Sunday Between February 11 and 17	Proper 1	Sixth Sunday of the Year	Sixth Sunday After the Epiphany
	Sunday Between February 18 and 24	Proper 2	Seventh Sunday of the Year	Seventh Sunday After the Epiphany
	Sunday Between February 25 and 29	Proper 3	Eighth Sunday of the Year	Eighth Sunday After the Epiphany
	Sunday Before Ash Wednesday	Last Sunday After the Epiphany		Transfiguration of Our Lord

[1]Easter can occur as early as March 22 and as late as April 25. When Easter is early, the number of Sundays after Epiphany is reduced as necessary, from as many as nine to as few as four.

	Date	Common	Roman	Lutheran
Lenten Season	Ash Wednesday	Ash Wednesday	Ash Wednesday	Ash Wednesday
	First Sunday in Lent	First Sunday in Lent	First Sunday in Lent	First Sunday in Lent
	Second Sunday in Lent	Second Sunday in Lent	Second Sunday in Lent	Second Sunday in Lent
	Third Sunday in Lent	Third Sunday in Lent	Third Sunday in Lent	Third Sunday in Lent
	Fourth Sunday in Lent	Fourth Sunday in Lent	Fourth Sunday in Lent	Fourth Sunday in Lent
	Fifth Sunday in Lent	Fifth Sunday in Lent	Fifth Sunday in Lent	Fifth Sunday in Lent
Holy Week	Sunday	Passion Sunday or Palm Sunday	Passion Sunday or Palm Sunday	Passion Sunday or Palm Sunday
	Monday	Monday in Holy Week	Monday in Holy Week	Monday in Holy Week
	Tuesday	Tuesday in Holy Week	Tuesday in Holy Week	Tuesday in Holy Week
	Wednesday	Wednesday in Holy Week	Wednesday in Holy Week	Wednesday in Holy Week
	Thursday	Maundy Thursday or Holy Thursday	Maundy Thursday or Holy Thursday	Maundy Thursday or Holy Thursday
	Friday	Good Friday	Good Friday	Good Friday
Easter Season	Holy Saturday	Easter Vigil	Easter Vigil	Easter Vigil
	Easter Morning	Easter Day	Easter Day	Easter Day
	Easter Evening	Easter Evening	Easter Evening	Easter Evening
	Second Sunday of Easter	Second Sunday of Easter	Second Sunday of Easter	Second Sunday of Easter
	Third Sunday of Easter	Third Sunday of Easter	Third Sunday of Easter	Third Sunday of Easter
	Fourth Sunday of Easter	Fourth Sunday of Easter	Fourth Sunday of Easter	Fourth Sunday of Easter
	Fifth Sunday of Easter	Fifth Sunday of Easter	Fifth Sunday of Easter	Fifth Sunday of Easter
	Sixth Sunday of Easter	Sixth Sunday of Easter	Sixth Sunday of Easter	Sixth Sunday of Easter
	Ascension Thursday	Ascension Day	Ascension Day	Ascension Day
	Seventh Sunday of Easter	Seventh Sunday of Easter	Seventh Sunday of Easter	Seventh Sunday of Easter
	Pentecost	Pentecost	Pentecost	Pentecost
	Trinity Sunday	Trinity Sunday	Trinity Sunday	Trinity Sunday
	Sunday After Trinity Sunday		The Body and Blood of Christ	

	Date	Common	Roman	Lutheran
Season After Pentecost[2]	Sunday Between May 29 and June 4	Proper 4 (if after Trinity Sunday)	Ninth Sunday of the Year	Second Sunday After Pentecost
	Sunday Between June 5 and 11	Proper 5 (if after Trinity Sunday)	Tenth Sunday of the Year	Third Sunday After Pentecost
	Sunday Between June 12 and 18	Proper 6 (if after Trinity Sunday)	Eleventh Sunday of the Year	Fourth Sunday After Pentecost
	Sunday Between June 19 and 25	Proper 7 (if after Trinity Sunday)	Twelfth Sunday of the Year	Fifth Sunday After Pentecost
	Sunday Between June 26 and July 2	Proper 8	Thirteenth Sunday of the Year	Sixth Sunday After Pentecost
	Sunday Between July 3 and 9	Proper 9	Fourteenth Sunday of the Year	Seventh Sunday After Pentecost
	Sunday Between July 10 and 16	Proper 10	Fifteenth Sunday of the Year	Eighth Sunday After Pentecost
	Sunday Between July 17 and 23	Proper 11	Sixteenth Sunday of the Year	Ninth Sunday After Pentecost
	Sunday Between July 24 and 30	Proper 12	Seventeenth Sunday of the Year	Tenth Sunday After Pentecost
	Sunday Between July 31 and August 6	Proper 13	Eighteenth Sunday of the Year	Eleventh Sunday After Pentecost
	Sunday Between August 7 and 13	Proper 14	Nineteenth Sunday of the Year	Twelfth Sunday After Pentecost
	Sunday Between August 14 and 20	Proper 15	Twentieth Sunday of the Year	Thirteenth Sunday After Pentecost
	Sunday Between August 21 and 27	Proper 16	Twenty-First Sunday of the Year	Fourteenth Sunday After Pentecost
	Sunday Between August 28 and September 3	Proper 17	Twenty-Second Sunday of the Year	Fifteenth Sunday After Pentecost
	Sunday Between September 4 and 10	Proper 18	Twenty-Third Sunday of the Year	Sixteenth Sunday After Pentecost
	Sunday Between September 11 and 17	Proper 19	Twenty-Fourth Sunday of the Year	Seventeenth Sunday After Pentecost
	Sunday Between September 18 and 24	Proper 20	Twenty-Fifth Sunday of the Year	Eighteenth Sunday After Pentecost
	Sunday Between September 25 and October 1	Proper 21	Twenty-Sixth Sunday of the Year	Nineteenth Sunday After Pentecost
	Sunday Between October 2 and 8	Proper 22	Twenty-Seventh Sunday of the Year	Twentieth Sunday After Pentecost
	Sunday Between October 9 and 15	Proper 23	Twenty-Eighth Sunday of the Year	Twenty-First Sunday After Pentecost

[2]The date of Easter determines the number of Sunday Propers after Pentecost. In addition, Roman Catholics delay the return to Ordinary Time by celebrating the Feast of the Body and Blood of Christ on the Sunday after Trinity Sunday.

	Date	Common	Roman	Lutheran
	Sunday Between October 16 and 22	Proper 24	Twenty-Ninth Sunday of the Year	Twenty-Second Sunday After Pentecost
	Sunday Between October 23 and 29	Proper 25	Thirtieth Sunday of the Year	Twenty-Third Sunday After Pentecost
	Sunday Between October 30 and November 5	Proper 26	Thirty-First Sunday of the Year	Twenty-Fourth Sunday After Pentecost
	Sunday Between November 6 and 12	Proper 27	Thirty-Second Sunday of the Year	Twenty-Fifth Sunday After Pentecost
	Sunday Between November 13 and 19	Proper 28	Thirty-Third Sunday of the Year	Twenty-Sixth Sunday After Pentecost
	Sunday Between November 20 and 26	Proper 29	Christ the King	Christ the King
Special Days	January 1	Holy Name of Jesus	Mary, Mother of God	Holy Name of Jesus
	January 1	New Year's Day	New Year's Day	New Year's Day
	February 2	The Presentation of Our Lord	The Presentation of Our Lord	The Presentation of Our Lord
	March 25	Annunciation	Annunciation	Annunciation
	May 31	Visitation	Visitation	Visitation
	August 15		Assumption	
	September 14	Holy Cross	Triumph of the Cross	Holy Cross
	November 1 or the First Sunday in November	All Saints Day	All Saints Day	All Saints Day
	Thanksgiving Day	Thanksgiving Day	Thanksgiving Day	Thanksgiving Day
	December 8		Immaculate Conception	

Year A

Sunday Between November 27 and December 3 (A)

First Sunday of Advent

Isaiah 2:1-5

Once there was a terrible war in a country called Vietnam. For years and years soldiers from America went to Vietnam to fight. Finally the last of our soldiers came home, but hatred often continues after wars end.

In 1981, long after the war ended, four Americans who had fought in Vietnam went back there to try to make friends with the people they had fought against. Their plane landed at the city of Hanoi in Vietnam, and a Vietnamese soldier came onto the plane to welcome them to his country.

When one of the Americans, a man named Tom Bird, saw the Vietnamese uniform, he boiled over with anger. He felt as if he were suddenly back in the war all over again and all he could think of doing was killing his enemies.

Tom Bird leaped out of his seat and charged down the airplane aisle toward the Vietnamese soldier. His friends had to grab him and hold him down in a chair until he could calm down. Over and over again during the next few days, the same thing happened. He would be calmly talking to some Vietnamese when all at once he felt like killing. The same thing happened to the other Americans, too. Their hatred for their enemies bubbled up inside them in ways that were disturbing and scary.

Slowly, very gradually, their feelings changed. By the end of their visit, the Americans and the Vietnamese were no longer enemies. How had it happened? Someone asked Tom Bird. He couldn't explain it. It seemed like a miracle to him. All he could say was, "Their friendliness won me over."

Today's reading from the Book of Isaiah tells us that God is going to do something wonderful like this, an even bigger miracle: Whole nations will be changed from enemies into friends.

Adapted from an interview with Tom Bird, *MacNeil/Lehrer Newshour*, December 28, 1981.

Sunday Between December 4 and 10 (A)

Second Sunday of Advent

Isaiah 11:1-10

Once long ago, over a hundred years ago, before your great-grandmother was born, there was a terrible war in America. War is always terrible, but this war was especially terrible. The people who lived in the northern part of the United States fought the people who lived in the southern part. The nation was divided and many families were divided: Cousins sometimes shot at their cousins.

This war, called the Civil War or the War Between the States, dragged on for over four years. Children who were one year old when the war started were five years old before it was over.

When the armies of the North marched into battle, their bands played "The Battle Hymn of the Republic":

> Mine eyes have seen the glory of the coming of the Lord;
> He is trampling out the vintage where the grapes of wrath are stored;
> He hath loosed the fateful lightning of his terrible swift sword;
> His truth is marching on.

And when the armies of the South marched into battle, their bands played "Dixie":

> Oh, I wish I was in the land of cotton;
> Old times there are not forgotten.
> Look away! Look away! Look away, Dixieland!

Naturally, everyone in the South hated their enemies' song, "The Battle Hymn of the Republic," and everyone in the North hated "Dixie."

Finally, after thousands of people had been killed, the North won the war. On the day the South gave up, a huge crowd of Northerners rushed to the White House to celebrate. Inside the White House was Abraham Lincoln, the president who had led the North during the war. President Lincoln's band leader got the army band ready to play "The Battle Hymn of the Republic." The band leader asked President Lincoln to come out and lead the crowd in singing the Northern battle song.

But Lincoln felt sorry for the people who had lost the war and wanted to make peace between the North and South. He said, "Will the band please play 'Dixie.' "

Today's Psalm is a prayer that God will teach the leader of the nation how to lead people with justice so that "the land may enjoy *shalom*"—peace. And today's Bible lesson is a promise that God will send a leader who is fair and who brings people together in peace, just the way Abraham Lincoln tried to bring enemies together in peace.

Sunday Between December 11 and 17 (A)

Third Sunday of Advent

Matthew 11:2-11

Once, over two hundred years ago in the land of England, there were a few rich people and very many poor people. The Church of England in those days had some beautiful places to worship God but did little to help the poor.

Then two brothers who were priests in the Church of England, John and Charles Wesley, felt God's love for them in a new way and knew at once that they had to show God's love to other people, especially those whom the Church of England ignored. They and a few of their friends went out to factories and mines to preach to the workers there. They built day-care centers to take care of the little boys and girls whose mothers and fathers had to work long hours in the mines and factories. They started classes to teach the poor how to read the Bible and how to write, how to pray and how to think for themselves, because in those days poor people were not allowed to go to school. They started free medical clinics for poor people who could not afford to pay a doctor.

Soon John and Charles Wesley and their friends knew that they wanted not only their Church but also their whole nation to change. They demanded that their government stop businessmen from buying and selling people from Africa as slaves. Since the slave-sellers also sold sugar, John Wesley urged everyone not to use any sugar in their tea until the slave trade was ended. The Wesley brothers demanded that the government stop throwing people into jail just because they were poor and could not pay money they owed. The Wesleys and their friends organized unions of workers and demanded that those who worked in mines and factories be treated fairly.

Of course, some people in England were upset by what the Wesleys were doing, but others saw these changes and knew that God was working through the Wesleys and their friends. Soon their movement, later called the Methodist movement, had spread to Ireland and Wales and America and Australia and other nations around the world.

In today's Bible lesson John the Baptist sends some of his followers to Jesus to find out if Jesus really is the special person sent by God whom John has been waiting for. Jesus answers, "Go and tell John what you see. Sick people are being made well. The people who have been ignored are being welcomed. Good News is being preached to the poor." When you see things like that happening, you can tell that God is at work.

Sunday Between December 18 and 24 (A)

Fourth Sunday of Advent

Romans 1:1-7

John Newton was a sea captain. His ship carried slaves—people who were kidnapped in Africa and locked and chained in the dark hold of the ship. The slaves were taken thousands of miles from their homes, separated from their families forever and sold like cattle. John Newton sailed his slave ship and never thought about whether what he did was right or wrong.

Then one night John Newton had a dream. He dreamed that a stranger came to him and gave him a magic ring. The stranger said that he would be safe and happy his whole life if he kept this ring. John guarded his magic ring for a while, but then another man came to him in the dream. This man laughed at John Newton for thinking any ring could be so important, so John threw the ring into the ocean. Right then a fire broke out on the mountains above him. It was a huge, raging fire, and he was sure it was going to swallow him up.

Just then a third person—or was it the first one again?—came to John Newton in his dream and asked him why he looked so sad. John told him the story, saying that he had thrown away everything that was of importance to him. The stranger dived into the water, swam further down than anyone could see and came back with the ring. But the stranger wouldn't give it back to John. He said, "I think it is better that I keep it for you. When you need the power of the ring, I will always be at your side."

When John Newton woke up and thought about this dream, he knew that he had thrown away everything important in life just to make money. He felt Jesus was coming to him just the way the stranger did in the dream, coming to show him that he had to change.

John Newton felt like a piece of wood rescued from a raging fire. He quit his job as the captain of the slave ship and became a pastor. He wrote several hymns, and one of them, called "Amazing Grace," became one of the most popular hymns of all time. It tells the story of his life and how he found God's grace: forgiveness that John Newton had not earned. It says,

> Amazing grace! How sweet the sound
> That saved a wretch like me!
> I once was lost, but now am found,
> Was blind, but now I see....
>
> Through many danger, toils, and snares
> I have already come.

'Tis grace hath brought me safe thus far
And grace will lead me home.

In today's Bible reading Paul tells his friends in Rome that "through Jesus Christ our Lord we have received grace." That is what is so amazing about grace: Jesus loves us without our deserving it any more than John Newton did. And we can sing for joy about God's grace the way John did.

December 24/25 (ABC)

Christmas (First Proper)/Mass at Midnight/
The Nativity of Our Lord, Midnight

Isaiah 9:2-7
Luke 2:1-20

The Old Testament lesson for today tells us about God's promise to send us a leader who will be called the Prince of Peace. The Gospel reading tells us that when Jesus was born, the angels sang about peace on earth. Let me tell you a story about someone who sang a song about the birth of Jesus and found peace.

It happened at Christmas, right in the middle of a war. Millions of soldiers fought in trenches dug into the dirt. The trenches stretched all the way from the mountains of Switzerland to the shore of the North Sea and, since the whole world seemed to be fighting, they called this the First World War. Each side had its own trenches, and between the two armies was a place called No Man's Land where no one dared go. The soldiers knew that if they got out of their trenches and walked into No Man's Land it would be easy for their enemies to shoot them.

On Christmas Eve the German soldiers crouched in their trenches on one side and the English soldiers crouched in their trenches on the other side. A soldier from England shivered in the cold night air and pulled his coat around himself tightly. He was very young, really still just a boy. "It's rotten," he said to himself.

"What's that you say, lad?" an older soldier asked.

"It's rotten to be here on Christmas Eve," the boy said.

"Right you are, lad. It's rotten to be in this stinking trench any day."

"But especially on Christmas Eve it's rotten!"

"Aye, lad, it is indeed."

They were quiet for a while, and then the boy asked, "What would you be doing now?"

"Say what?" asked the older man.

"What would you be doing now if we were back home?" the boy asked.

"I'd be sitting in front of a roaring fire in the fireplace and not in this cold, muddy trench, that's what!" said the older soldier. "I'd be eating a real Christmas dinner and singing Christmas carols with my family. I'd be bouncing my little boy and girl on my knees. I'd be... Oh, I don't want to think about it. Just makes us more miserable here."

"Aye," sighed the boy, "I suppose you're right." But he went on thinking about home just the same. He thought about how far he was from the people he loved. They were both quiet for a long time.

Then, far down the trenches, someone started singing. "Listen," the boy said, and the English soldiers around him listened. They couldn't hear the words, but they could tell that the song was "Silent Night." Far away, one voice after another joined the singing. The song grew louder and louder, and the English soldiers listened happily.

Then, suddenly, the young soldier was able to hear the words:

Stille Nacht, heilige Nacht!
Alles schläft, einsam wacht....

Someone was singing "Silent Night" in German! "It's the Germans singing!" he shouted in disbelief. "The Germans!"

The other English soldiers couldn't believe it at first: Their enemies were singing the same Christmas song that they loved to sing! They listened for a while. Then one of the English sang,

Silent night, holy night,
All is calm, all is bright....

Another English soldier started singing with him, then another and then another. Soon up and down the trenches everyone was singing in English and German at the same time. Together they sang:

Sleep in heavenly peace,
Sleep in heavenly peace.

And then the English boy did something very brave. He stood up and dropped his rifle.

"What are you doing, lad? Sit down! You'll get shot!" shouted the older soldier.

"I have to see who is singing to us," the boy said. He climbed out of the trench and walked into No Man's Land. On the other side the German soldiers watched tensely. What should they do?

Then a German soldier got up out of his trench, threw his rifle down and walked into No Man's Land. Slowly, he reached out to the English boy and shook his hand. One man after another dropped his gun and went out to meet the soldiers who had been his enemies.

They shook hands. They told each other their names. They shared food and other gifts with each other. They showed pictures of their girlfriends and their wives and their children back home. They hauled little trees into No Man's Land and decorated them and sang more Christmas carols together. They even played a soccer game, right in the middle of No Man's Land. For a while at least, the war stopped.

Once, in the middle of a terrible war, enemies sang a Christmas song and became friends. Soldiers heard each other sing about peace on earth, and they threw down their guns. Once there was a Christmas which was like the song the angels sang when Jesus was born: There was peace on earth.

And if this happened once, it can happen again. Right now, across the continent of Europe, soldiers are being sent home and walls that divided people are being torn down and nations who were enemies are becoming friends. It is just as the angels said when Jesus was born: There will be peace on earth for the people with whom God is pleased.

An earlier, illustrated version of this story can be found in the Upper Room's *Pockets*, December, 1982. An abridged, illustrated version appeared in the United Methodist Church's *Invitation*, Winter 1988/89.

December 25 (ABC)

Christmas (Second Proper)/Mass at Dawn

Luke 2:8-20

The shepherds who were taking care of their sheep must have been really surprised when they were told that their Savior would be seen by poor people like them. And they must have been even more surprised when they found the baby Jesus in a manger—a feed trough—with all those animals around him. What a place for God to be born!

One year in Canada some teenagers put on a Christmas play in their church. They decided to show what it might be like for Jesus to be born today. In their play, Mary and Joseph were a poor couple on a long trip and Jesus was born in the home of a poor family. Nobody knew they were anyone special. Then one day, Mary, Joseph and Jesus went into a McDonald's. They were hungry and didn't have any money for the food, but an old woman saw them and bought them lunch. Just like Anna in next week's Bible lesson, this old woman recognized who this baby was.

While the young people in the church were watching this play, a young man stood up. Because he was mentally retarded, he usually could not think very fast. As he stood up he shouted, "Oh, wow! I can't believe it! God could be in McDonald's! Far out!"

And he was right. God could be in McDonald's. God is often among the poorest people, just as the shepherds learned when Jesus was born. God can be anywhere.

December 24/25 (ABC)

Christmas (Third Proper)/Mass During the Day/
The Nativity of Our Lord, Morning

Isaiah 52:7-10

In the year 1900, two countries in South America were headed for war, and it seemed that no one could stop them. The rulers of Argentina and Chile both claimed they owned some land high in the Andes Mountains between their two countries, and both were determined to fight to get it. Forts and warships were being built. Men and boys were being trained to be soldiers and sailors. Children in both countries had less food to eat because of all the money being spent on guns and bullets and battleships.

Then Bishop Benavente of Buenos Aires, the leader of most Christians in Argentina, preached a sermon in the biggest church in Buenos Aires. He said, "O my people, I beg you—stop building warships and training armies. Suppose Argentina and Chile do go to war. Killing fathers and brothers in two countries will not tell us which country was right.... Let us ask the king of England to hear both sides and tell us what to do. Let us remember the teaching of Jesus, the Prince of Peace."

When Bishop Java in Chile heard about this sermon, he knew that he and Benavente had a chance to prevent a war. Bishop Java preached to the people of Chile, "We, too, call ourselves followers of the Prince of Peace. Let us then not work for war, but for peace."

The two bishops traveled throughout their countries urging people to pray for peace between Chile and Argentina and to work for peace. Slowly people in both countries began to realize that killing each other over this argument would be a terrible mistake. Finally, the rulers of Chile and Argentina agreed to ask the king of England to help them settle their dispute.

The king sent surveyors to make maps of the land which both countries had said was theirs. He listened to the reasons Argentina or Chile thought this bit of land or that bit of land should belong to them. Finally he divided the land they had been arguing about.

The people of both Argentina and Chile rejoiced that there would be no war. Now their soldiers could go back to work in their farms and factories. Now there would be more money for food and clothing for children.

Then Bishop Benavente had another idea for a way both countries could remember the time they had chosen peace instead of war. Why not melt down the bronze cannons both countries had built for war? And they could use this bronze to make a statue of Jesus, the Prince of Peace!

People in both countries thought this was a great idea. People gave money, the cannons were melted down and a huge statue of Jesus was created by a sculptor. Then the statue was hauled up to the highest peak in the Andes Mountains, a mountaintop high above both Chile and Argentina. First it was carried by train, next by a team of mules and finally it was dragged up to the top by soldiers and sailors.

Three thousand people from both nations climbed to the top of the mountain and camped out together around the statue. They sang songs from both lands, they worshiped God together and they prayed that someday the whole world would live in peace.

In today's reading we hear the prophet Isaiah tell how wonderful it is to see on the mountain the feet of the messenger who brings good news of peace. Through the work of people in Argentina and Chile there was good news of peace, and the feet of the Prince of Peace were planted high upon a mountain. The statue "Christ of the Andes" still towers over the border between Chile and Argentina today.

Sunday Between December 26 and January 1 (A)

First Sunday After Christmas/Holy Family/
First Sunday After Christmas

Hebrews 2:10-18

Have you ever been embarrassed by something a friend of yours did? Or felt ashamed because of something your brother or sister did? Sometimes even when you don't do anything wrong yourself you can feel embarrassed by someone else. It even happens to grown-ups.

Once a new girl came to a school. She was shorter than the other children her age and her mommy and daddy were very short. They were dwarfs—not the pretend dwarfs in fairy tales, but real dwarfs, people who never grow to be very tall. One day this new girl and her mother got on the school elevator with a class of kindergartners. Most of the children had never seen a dwarf before, and some of them started giggling. Soon they were laughing and pointing at the new girl's mother, and saying "Look at that funny lady!"

The kindergartners didn't mean to hurt anyone's feelings, but that's exactly what they did. It's bad enough to have people laugh and point at you but even worse if you are in an elevator and can't get away from them. The girl's mommy was nearly in tears.

You can imagine how embarrassed the teacher was that the children had hurt this woman's feelings. And one little boy was embarrassed, too. He tried to pretend he didn't know these other kids from his class. He wanted to run away from them. He said he wished he could disappear.

That's how most of us feel when we are ashamed. Today's Bible lesson has some good news for us, though. Jesus is not ashamed to be our brother. He will not run away from us, even when we have done something wrong. Jesus has been a human being like you or me. Because he knows what it is like to be tempted to do wrong, he can help us when we do wrong and he can help us when we are tempted to do the wrong thing.

Sunday Between January 2 and 5 (ABC)

Second Sunday After Christmas

Ephesians 1:3-6, 15-18

One Monday morning a teacher asked two children in his class what they had done the day before.

"Oh, I just walked through the east woods," Billy said. "I climbed a hill and came through a meadow. It was boring. I didn't see anyone to play with."

"How about you, Dalia?" the teacher asked. "What did you do yesterday?"

"Oh, I had a great time!" she answered. "Look at all the stuff I found! I saw this green thing growing on a tree," she said, holding up a piece of mistletoe. "Can you tell me what it is? And look: I found these strange flowers among the trees. Then I chased a butterfly until I fell into a stream and got all wet!" she added, laughing. "Then I met an old woman who was gathering firewood. She told me about all kinds of trees and gave me this neat piece of bark. Then I climbed up a hill to have a look around. I remembered that my uncle calls it Fort Hill, so I dug around in the dirt and found this arrowhead! It was a really good day!"

Their teacher looked at all the things that Dalia had found and talked about them. Later, when he noticed Billy looking at the arrowhead, the teacher said softly to him, "You know what, Billy? You went the same places yesterday that Dalia did! You were bored—but look at what Dalia found!"

And that's the way it is: Some people see lots of things, while others act as if their eyes were shut most of the time. In today's Bible lesson Paul tells his friends that he hopes they will have "the eyes of their hearts opened." Paul wants us to see how much God loves us, how wonderful Jesus is and how beautiful the world around us can be. He wants us to see all these things, just the way Dalia discovered all sorts of wonderful things on her walk.

January 6 or First Sunday in January (ABC)

Epiphany

Matthew 2:1-12

Once upon a time there was a little rabbit who lived near a tall palm tree. One day a coconut fell from the palm tree and landed right behind the rabbit with a loud thud.

The loud noise scared the little bunny so much that he took off running. A deer saw him running and asked, "Brother Rabbit, why are you running so fast?"

"Thud is coming!" shouted the rabbit.

The deer started running, too, and when a wild pig saw the deer and the rabbit she called out to them, "Why are you running?"

"Thud is coming!" yelled the deer. "Run for your life!"

The pig started running as fast as her little legs would carry her and before long they all passed a panda. "Why are you running?" asked the panda.

"Thud is coming!" squealed the pig, so the panda started running, too.

Before long all the animals in the forest were running, bellowing about the terrible Thud that was behind them. Finally the herd of terrified animals came toward a lion. "Why are you running?" she asked.

"Because Thud is coming!" the animals roared.

"And just who is Thud?" asked the lion.

Well, the animals looked at each other and finally turned to the rabbit for an answer. "I don't know," he said, "but I heard him!"

"Well, then," asked the lion, "where does Thud live?"

"Back by the coconut trees," answered the rabbit.

"I see," said the lion, thinking for a minute. Then she led the animals back toward the coconut tree—at least those who were brave enough to go with her. She told the animals to sit down and watch the palm trees and wait. After a while another coconut fell from a tall palm tree and landed on the ground with a thud.

"There," the lion said, "is your terrible Thud. You have been running from a coconut like crazy people."

People in China tell this story to remind themselves how we sometimes run around acting crazy when something new scares us. Today's Bible lesson tells us that when King Herod heard that Jesus had been born, the king was very worried. Herod was afraid something new might happen: Even a king was worried about the changes Jesus might bring.

Sunday Between January 7 and 13 (A)

Baptism of the Lord/Baptism of Our Lord/
First Sunday After the Epiphany

Isaiah 42:1-7

Today's lesson tells us that God will send leaders to bring us justice and righteousness, which means that things will be made right and fair. Last month Jewish families celebrated a time when this happened. Their celebration goes on for eight days, and it is called Hanukkah. Hanukkah is a time for singing special songs, saying special prayers, giving gifts, eating special foods and playing special games. This is the story which Hanukkah celebrates:

A long time ago a king in the country of Syria ruled over many Jewish people. His name was Antiochus IV. He decided that he wanted everyone in his kingdom to worship the gods he worshiped. He said he would not let the Jews pray to God their own way—in their own Temple and in their own language.

Some of the Jews did what Antiochus told them to do, but others wouldn't give in. An old Jewish priest named Mattathias and his children ran off to the mountains and fought against King Antiochus's army.

Many Jewish people, led by Judah Maccabees, fought bravely against the king's army. Finally, Antiochus gave up and said the Jews could worship God in their own way. The Jews went to their Temple in Jerusalem to thank God for their freedom.

But when they saw the Temple, oh, they were sad! It was a mess. Antiochus's soldiers had burned the gates to the Temple and upset the altar and put up idols, statues of Greek gods. Oh, it was terrible!

But the Jews got to work to clean up the Temple. They took down the idols. They built a new altar. They made everything nice, just the way they thought God would like it to be. When the Temple was all fixed up, they had a huge feast to celebrate their freedom, and it went on for days and days.

And ever since then, Jews have celebrated Hanukkah, the Feast of Remembering. They remember Judah Maccabees and the brave people who helped him. They remember how God sent them someone to make things fair and right.

Sunday Between January 14 and 20 (A)

Second Sunday After the Epiphany/Second Sunday of the Year/ Second Sunday After the Epiphany

Isaiah 49:1-7

In today's reading from the Book of Isaiah the people of Israel hear that God wants them to be "a light to the nations" so that God's salvation can reach to the ends of the earth. Have you ever thought about how important a light can be to people who are lost? Let me tell you about a light in Hawaii that guides people.

Near the Makupuu Peninsula on the island of Oahu, the ocean currents are fast and dangerous. Year after year many ships lost their way here at night as they sailed between the island of Oahu and the island of Molokai. The swift currents drove these ships right into the rocks and many people were hurt.

Finally the Coast Guard built a lighthouse on the peninsula so ships could see where they were going at night. And the very first light in that lighthouse was a lamp named Lisa.

When the Coast Guard finished building the lighthouse, they had a big party to celebrate. Lots of people came to the party because they were so happy that Lisa was there to protect the ships and sailors. They shared food and speeches and singing and dancing. Lisa was proud of the fine things everyone said about her.

When evening came, though, the people went home and Lisa was left alone in the lighthouse. It had been a beautiful day—clear and sunny, with only wispy little clouds in the sky—but as the sun went down, storm clouds began to cover the sky. Rain started to pour and the wind began to blow. Waves pounded the rocks near Lisa and, to tell you the truth, she was lonely and scared.

Then Lisa looked out to sea and saw a ship trying to return home in the storm. The waves tossed the ship so violently that the captain could hardly tell where he was. He was headed right toward the rocks! "I hope he will turn," Lisa thought, but the ship kept coming. "Turn!" she called out, but the captain could not hear her over the wind and the waves. "Turn!" Lisa shouted with all her might, but the storm raged so fiercely that no one could hear her. "Help!" she cried. "Someone help! They're going to crash!"

Then Lisa remembered that *she* was someone who could help. She remembered that she was a powerful light.

Lisa started shining. She shone as brightly as she could. She shone with all her strength. Her powerful beam cut through the night as she spun around and around. Just in the nick of time the captain saw the light and saw the rocks in front of his ship. He grabbed the wheel and turned the ship. Lisa saved his ship and the sailors.

God wants us to be like a light that helps other people see the way. God wants you and me to shine wherever we can.

Sunday Between January 21 and 27 (A)

Third Sunday After the Epiphany/Third Sunday of the Year/ Third Sunday After the Epiphany

Matthew 4:12-23

A long, long time ago there were no colleges or universities. In those days a teacher would just gather grown-up students who would follow the teacher around.

In the country called Greece there was a great teacher named Socrates. One day Socratesmmet a man named Aeschines. Aeschines told Socrates, "I want to be your student, but I am a poor man. I can't pay you anything to teach me. I have nothing to give you but myself."

"Ah," said Socrates, "don't you see that you are giving me the most important thing of all? Come and be my student."

Another time, Socrates was walking down a narrow alley with a long walking stick when he saw a young man names Xenophon. Socrates blocked the alley with his walking stick and said, "Sir, can you tell me where I can buy some food?"

"Yes," answered Xenophon, a little suspicious of this stranger, "you can buy food at the market. It's up this street and to the left."

"Sir," Socrates continued, "can you tell me where ships are built?"

"Why certainly," answered Xenophon. "Ships are built down at the shipyards near the harbor."

Socrates kept asking Xenophon where he could buy this and that, and where one thing or another was made. When Xenophon was worn out from all these questions, Socrates finally asked him, "Do you know where people are good and virtuous?"

"No," answered Xenophon.

Then Socrates said as he picked up his walking stick, "Follow and learn." And that is just what Xenophon did.

In today's Bible lesson Jesus calls some fishermen to become his students, his disciples. He says to them what I think he still is telling us, "Follow and learn."

Sunday Between January 28 and February 3 (A)

Fourth Sunday After the Epiphany/Fourth Sunday of the Year/ Fourth Sunday After the Epiphany

Matthew 5:1-12

Long ago soldiers from Spain came to Central America. They stole land from the natives who lived there, killed many natives and made the others slaves. The soldiers did not think this was wrong, because they did not think of the natives—whom they called Indians—as being people like themselves. And some Spaniards thought that after the soldiers conquered the natives, priests from Spain could force them to become Christians.

Then in the year 1535 a Roman Catholic priest named Bartolomé de Las Casas came from Spain to the part of Central America which is called Nicaragua. He learned that the Spanish governor was planning to send his soldiers to enslave the last free natives of Nicaragua. Las Casas preached sermons saying that this was wrong and soon the soldiers did not want to conquer anyone.

The governor was so angry that he made Bartolomé and his friends leave Nicaragua at once. Bartolomé and his friends fled to the town of Santiago in the part of Central America which today is called Guatemala. In Santiago Bartolomé told the Spaniards that they must not try to force the natives to become Christians. "We cannot teach them anything about Jesus," he insisted, "until we have made peace with them."

"If that's what you think," the other Spaniards laughed, "go to Tuzulután!"

Tuzulután was a part of Guatemala with thick jungles, steep mountains, huge snakes and ferocious animals. And the natives who lived there killed people to worship their gods. The Spanish soldiers had never been able to defeat the fierce warriors of Tuzulután. They had fought such terrible battles with the natives there that they gave Tuzulután a nickname in Spanish: *Tierra de Guerra*, "Land of War."

But Bartolomé de Las Casas believed that God could help him make peace even in the Land of War. He and his friends decided to go to Tuzulután.

First, Bartolomé asked the governor to promise not to send his troops into Tuzulután for five years while Bartolomé and his friends worked there. Amazingly enough, the governor said "Yes." Maybe the governor wanted to get rid of Bartolomé for a long time. Maybe the governor thought the natives would kill Bartolomé and the other priests—or at least send them running home in no time.

Bartolomé and his friends began getting ready for their dangerous work in the Land of War. First, they prayed for several days, asking God to help them make peace with the natives of Tuzulután. Next they made up songs about how God made the world, how Jesus was born and about what Jesus did. Then they found some natives from another part of Guatemala who were already Christians, natives who were merchants and who traveled into Tuzulután to buy and sell things. Bartolomé and his friends taught their new songs to these native merchants.

The merchants headed right for Atitlan, the village where the High Chief or *Cacique* of Tuzulután lived. The merchants bought and sold things in the village during the day. Then, when it got dark, they began singing the new songs.

"Say, I've never heard a song like that," a little girl said. "Could you sing it again?" Soon nearly everyone in the village was crowding around to listen. Even the High Chief, the Cacique, came.

"Who is this God who made the world?" a mother asked. "Tell us more about this man named Jesus," a father said.

"You'll have to ask the missionaries," the merchants answered, as they played another song. They sang their songs for eight nights in a row, but whenever someone asked a question, the merchants just said, "The missionaries can tell you more about that."

Finally the Cacique asked, "What are missionaries?"

"They come from Spain and live near here, but they do not carry guns or kill natives the way the other Spaniards do. They do not steal our land and they are not interested in taking our gold or our jewels. They know more about Jesus than even the King, the Cacique of all the Spaniards."

"Where can we find these people?" the Cacique asked.

"Just ask them to come here!" said the merchants.

So the Cacique sent his brother back to Santiago with the merchants to invite Bartolomé and his friends to visit the village. "But first," he told his brother secretly, "find out if they are as good as these merchants say they are!"

The chief's brother went to Santiago and watched Bartolomé and his friends very closely. *These* Christians, he decided, really were the way the merchants said they were. Bartolomé and the other priests were overjoyed when the chief's brother invited them to visit Atitlán.

Bartolomé and his friends sent just one priest, Father Luis Cáncer to Atitlán at first. When Father Cáncer got to Atitlán he found the natives had prepared a big party and a huge flower-covered doorway to welcome him to their village. And when the High Chief learned from his brother that Bartolomé had made the governor promise to keep his soldiers out of Tuzulután for five years, he asked Father Cáncer to have a Christian worship service in his village and to show them how to build a church building.

Father Cáncer told the villagers all he could about Jesus. Many natives, including the Cacique, became followers of Jesus and were baptized as members of the Church. The Cacique told his people to stop killing people to worship their old gods. He invited Bartolomé and his friends to travel throughout Tuzulután telling the natives about Jesus.

And so, thanks to Bartolomé de Las Casas and his friends, the fierce warriors of Tuzulután became followers of Jesus, the Prince of Peace, and peace came to the Land of War. Today's Bible lesson says, "Happy are the peacemakers!" Bartolomé and his friends were certainly happy to make peace in the Land of War.

An illustrated version of this story will appear in the Upper Room's *Pockets*. Another version of this story for older students appeared in *With*, September, 1984.

Sunday Between February 4 and 10 (A)

Fifth Sunday After the Epiphany/Fifth Sunday of the Year/
Fifth Sunday After the Epiphany

Isaiah 58:3-9a

Easter can occur as early as March 22 and as late as April 25. When Easter is early, the number of Sundays after Epiphany is reduced as necessary, from as many as nine to as few as four. In addition, the Protestant lectionaries observe the Transfiguration of the Lord on the Last Sunday After Epiphany.

Once, long ago, there was a boy named William who got into trouble. He didn't do anything bad, but sometimes you can get into trouble because other people are doing wrong and you decide to do what is right.

William Penn's father was a rich man in the country of England and an admiral in the British Navy. His father hoped that William would be just like him when he grew up, but William had his own ideas about what he wanted to do.

These ideas got him into trouble. His father sent William to a famous school in Oxford, but William got in trouble at school because he had his own ideas about God and about how he wanted to worship God. His teachers all belonged to the Church of England and, in those days, if you lived in England and didn't belong to the Church of England and say you believed what the people in that Church believed, you might be thrown in jail or even killed.

William was a very brave boy, though. He wouldn't lie about what he believed. So his teachers threw him out of school.

"What am I going to do with that boy?" his father thought. His father sent William off to France to spend some time with the king of France, hoping that if William got to know the rich people at the king's court then William would want to become rich himself.

But it didn't work. Soon William left the king's court and went to a Church school in the city of Saumur to learn more from people who had their own ideas about God. "What am I going to do with that son of mine?" his father moaned.

When he was twenty-one years old, William went back to England and entered law school. "A lawyer!" thought his father. "Now that's a good job. My son will be a lawyer!" But William never finished law school or became a lawyer.

The next year William went to Ireland to take care of some farmlands his father owned. "Well, maybe he will finally settle down," his father told himself. But only a year later William joined a group of people called the Quakers.

They were a very brave group of people. They had to be brave because you could be thrown in jail if you worshiped a new way. Sure enough, as soon as William joined the Quakers, he was thrown in jail. I bet that when his father heard this, he yelled and screamed and cried.

Some people are scared by getting into trouble, but when William got out of jail he traveled all over Europe telling others what these Quakers believed. Next, he helped some Quakers move to New Jersey where they could start their own towns, to live and worship the way they wanted without anyone bothering them. The king of England owed William Penn a lot of money, but William asked the king to give him land in America instead. The king agreed and called this land Pennsylvania, which means "Penn's Woods."

William Penn sailed across the Atlantic Ocean to Pennsylvania and bought land there from the Indian tribes of Pennsylvania. Then he told people in many different countries that they could come to Pennsylvania to worship as they wished. In Germany people who belonged to the Mennonite Church were suffering because of their beliefs. When one Mennonite family in Germany heard about this new land, they wrote this letter to their son in Pennsylvania:

February 6, 1681

Dear Son:

Your letter from faraway America reached us today...and gave us great joy.... America, according to your writing, must be a beautiful land. We rejoice greatly that your home is with such good God-fearing people, and that the Indians in your community are a peace-loving people.

Dear Henry, since you have been away from us conditions in South Germany have become very much worse. The French armies have wrought much devastation.... Thousands would gladly leave the fatherland if they had the means to do so. A merchant from Frankfurt was with us last week and informed us how along the Rhine a number of families have banded together to accept the invitation of an Englishman, named William Penn, who had recently visited that community, to settle in that beautiful land and there establish new homes.... We, as also the Plattenbach family, are only waiting for a good opportunity when the dear Lord will bring us to you....

America is the only dream of your sister Elizabeth. Your sister Catharine, only six years old, asks us daily, "Will we soon be going to our brother in America?"

Your dear mother, as also your brothers and sisters, greet you heartily and pray to the dear Lord that he may protect and ever keep you.

From your loving father,

Heinrich Frey

Today's Bible reading from the Book of Isaiah tells us that what God wants us to do, more than anything else, is to be kind and fair. God wants us to help people be free, to share food with people who are hungry, to share clothes with people who do not have enough and to make homes for people who don't have anyplace to live. That's exactly what William Penn did.

This story might also be told on a Sunday near the Fourth of July to celebrate the freedom many immigrants found in the United States. An earlier, illustrated version of this story appeared in *On the Line* (Mennonite Publishing House), March 21, 1982.

Sunday Between February 11 and 17 (A)

Proper 1/Sixth Sunday of the Year/Sixth Sunday After the Epiphany

Deuteronomy 30:15-20
Sirach (Ecclesiasticus) 15:15-20

Once there was a little red hen who scratched around in the dirt and found some grains of wheat. Suddenly she had an idea: She could plant the wheat seeds and grow a whole lot of wheat. "Who will plant this wheat with me?" she asked.

"Not I," grunted the pig.

"Not I," quacked the duck.

"Not I," purred the cat.

So the little red hen planted the grains of wheat all by herself. "Who will help me water the wheat plants?" she asked.

"Not I," grunted the pig.

"Not I," quacked the duck.

"Not I," purred the cat.

So the little red hen watered the wheat plants week after week, while the pig just wallowed in the mud and the duck just swam in the pond and the cat just slept in the sunshine. The little hen kept working, though, and soon the wheat was tall and golden and ripe. "Who will help me cut down the wheat?" she asked.

"Not I," grunted the pig.

"Not I," quacked the duck.

"Not I," purred the cat.

So the little red hen cut down the wheat all by herself. Then she asked, "Who will help grind these grains of wheat into flour?"

"Not I," grunted the pig.

"Not I," quacked the duck.

"Not I," purred the cat.

So the hen ground the wheat into flour all by herself. Then she asked, "Who will help bake this flour into bread?"

"Not I," grunted the pig.

"Not I," quacked the duck.

"Not I," purred the cat.

So the little red hen baked the bread all by herself. The wonderful smell of bread baking soon brought the pig and the duck and the cat to the kitchen just as the hen was taking the beautiful, crusty, golden-brown loaf out of the oven.

"So you think you're going to eat it now, do you?" the hen said. "You had your chance to help, but you would not plant the seeds or water the plants or cut the wheat or grind the flour or bake the bread, so you will not eat the loaf. I will eat the loaf all by myself."

And that is just what she did.

Today's Bible lesson tells us that we must choose whether or not we will help do the things God wants us to do, just as the animals decided whether or not to help. And what we choose makes all the difference in the world.

Sunday Between February 18 and 24 (A)

Proper 2/Seventh Sunday of the Year/
Seventh Sunday After the Epiphany

Psalm 62:5-12

You know how hard it can be for a class of children to be quiet when their teacher asks them to be quiet? One day a teacher took his kindergartners way up in the tall tower of the Riverside Church in New York City. They had just been on the playground for an hour and everyone was still excited and loud as they crowded into the elevator and rode all the way up to the twentieth floor of the tower. And it's almost impossible to stand still when other kids are pushed against you and stepping on your toes, isn't it?

When the class got to the twentieth floor they could see so far up the Hudson River and down the Hudson River and all the way to New Jersey that they were yelling and pointing here and there as they told each other, "Look, there's the George Washington Bridge!" and "Hey! There's the little red lighthouse! I can see it!" and "Wow! I can see all the way to the World Trade Center!"

And as the children crowded back into the elevator and rode down they just couldn't be quiet, even though their teacher told them to. But then the elevator door opened and the children walked out and right into the great big sanctuary of Riverside Church. And do you know what happened?

Suddenly a hush fell over all those wild, noisy boys and girls. The children walked very quietly down the center aisle and found places to sit. They silently looked around at the altar and the stained glass windows and the great big pipe organ. Then someone started to play the organ and the whole class listened, perfectly still. You see, as soon as they walked into the sanctuary they knew they were in a special place, a place where people come to pray to God and to worship God. Without their teacher saying a word, they all realized at once that this was a place to listen and wait and wonder.

Today's Psalm talks about waiting for God in silence. And that's a very important way to pray: to spend time silently with God. Maybe you would like to do so, to pray and listen silently to God, the next time you come into this sanctuary. Maybe you would do that with me now.

Sunday Between February 25 and 29 (A)

Proper 3/Eighth Sunday of the Year/Eighth Sunday After the Epiphany

Matthew 5:38-48

In today's Bible lesson, Jesus tells us to love our enemies and pray for those who are mean to us. It isn't easy to love your enemies, to pray for them instead of hitting them. You have to be brave to love people who are mean to you.

Look what happened to some people who were brave enough to do what Jesus taught: Long ago, the people of India were trying to win their independence from England. They wanted to run their own country. They did not want England telling them what to do. Their leader, a man named Mahatma Gandhi, told the people of India that they could do what Jesus said, they could love their enemies. Gandhi told Indians to use something called nonviolence to win their independence without killing or hurting others. Besides, Gandhi said, it is better to *change* your enemies than to defeat them.

Some of Gandhi's followers were Sikh warriors. They were huge, many of them over six feet tall, and they wore big turban hats with knives stuck in them. They carried long curved swords that were taller than any of you are. Before they became followers of Gandhi, the Sikhs had been the bravest, fiercest fighters in all of India.

One day Mahatma Gandhi led a big protest march to demand that England give India its independence. The English government said they would not allow any march. Gandhi said that they would march anyway. The English government said that any protest marchers would be arrested and put in prison. Gandhi said that they were coming all the same—and he asked the Sikh warriors to march at the front.

When the English soldiers saw thousands of people coming toward them, they were worried. And when the soldiers saw the huge Sikhs coming toward them, they were really scared. "Arrest them!" shouted the English officers to their frightened troops. The protesters were very brave, though, and refused to go. Then the scared English soldiers started hitting the protesters with long clubs.

Now, it would have been easy for the Sikhs to fight back with their swords, but then the soldiers would have fired their guns and many people would have been killed. The Sikhs were certainly brave enough to fight, but they were even braver than that: They were brave enough to stand their ground and not fight back.

One after another, the Sikhs were knocked to the ground by the soldiers. One after another, other Sikhs stepped up to take their places. For the longest time, the soldiers kept clubbing the Sikhs down and the Sikhs kept being hit without hitting back. This went on until many of the English felt sick inside about what they were doing.

When people around the world saw pictures of these soldiers attacking people who didn't fight back, they were shocked. And when people in England saw the bravery of these Sikhs, they, too, felt sick inside, and they were deeply ashamed of what their government was doing in India. From that moment, many people in England, as well as other people all over the world, started demanding that England give India its independence.

Gandhi turned out to be right: If you love your enemies, as Jesus tells us to do, you often can change them. Nonviolence slowly changed the English. Because of the bravery of people like Mahatma Gandhi and the Sikhs, the people of India won their freedom without war or killing.

Sunday Before Ash Wednesday (A)

Last Sunday After the Epiphany/Transfiguration of Our Lord

Psalm 2:6-11

Today's Scripture reminds even rulers that they are not more powerful than God. There is a story from the Bible about a king who learns this from a witch.

Long ago there was a king of Israel whose name was Saul. He had driven out of Israel all the witches and wizards and mediums (people who talk to the dead). He said he didn't believe in their magic and witchcraft. But then Saul's enemies, the Philistines, sent a huge army to kill Saul and the army of Israel. When Saul saw the army of the Philistines he was really afraid.

"What is going to happen to me?" Saul asked God, but God wouldn't tell Saul what would happen. Neither did God send Saul a prophet or a dream to tell him what would happen. Saul became even more afraid.

So Saul said to one of his servants, "Go find a witch for me, so I can ask her what is going to happen." Saul's servant went off and looked for a witch. Soon she returned to the king and said, "There is a witch near here, in the town of Endor. She can talk to the dead."

Saul didn't want anyone to know that he would go to a witch for help, so do you know what he did? He took off his royal robes and put on other clothes to disguise himself. Then he went to see the witch of Endor late at night, when no one was watching.

"I want you to help me speak with someone who is dead," Saul told the witch.

"I can't do that!" the witch shrieked. "Don't you know that the king has said no one may practice witchcraft in his kingdom? He could have me killed!"

"As God lives," Saul swore, "no one will punish you for doing this."

"OK," the witch said. "To whom do you wish to speak?"

Saul thought about his old friend who had died, the prophet Samuel. Samuel always knew what would happen next. Samuel knew what God wanted people to do. If only he could talk to Samuel! "I want to talk with Samuel," Saul whispered.

"Why did you trick me?" the witch howled. "You must be Saul—the king who hates witches!"

"Don't be afraid," Saul begged. "Please, tell me what you see."

So the witch of Endor told Saul what she saw: She saw the prophet Samuel coming. The witch helped Saul to talk with Samuel, and Samuel told Saul he was in big trouble because the king had not done what God wanted. Samuel spoke to Saul, "You and your army are going to lose."

When King Saul heard this, he threw himself on the ground, filled with fear. He was so afraid he was trembling. Besides, because he had been too worried to eat anything all day, he was now weak from hunger.

When the witch saw how frightened Saul was, she forgot how afraid she herself was of the king. "I have listened to you," the witch said. "Now listen to me. I'm going to give you some food and I want you to eat it."

Saul didn't want to eat, but finally he agreed. The witch got some food for Saul and he ate it. It gave him back his strength. Saul got up and went back to his army.

And that was how a witch helped a king accept what God was going to do. Saul realized that he was not stronger than God.

This story might also be used for Halloween or the Sunday nearest it. Children are fascinated to learn that there is a witch story in the Bible—and amazed to find that the Witch of Endor is not an evil figure but one who helps a king accept the inevitable.

Ash Wednesday (ABC)

Joel 2:1-2, 12-17a

Once, long ago, there was a slave named Callistus (or Calixtus or Kallistos) who lived in the city of Rome. He was a Christian, a follower of Jesus, but he got into lots of trouble. He lost some of his master's money and was punished. Then somebody said, "Hey, there's Callistus! He's a Christian!"

In those days it was against the law to be a Christian. Callistus was arrested and sent to work in the mines on the island of Sardinia. The jobs that Christians were forced to do in the mines were terrible. But before long, a woman whom the emperor in Rome loved told the emperor that she felt sorry for the Christians who had been sent to the mines. "The work they must do in the mines is so dangerous," she said. "No one should be forced to work there. Please, free them." And the emperor did just that.

When Callistus was set free he went home to Rome. In Rome another wonderful thing happened. Though he had been a slave, he was picked by Pope Zephyrinus to be his helper. And when Zephyrinus died, the former slave Callistus was chosen to be the new pope.

Before long, Callistus had to make a decision. Some people who had done bad things were being told that they could not come to Communion. They were told they couldn't belong to the Church anymore—no matter how sorry they were about what they had done.

You can imagine how awful it made people feel for their friends to tell them, "You can't share Eucharist with us. You don't belong to the Church anymore." But Callistus reminded Christians that God is loving and forgiving. He insisted that there is room in the Church for people who have sinned, because none of us is perfect and all of us need God's forgiveness. He said, "If you repent—if you tell God you are sorry for what you have done and ask God to help you to do better—you are welcome in our Church."

A woman's kindness got Callistus out of the mines. A pope's kindness made him a leader of the Church. Perhaps because people had been kind to him, Callistus knew that the Church had to be kind to those who had done wrong. Today's reading from the Book of Joel tells us that God is full of faithful love for us. Because God is like this, we can trust God when we are sorry about the things we have done wrong. Callistus reminded Christians that we should give thanks for God's forgiveness and show it to others.

First Sunday in Lent (A)

Matthew 4:1-11

Today's Bible reading tells us about a time when Jesus was tempted. He wasn't tempted to something *bad*. He was tempted to be the sort of leader other people wanted instead of being the leader God wanted him to be. The Book of Esther tells us about a girl named Esther who was tempted not to be the leader God needed her to be. Every spring Jewish people around the world remember her when they celebrate the holiday called Purim. Listen to her story.

Long ago, many Jewish people were taken as prisoners of war to the land of Persia. These Jews lived in Persia for many years. One young Jewish girl named Esther was picked by the emperor of Persia, King Xerxes, to be his new queen. King Xerxes had no idea that Esther was Jewish, though, and she kept this secret, for it was dangerous to be a Jew.

Soon after Esther became Queen she learned that something terrible was going to happen. Evil men were plotting to murder every Jew in Persia, and they had gotten King Xerxes to order his army to help kill the Jews.

What was Esther going to do? If she did nothing, her people would be murdered. But if she tried to help them, others might find out that she was Jewish and kill her, too. Esther wanted someone else to confront the emperor about the evil he was going to commit, but there was no one else but her to do what God needed someone to do. Would she be the one to risk her life? Certainly Esther must have been tempted to remain silent, to do nothing, to try to save herself.

But Esther was very brave. She decided to run right into the emperor's court and demand to see him.

Now, to do this was very dangerous. No one was supposed to come near the emperor, not even his wife, until *he* invited them to come near. There were guards who stood in front of King Xerxes to protect him. And if anyone entered his court without being invited, the guards were supposed to kill that person at once.

Esther put on her royal robes. She went to the palace and ran right into the emperor's court. A guard saw her and raised his huge sword, ready to kill her. "Stop!" shouted King Xerxes. "Put away your sword!" he commanded the guard, still shaking from his fear that his beautiful wife might have been killed. "My queen," he asked, "why did you come here like this? Why did you risk your life?"

"Because I must talk to you at once," Esther answered.

"But what can be so important?" King Xerxes asked her.

"I have come to ask a favor," Esther said.

"But what can you want so badly, my queen?" the emperor begged. "Tell me what you want and you will have it—even if it is half my empire!"

"What I want," Esther replied, "is for my people—the Jews—to live."

"*Your* people!" the king sputtered, unable to believe his ears.

"Yes," she said, "*my* people. I have kept it a secret for a long time but I cannot hide who I am any longer. I cannot stand by and do nothing while your soldiers kill my people. Please, spare the lives of my people."

King Xerxes granted Esther's wish. Because of her courage, because she did not give in when tempted to remain silent, her people lived. That is exactly how brave Jesus had to be when he was tempted. Jesus had the courage to risk his life to be the sort of leader God wanted.

Second Sunday in Lent (A)

Genesis 12:1-4a (4b-8)

Mathilda Wrede was a rich young woman only twenty years old when she began going to prisons. Now why would she do that, do you think? Mathilda knew that God wanted her to help change the terrible prison conditions that existed in her nation, Finland, and in many other countries, too. So Mathilda started visiting jails and prisons and worked to make them better—and to help prisoners change for the better.

Mathilda spent one Christmas Eve going from cell to cell wishing the prisoners a Merry Christmas. Suddenly she heard wild shrieks. A prisoner was raging around his cell, waving a knife and bellowing that he would kill the next person who came into his cell.

All the guards were afraid to face him, but Mathilda was braver than any of them. She quickly prayed to God and then walked calmly into the cell where the crazy man was charging back and forth. "Please give me the knife," she politely asked.

"A man should always keep his word," he roared, "that's what you tell us. And I have sworn not to give it up!"

"I am glad that you mean to keep your word in the future," Mathilda answered. "But won't you give me that knife as a Christmas present?"

But the prisoner just pushed her out of the way and went on yelling and screaming and waving his knife around. "Then I must take it," Mathilda said softly. "Put out your hand and I will try."

The huge man looked at young Mathilda in disbelief. Then he held out his strong fist, clenched tightly around the knife. Mathilda made a game out of opening up his fist as if he were a little boy. One finger at a time, she pulled his hand away from the knife. Then she sat with the man and talked and talked with him until his fit of madness was gone and he was calm again.

Mathilda Wrede knew that God wanted her to go someplace new: God wanted her to visit prisons in Finland—and later in other nations, too. Today's Bible lesson tells us how, long ago, Abraham and his wife Sarah went where God told him to go. People like Abraham and Sarah and Mathilda Wrede go to new places because God wants them to go there and because they have faith in God. They trust God to lead them.

Third Sunday in Lent (A)

John 4:5-26 (27-42)

Once there was a little girl named Mary Slessor, who grew up in Scotland. When she became a young woman she discovered that God wanted her to be a missionary. She went to Africa, where she became one of the greatest missionaries who ever worked in that continent.

You have to be brave to make a long journey such as this, but Mary had to be particularly courageous. Her Protestant Church did not have any nuns and the men in her Church thought that women should not be missionaries, especially women such as Mary who were not married. But Mary Slessor was strong enough and brave enough to travel alone thousands of miles from Scotland to Africa to tell people about Jesus. She had all sorts of adventures in Africa, including this one.

One day Mary Slessor was traveling up the Creek River in a boat to an area where none of the natives had ever seen a woman from Europe. Suddenly a canoe shot out from the river bank and headed right for Mary's boat! Were they going to attack Mary? Rob her? Or kill her? Should she try to escape?

Mary decided to wait calmly for the canoe. Much to her surprise, the men in the canoe asked politely, "Will you please come with us to our village? Our chief has heard about you. He wants to meet you."

Mary had no idea what the chief wanted, but she decided to go with the natives in their canoe. They took her to their chief's home and said, "This is our chief, Onoyom."

Onoyom told Mary that another Christian had come to the village earlier. "He was not a good man," Onoyom explained. "He got drunk all the time and did many bad things. We were glad when he left our village. But sometimes this bad man used to talk about a very interesting person, someone called Jesus. Do you know him? Can you tell me more about this Jesus?"

Mary Slessor was overjoyed to hear this. She told the chief and his wife story after story about Jesus. Soon Onoyom and his wife decided to become Christians—followers of Jesus. They gave Mary money to build a church in their village. Soon many of the people in the village had become Christians.

The chief was wise enough to know that even though the first Christian he met was a bad man, the things he said about Jesus were important. And today's Bible lesson tells us how a woman who was a sinner became the first missionary to the Samaritans, telling her neighbors about Jesus. God can use even bad people to do good things.

Fourth Sunday in Lent (A)

1 Samuel 16:1-13

Once there was a young man in France who couldn't do anything right. John Vianney was drafted into the army but got sick for three months. When he was well, he was told to go join another group of soldiers—but he walked so slowly that he never found them.

John Vianney came home and went to school to become a priest. But he wasn't very smart and he had a hard time in school. The first time he took the test to become a priest he failed. When he finally became a priest, he couldn't preach a sermon very well. He never worked in a big, rich church. He worked only in a small, poor village. In many ways John Vianney was a failure. He didn't amount to much.

But one thing that John Vianney could do was listen. He listened to the people in his village tell about their problems, the mistakes they had made, the things they had done wrong. He knew how to find out what was bothering people. He told them how God could help them solve their problems. He listened so well that people started coming to talk with him from miles around. Twenty thousand people came in just one year to talk with John Vianney.

Who would ever have believed that God could work through a failure like John Vianney? Today's lesson tells us how David was chosen by God to do very special things for God. But David is almost overlooked. No one thinks he is old enough to do anything important. God says in this story, "I don't see the way people see. People see only what someone looks like. I see what someone is like inside." God often uses people that you and I overlook.

Fifth Sunday in Lent (A)

Ezekiel 37:1-14
John 11:(1-16), 17-45

Today's readings tell us that God is more powerful than death. That doesn't mean that dying is easy. Death can be scary sometimes. But I want to share with you something that happened once in our family.

Once my wife Karen and I moved from Hawaii to New York City. Karen flew to New York before I did and found an apartment for us to live in. She called me on the telephone and told me she had found an apartment. Then I took our two cats to the airport. They were put in two little cages and put on a great big jet. They meowed and meowed. The jet was so big and they were so tiny. They didn't know where they were going. Were they ever scared!

When the airplane landed in New York, Karen was waiting to pick up our cats. For hours and hours the two little cats had been inside the dark, bumping, rumbling jet. Were they ever glad to see Karen! The cats didn't know where she was going to take them, but they knew that they were with someone they loved and trusted. The cats meowed again, but this time they were happy meows.

We are a little like those cats. We're scared of dying sometimes, because we don't know what it will be like after we die. But God is stronger than death, and we will be with God and with those we love.

Passion Sunday or Palm Sunday (A)

Matthew 26:14—27:66 or Matthew 27:11-54

Once a preacher was trying to figure out what he would say on the coming Sunday. He was going to preach a sermon about the story of Jesus' death. He couldn't figure out himself why Jesus had to come to earth even though it meant he would be killed. Why did God have to become a human being in the first place, he wondered.

This preacher stayed up late into the night studying the Bible. As he was studying, a huge storm came up. The storm confused some birds that had been flying by. The birds saw light inside the preacher's house and wanted to get inside to get away from the storm. And the birds couldn't see the big glass windows on the side of the house.

The birds started flying right into the big glass windows, crashing right against them. The preacher ran outside and tried to stop the birds from hurting themselves, but the birds kept right on crashing into the windows. Many of them fell to the ground with their wings and necks broken, dying.

"Stop!" the preacher called out, but the birds couldn't understand him and kept crashing into the windows. "Stop!" he called out as he fell to the ground on his knees, crying.

"If only I could tell them to fly around the house!" he cried. "If only I could become a bird so I could save them."

Suddenly the preacher knew why God had to send Jesus into our world: The only way God could save us from destroying ourselves was to become a human being just like one of us. God wanted so much to save us that God was willing to send Jesus, even if it meant Jesus would be killed. That is how much God loves us.

Monday in Holy Week (ABC)

John 12:1-11

In today's Gospel lesson we hear how a woman named Mary poured sweet-smelling perfume on the feet of her friend Jesus. Why would she do a thing like that?

There is another woman who has spent nearly her whole life doing things that other people could not imagine themselves doing. She was born in Albania in Europe and became a nun when she was still a teenager. As a young sister, she became a teacher in India and taught geography to girls at a high school in Calcutta. Near the school she saw many poor and starving people every day. One day, while riding a train, this young woman suddenly knew what she had to do. She had to work among these sick and starving people.

So this young woman left her school and trained to be a nurse. Then she started a school in the poorest part of Calcutta, where many of her former students joined her. This group of nuns became known as the Missionary Sisters of Charity, and she became known around the world as Mother Teresa.

Mother Teresa's nuns bring the sick people who are dying on the streets of Calcutta into their hospitals to care for them with love, so that they can live their last days among friends. Mother Teresa says that the most terrible poverty of all is loneliness and feeling unwanted.

When people ask Mother Teresa why she spends so much time helping these poor, dying people, she tells them that it makes her happy to do something beautiful for Jesus. She has started other hospitals in India, in New York City and in other places around the world, caring for the poorest and sickest people in order to do "something beautiful for Jesus."

I guess that is what Mary of Bethany wanted to do: to do something beautiful for Jesus because Jesus had shown her how much God loved her. Mother Teresa has shown the whole world how we can do something beautiful for Jesus today: care for the sick and the poor.

Tuesday in Holy Week (ABC)

Psalm 71:1-12

During World War II, the Nazis set out to kill all the Jews in Europe and many other people, too. They were powerful and conquered nation after nation, but some people were brave and resisted the evil they were trying to do. In one village in France a group of boys had the courage to do what was right.

The little village of Le Chambon-sur-Lignon became famous for sheltering Jews, gypsies and other people who were fleeing the Nazis. Led by their pastor, the Rev. André Trocmé, the people of Le Chambon fed and clothed the refugees and set up orphanages for the children whose parents had been killed by the Nazis. From Le Chambon, brave women of a secret organization called CIMADE guided the refugees on foot over high mountain passes to safety in Switzerland.

This infuriated the Nazis and those who collaborated with them. Georges Lamirand, whom the Nazis had made the French Minister of Youth, wanted to turn all the boys and girls of France into little French Nazis who would hate the people the Nazis hated. He particularly wanted to control the boys and girls of Le Chambon.

On August 15, 1942, Lamirand came to Le Chambon hoping to inspire boys to join the Companions of France, a group like the Nazis' Hitler Youth. But the French Boy Scouts refused to join the Nazis and a dozen students from the high school bravely stood up to Lamirand and told them they were sheltering Jews and would never turn the refugees over to him.

Pastor Trocmé knew that the Nazis would soon invade the village, so he met with the Boy Scouts and other villagers and made a plan to protect the Jews. When the Nazis came two weeks later, someone shut down all the lights in the village and the Boy Scouts and other villagers sprung into action. All night long, they led the Jews from their homes deep into the woods that they knew well. And from these hiding places the CIMADE women took them to Switzerland.

The Nazis spent three weeks searching the village and the whole area with little luck. In one night these Boy Scouts and the other villagers saved the lives of eighty people.

Today the psalmist says that he takes shelter in God and asks God to rescue him from the wicked. In Le Chambon, God worked through Pastor Trocmé, the brave women of CIMADE, many courageous villagers and a group of Boy Scouts to rescue refugees from wicked people.

This story could also be told on Boy Scout Sunday, which is usually the second Sunday in February. A version of this story for older children appeared in *Boys' Life*, August, 1986.

Wednesday in Holy Week (ABC)

Isaiah 50:4-9a

In today's Scripture reading, the Servant of God says that God has given him the ability to comfort with one word those who are weary. And do you know what? Sometimes you really *can* help others by saying just one word. Once a little boy and a little girl did that for me.

Several years ago my wife's father died. I was feeling very sad that I would not be able to see him anymore. We had a funeral at his church—a worship service where people who knew him got together to remember things about him, to thank God for his life and to try to help each other feel a little better. After the funeral service I felt a little better, but I still was sad.

I went out for a walk, hoping that the sunshine and the fresh air would cheer me up. But I felt awfully lonely as I walked down streets where I didn't know a single person. Then the clouds moved in and covered the sun and it started raining. "Oh, no," I muttered to myself, feeling even worse, "this is all I need! Now I'm going to get all wet!"

But just then two little children did something that made me feel better. Can you guess what it was?

From across the street I heard someone say, "Hi!" I looked up, but didn't even see them at first. "Hi!" they called again. Then I saw a little boy and a little girl sitting on the front steps of their house, waiting for the rain to stop, waving at me and calling out just one word: "Hi."

I smiled at them and they smiled back. I shouted out "Hi!" and waved back to them. And suddenly I didn't feel so bad anymore.

That was all it took to make me feel better, to make me feel welcome in a town where I hardly knew anyone: just two children waving and saying "Hi!"

Often, it seems, God sends us people who can comfort us when we are sad or weary. And sometimes it only takes them a single word to help us feel better. You, too, can be someone who does this work for God. With a single word—by just saying "hi"—you may be able to comfort someone who needs cheering up.

Maundy Thursday or Holy Thursday (A)

John 13:1-15

Billy was in a bad mood when he came to class. He did not like the song his teacher wanted the class to sing, so Billy started singing his own song. Billy thought this was pretty funny, and so did Andy and Suzy, but his teacher got mad. When his teacher, Mr. Barnes, told the class a story about Palm Sunday, Billy whispered a joke to Joe. Mr. Barnes asked Billy to stop talking, but he went on telling jokes instead of listening. And then Billy poked Melissa and she hit him back. Mr. Barnes had to stop his story and pull the two of them apart.

Mr. Barnes was very frustrated; he really did not know what to do with Billy. Then he got an idea. "Come sit in my chair," Mr. Barnes told him.

Now I'm really in trouble, Billy thought. What would Mr. Barnes do to him?

"Please take your shoes off," Mr. Barnes said.

"Why?" Billy demanded, frightened even more.

"You'll understand later. Just take your shoes off."

Billy was too scared to say no.

"Now take your socks off," Mr. Barnes told him.

Then Mr. Barnes said as he got up and took off his coat, "During the last meal that Jesus ate with his friends he did something that really shocked them: He got up, took his coat off, and got a bowl of water and a towel." Then Mr. Barnes poured water into a big bowl, walked up to Billy and knelt in front of him with the water. "Maybe his disciples had been arguing and fighting among themselves, or maybe Jesus had another reason for what he did. But this is what Jesus did at that Last Supper: He did a job that slaves did, or that little boys and girls could be forced to do. He washed their feet." And with this, Mr. Barnes plunged Billy's feet into the water, washed them and dried them with the towel.

"Why—why are you doing this?" Billy asked.

"Because we all need to be loved. We need to wash away each other's mistakes, just the way Jesus told his friends to do."

Suddenly Billy started crying. He told his teacher how sorry he was about the way he had been acting. "I'm sorry I didn't see how unhappy you were when you came here this morning," Mr. Barnes replied. "You know, sometimes the men who followed Jesus wanted to show off so much that they didn't listen to Jesus either."

Mr. Barnes washed Billy's feet when he was being a real show-off. And I think Jesus washed the feet of those men to show them that if they really wanted to be important, they should serve others.

This would be a time to do foot-washing with children. For more information, see my article "A Place for Children at the Basin" in *Service* (Paulist Press), Number 1 (January-March), 1986, pp. 41-42.

Good Friday (ABC)

John 18:1—19:42 or John 19:17-30

Today's Gospel tells about how Jesus was killed and how Jesus loved us so much that he was willing to give up his own life to save us. Can you imagine loving people enough to die in order to save them? Over a hundred years ago a woman named Mary Dodge wrote this story about a little boy who loved people that much.

Once there was a little boy named Peter. He lived in the country called the Netherlands, which means "the lowlands." It is called that because much of the land in that country is even lower than the level of the sea. The clever Dutch people of the Netherlands built huge walls called dikes that hold back the North Sea so they can farm the lowland near the sea.

One night there was a terrible storm over the ocean. Peter and his sister were frightened by the flashes of lighting and the rolling boom of thunder. The wind howled and the rain pounded against their bedroom window. They heard their mother in the kitchen asking, "Will the storm break the dike?" and they heard their worried father reply, "If it does, our home will certainly be flooded."

But the next morning the storm ended and the sun came out and it was a beautiful day. That afternoon Peter bicycled to a friend's house in the next village while his sister went off to play with someone else. Later, Peter pedaled toward home on a road that ran along the top of the dike. He passed homes with smoke curling out the chimneys as families sat down for dinner and he bicycled past farms where girls were bringing cows into the barn for the night.

Then, down at the bottom of the dike, Peter saw something else: a stream of water. He hopped off his bicycle and climbed down the dike for a closer look. Sure enough, there was a hole in the dike! Water was gushing through! "I had better fix it," he told himself.

Little Peter found a small stone and stuck it into the hole. But the sea was powerful and shot it out again. Peter found a bigger rock and jammed it into the hole, but the rushing water pushed it back out. Peter saw that the hole was getting bigger and that more and more water was pouring through the dike.

"Help!" he called, but there was no one near enough to hear Peter or to see the surging water. "Maybe I should bicycle home and tell Mommy and Daddy," he thought, but he realized that by the time he got home the dike might break, flooding all the farms and homes nearby. "Help!" he screamed with all his might, but nobody heard.

And then do you know what this little boy did? He stuck his finger into that hole and held it there with all his strength. It worked! His finger plugged the hole.

As long as he held it there, his neighbors were safe!

The sun went down and it became very dark. A cold wind started to blow.

"Will wild animals attack me here?" Peter worried. "Will I die here in the cold?"

Peter knew that if he got up now he had enough strength left to make it home. But he also knew that if he pulled his finger out, the water would rush through again and the dike might break, killing many people. He bravely decided to keep his finger in the dike, even if it killed him.

In the morning Peter heard the sound of a jangling bell and saw a girl leading a cow out to the pasture. "Help!" Peter called, and she came running. Peter told her to hurry to the nearest town and bring back everyone to patch the dike. Soon he was surrounded by a crowd of people with tools and his sister and his mommy and daddy—who had been frantically searching for him all night long.

Because he risked his life, Peter saved other people. Today's Bible lesson tells us that Jesus loved us the same way. He, too, was willing to die in order to save us.

Easter Vigil (ABC)

Isaiah 54:5-14

Once, not long ago, a young boy took a long train ride. At one station a woman got on the train when it stopped. She sat down across the aisle from the boy. The train started moving again. After a while the boy noticed that the stranger was very nervous. She kept fidgeting and wringing her hands. The boy wondered what was bothering the woman. Finally he decided to ask her. "Excuse me, Ma'am," the boy said. "Are you OK?"

The woman started to say something, then stopped. She thought a moment and then spoke again, as if she just had to tell someone. "I'm going home," she said softly, "only I don't know if they want me."

"Why wouldn't they want you?" the boy asked.

"I've been in prison the past two years," the woman said. "I don't know if my husband wants me back." The little boy didn't know what to say, so he just listened. "Just before they let me out of prison, I wrote a letter to my husband. I told him that if he wanted me to come home, he should tie a yellow ribbon to our oak tree. It's down by the train tracks. That way I can see it just before the train stops at the station near our home. I told him that if I didn't see a yellow ribbon, I would just stay on the train until I was far away. Now we're coming near home, and I'm too afraid even to look."

The boy thought for a moment, then suggested, "Maybe I could watch for you."

"Oh, would you?" the woman said. "Thanks," she whispered, and then looked away. She became more and more worried as the train neared her home. The boy watched out the window and prayed very hard that there would be a yellow ribbon.

As the train slowed, the boy shouted to the worried woman. "Look! Look!"

"What is it?" the woman asked, afraid to look.

But the boy was too excited to say anything. He just pointed out the window and shouted, "Look!" There wasn't one yellow ribbon—the tree was *covered* with yellow ribbons, hundreds of bright, beautiful yellow ribbons. Every single branch had a ribbon tied on it.

The boy and the woman cried for joy. The woman hugged him and ran to the train door. As the train pulled away from the station, the boy saw the woman race toward the open arms of a husband who wanted her back very much.

Today's reading from Isaiah tells us that God loves us just as much as that husband loved his wife.

There are, of course, countless versions of this tale. Mine is loosely inspired by the folk song, which was probably itself inspired by Richard Pindell's short story, "Somebody's Son." Perhaps my version will inspire you to make this tale your own in some way.

Easter Day (A)

John 20:1-18

Once there was a young soldier named Juan Ponce de León. He was an officer in the Spanish army, and he became rich through his many exploits as a soldier. His friend, the king of Spain, made him the governor of the land that is today called the Dominican Republic, but being rich and being governor wasn't enough for Ponce de León.

Ponce de León heard that there was gold and other wealth on a nearby island which today is called Puerto Rico. He talked the king into making him governor of Puerto Rico. He then sailed to Puerto Rico with eight big warships and hundreds of soldiers.

The native people of Puerto Rico welcomed the Spaniards at first and helped them and tried to be their friends. But Ponce de León and his men stole the natives' land, stole their gold, killed thousands of natives and tried to make all the others slaves. Ponce de León was now ruler of Puerto Rico and richer than ever before.

But Ponce de León was still not happy. By the time he was fifty years old, he was a miserable old man. Then one day he overheard a slave girl say, "No one ever grows old in Bimini."

"Where is this place Bimini?" Ponce de León wanted to know.

"My parents have said that it is far, far to the north," the native girl answered. "There is a fountain there, a spring which bubbles up delicious clear water. Whoever bathes in that fountain will become young and strong. If you drink the water from that magic fountain, you will never grow old and die."

I don't know if the girl really believed it, but maybe she was smart enough to figure out that this was one way to get rid of this cruel, evil governor.

Ponce de León was determined at once to find this Fountain of Youth. He asked the king of Spain to let him conquer Bimini, wherever it might be. Ponce de León took three sailing ships and many soldiers and sailed north. (And I'll bet the natives of Puerto Rico were glad to see him go!)

When Ponce de León got to the islands which we call the Bahamas, he asked the natives if they knew where Bimini was. "Yes," a girl told him, "I have heard of Bimini and the magic fountain, but it is far north and west of here."

So Ponce de León sailed on farther, and the natives of the Bahamas breathed a sigh of relief to see him go.

Ponce de León sailed on. Then, on Easter Sunday, one of his sailors spotted land ahead. Soon they reached a beautiful, green land which Ponce de León named Florida. Ponce de León asked the natives in Florida where he could find the Fountain of Youth, and they told him about a spring of clear water. He went there and started the town of St. Augustine, the oldest city in the United States. Ponce de León drank from this fountain and bathed in it, certain that this must be the Fountain of Youth.

But Ponce de León did not become a young man again after bathing in these waters. He spent the rest of his life searching all over the southeastern part of America for the magic fountain that would keep him from growing older, but he never found it.

All around the world people know stories like this about people who looked for magic ways to keep from growing old and dying, but the magic never seems to work. In today's Gospel, however, we learn how Mary Magdalene discovered that God is stronger than any magic: The power of God brings new life to Jesus and raises him from the dead. God is even stronger than death: This is what we celebrate every Easter.

Easter Evening (ABC)

1 Corinthians 5:6-8

Once, long ago in the land of China, there was a huge lion who lived near a little bunny rabbit. The big lion was always boasting because he was very strong and thought he was better than other animals. "I'm so powerful I could crush you with one paw!" the lion snarled at the poor little bunny rabbit one day.

"I could eat you with one snap of my jaws!" the lion boasted the next day. "Maybe I'll rip you to shreds with a swipe of my sharp claws!" the lion told the rabbit the following day.

The little bunny was weak, but she was also smart. Afraid the lion really might kill her someday, she told him, "I met another lion who says he is even stronger than you are."

"Oh, yeah?" roared the lion. "Where is this guy? I'll show *him* who's boss!"

"Oh, I don't think you should go near *that* lion," said the rabbit. "He looks as big and as ferocious as you are!"

"Let me at him!" roared the lion. "Show me where he is and I'll tear him apart!"

So the rabbit led the lion to the edge of a well that had a pool of water at the bottom. The lion peered over the edge and saw a lion's face at the bottom of the well. Of course, it was his own face he was seeing reflected in the water, but he didn't know this.

The lion growled and heard a growl echo back from the bottom of the well. He bared his sharp teeth and saw his reflection at the bottom of the well baring his teeth. He swung his claws fiercely and saw the other lion do the same thing. Finally, roaring with anger, the lion leapt down into the well at his own reflection and drowned. The conceited lion died fighting himself.

Today's lesson warns us that we should not boast the way that lion did, as if we are better than others. On Easter we should celebrate what God has done without acting as if we are better than everyone else.

Second Sunday of Easter (A)

1 Peter 1:3-9

Once there was a king and a queen who had twelve sons. The queen was expecting a baby, and the king told her, "I want a daughter. If our thirteenth child is a girl, I will kill all our boys and let her inherit our kingdom and all our riches all by herself."

The queen was horrified but afraid to do anything to stop her husband. Their youngest son, Benjamin, learned about his father's plan. When a girl was born, the boys all escaped and hid deep in the woods. The twelve brothers were so angry they vowed they would kill the first girl they met.

For ten years the little girl grew up in the castle while her brothers lived in a cottage they had found in the woods. (It was an enchanted cottage, but they did not know this.) Then one day the girl found twelve little shirts in the castle and learned about the terrible injustice her father had done to her brothers. Giving up all the land and all the wealth she would inherit, the girl left the castle with the twelve shirts and went searching for her brothers.

She found the enchanted house one day while Benjamin was alone at home and the other brothers were out hunting. When Benjamin heard that she was looking for twelve brothers and saw the twelve shirts, he realized that this was the sister he had never seen before. They hugged and kissed. Then, remembering the horrible promise the brothers had made, Benjamin hid his sister under a big tub.

Soon his older brothers returned from hunting and sat down to eat the dinner Benjamin had cooked for them. Benjamin asked if they had heard any news while out hunting. No, they hadn't, they answered.

"You have been out in the world while I stayed home taking care of the house," Benjamin said with a smile, "yet I know something you don't."

"What is it?" his brothers begged him. "Please tell us!"

"I will tell you," Benjamin said, "only if you end the promise to kill the first girl we meet." They agreed. "Our sister is here!" he shouted, lifting up the tub over her. They all hugged and kissed and begged her to stay with them.

But one day the girl picked some flowers in the garden near the enchanted cottage, not knowing that there was a curse on the flowers. As she picked twelve flowers, each of her brothers was turned into a raven. Suddenly the cottage disappeared and the ravens flew away. The girl was struck with sorrow.

Then a wise woman told the girl that the only way to break the magic spell was for her to remain silent for seven years. If she spoke a single word a minute before the seven years had passed, her brothers would die. The girl vowed to keep silent all those years.

Now it happened before long that a young king rode through the woods, met the girl and fell in love with her. He asked her to marry him and become the new queen. She nodded her head yes, but said not a word.

The two of them lived happily in the castle for several years, but then the king's mother falsely accused the girl of having done all sorts of evil things.

The girl, however, would not say a word in her defense.

She was condemned to death, but still would not say a thing, for the seven years had not yet passed. She was tied to a stake in the courtyard of the castle and wood was piled around her to burn her up, but still she would not say a word. The fire was lit. As the flames began to creep toward her, there was the sound of wings in the sky. Twelve ravens came flying into the courtyard, and as each touched the ground it turned into one of her brothers. Her twelve brothers raced into the fire, kicked the wood aside and untied her.

Now their sister could tell everyone that she had done nothing wrong, that she had remained silent only to save her brothers. Her husband the king rejoiced, and he and the sister and her brothers lived happily together in the castle for a very long time.

Through many trials, the little girl's trust and love for her brothers was proven to be real. The Bible lesson for today tells us that the trials we suffer prove that our trust in God is real.

This folktale is common throughout many nations of Europe, where it is known as "The Maiden Who Seeks Her Brothers." The Grimm brothers included it in their collection, calling it "The Twelve Brothers"—although the focus of the tale is clearly on the faithful sister, not her brothers.

Third Sunday of Easter (A)

1 Peter 1:17-23

Once there was a woman named Thelma Marr who was worried. Her husband was out of work after being hurt in an accident on the job. The family got only $18.08 a week in disability pay, which was not very much money, not even back in 1953. She wondered how she would be able to get Christmas presents for their seven children.

Thelma heard that some firefighters nearby were collecting old toys and fixing them up to give to needy children at Christmas. And so, day after day, she walked three miles from her home in Thomaston, Maine, to the Camden Fire Station to help the firefighters repair toys, and she took some home for her own children.

Thelma Marr kept helping the firefighters repair toys for fifteen years. Then, in 1968, she moved the toy project into her own home. There she now collects and cleans and repairs toys for boys and girls. She also collects hats and mittens and canned food for those who have no money for food or for clothes to keep warm in the winter.

Why does she keep doing all this work? Recently she told a newspaper reporter, "It's such a good feeling knowing you're doing something for others and not for yourself, knowing that little children will have something under the tree."

Today's reading from 1 Peter tells us to "love one another earnestly from the heart." That's what Thelma Marr does. And she knows how good it feels to love this way.

Fourth Sunday of Easter (A)

Acts 2:42-47

Once there was a terrible hunger in a land far away. Everyone worried about where their next meal would come from. They hid what food they had and would not share it. Then one day three people wandered into a town and saw that there was no food for them to eat.

So these three walked to the center of town and announced: "We can make stone soup."

"Stone soup?" the people of the town asked. "How can anyone make soup from stones?"

"Bring us a huge soup pot!" said the three strangers. "Bring us some water! Bring us firewood and we will make stone soup for the whole town."

So the townspeople brought the biggest pot in town, filled it with water and put it on a fire. The three travelers carefully selected three round, smooth stones for the soup. They brought the water to a boil and tasted it. "Ah, good, but it needs some salt and other spices."

"Oh, we have some salt," said a little girl who ran home to get it to put in the soup.

"And we have garlic," said a woman, who hurried off to fetch it. Soon other townspeople had brought other spices, too.

The three strangers tasted the soup again. "Well, it is all right, but it is a bit plain. Some onions would help."

"Oh, I have onions growing in my garden," said a little boy, who gathered up a bunch for the soup.

"It's good," said the travelers as they tasted the soup again. "Ah, but it's still a bit thin. If only we had some carrots or potatoes."

"I know where there are some potatoes!" a girl shouted, remembering where her father had hidden them in his closet.

"I've got carrots and celery!" a boy said, bringing the vegetables his parents had hidden under the stove.

"Now this is an excellent soup!" pronounced one of the strangers. "Why if it had a little beans and barley, it would be fit for a king."

"Oh, but a king must have tomatoes for his soup," another of them objected.

"Ah, right you are, but I'm afraid we have no tomatoes," said the three men.

"Well, I have a few you might as well have," said the mayor begrudgingly.

"And I have some beans," the banker said.

"I suppose we can spare a little barley," offered a farmer.

So they stirred all of these into the soup, let them cook a while, then gave it a taste and exclaimed, "A soup fit for a king!" Carefully they removed the three smooth round stones from the soup. "Bring bowls and spoons everyone! Bring chairs and bread!" they called out.

And the whole town feasted on the soup. Now some said these strangers had tricked them, but others knew they had worked magic, for when everyone shared what little they had, everyone had plenty to eat.

Today's Scripture lesson tells us about a time at the very beginning of the Christian Church. The first Christians shared everything they had. They ate together and shared their food happily and freely while praising God. And just like the people who made stone soup, when they shared their food, everyone had plenty to eat.

Fifth Sunday of Easter (A)

Psalm 31:1-8

Marian Anderson is remembered by many people as the greatest singer they ever heard. When she was a little girl, she loved to sing at school and at her church. She wanted more than anything else to spend her whole life singing. When she graduated from high school, she wanted to go to a music school near her home in Philadelphia, but the school refused to accept her as a student just because she was black. Can you imagine how much it must have hurt her to be rejected just because of the color of her skin?

Marian's mother Annie Anderson was a woman of deep Christian faith. Her mother told her to keep on singing and calmly assured her that "someone would be raised up by God" to help her. Sure enough, a few weeks later Giuseppe Boghetti, one of the best singing teachers in Philadelphia, heard Marian sing. He knew at once that she had tremendous talent and said that if no music school would let Marian in, he would be her teacher.

Marian worked very hard practicing her singing and studying music. When she began to sing in concerts, some people insulted her just because of the color of her skin, but her trust in Jesus helped Marian to keep on singing.

Maybe the worst hurt of all came in the year 1939. She wanted to sing in Washington, D.C., the capital of our country. She wanted to sing at Constitution Hall where all the big concerts were held in those days. But the people who owned Constitution Hall said they couldn't let a black person sing in their building.

Some people might have given up, but Marian Anderson knew that she had to sing and she had to sing in our nation's capital. So she decided to have her concert anyway: She would sing outdoors by the statue of Abraham Lincoln, the president who freed the slaves, and invite everyone to come for free.

On Easter Sunday, 1939, a huge crowd of 75,000 people, about half of them black people and the other half white and every other color, came to the Lincoln Monument to hear Marian Anderson sing and to show that they wanted black singers to be treated fairly. Everyone said that it was one of the greatest concerts they had ever heard. Marian began by singing "America," which asks God to make all Americans brothers and sisters, "from sea to shining sea." And she ended her songs with one called "My Soul Is Anchored on the Lord."

This concert changed both Marian Anderson's life and our nation. It made her more famous, and eventually she sang for the president of the United States in the White House. She sang with the Metropolitan Opera in New York and she was chosen by the president to be a delegate from the United States to the United Nations. This concert also made many Americans start to think about how rules that were unfair to black people had to be changed.

Today's Psalm reminds us that God sees our suffering and knows our troubles. God can be like a rock that we hang onto for safety. Marian Anderson held onto Jesus the way a boat is held by an anchor to a rock when the seas are stormy. Her soul was "anchored on the Lord." If we follow Jesus and keep on trusting him the way Marian Anderson and her mother did, we will be able to do great things.

Sixth Sunday of Easter (A)

1 Peter 3:13-22

Today's Bible lesson tells us to be "zealous for what is right." I think that means to try hard to do right, even if we have to suffer because we are doing the right thing. Rosa Parks was brave enough to suffer to do right.

In the 1950's there were laws in many places in America that kept white people and black people apart. In one city called Montgomery, there was a law that said black people had to ride in the back of the buses. Even if you were old or had bags in your hands or a baby in your arms, if you were black, you had to walk to the back of the bus. If there were seats up front and none in the back, black people had to ride standing up in the back.

Rosa Parks, a Christian living in Montgomery, knew that God loved black people as much as white people. She knew that black people should be able to do anything white people were allowed to do. She knew that Jesus loved all people. Day after day, year after year, she had to sit apart from white people on the bus. She knew this was not right.

Finally, Rosa Parks knew what she had to do. She got on the bus one day and saw a seat up front. Quietly, she sat down in the seat. "What's wrong with you?" people next to her asked. "Move to the back of the bus!" But she wouldn't move. "Move to the back of the bus!" the bus driver shouted. But she knew she was right, so she just sat there. "Move to the back of the bus, or I'll have you arrested!" shouted the driver. But Rosa Parks sat right where she was.

When the police arrested her, the Rev. Martin Luther King, Jr., organized a boycott. Thousands and thousands of people in Montgomery said they would not ride the buses again until black and white people were treated the same. The buses were so empty that the law was changed in Montgomery. And slowly but steadily laws like this were changed all across America.

A Christian woman named Rosa Parks helped to bring blacks and whites together just as Jesus helped bring different kinds of people together as friends. Because of people like Rosa Parks who were "zealous for what is right," unfair laws were changed.

Ascension Day (ABC)

Acts 1:1-11

Once long ago there was a woman named Lydia. She sold beautiful purple cloth, cloth that was made into clothes for very rich people. She was a very good merchant. She made lots of money and bought a nice home in a big city in Greece called Philippi. But Lydia still wasn't happy.

Lydia had grown up worshiping the Roman gods and Greek gods, but she knew somehow that they were not real. She began visiting a Jewish synagogue to learn about the God they worshiped. She was most impressed with everything she heard there about this one God who made heaven and earth, who led the children of Israel out of slavery, who spoke through the prophets. Lydia went back over and over again to the little synagogue by the river, just outside the city walls of Philippi, and she began to worship this God herself.

Lydia was happy to be learning about God and worshiping God, but there was still something very sad. Back in those days women could not speak in a synagogue. Worse yet, there was a special way of welcoming a boy or a man into the Jewish community with a worship service and a big party, but in those days there was no way to show a girl or a woman that she was now a part of the Jewish community. Lydia loved the synagogue, but she must have wondered if she really *was* a part of the people who worshiped there.

Then one Saturday someone new came to the synagogue. He was a Jewish rabbi, or teacher, whose name was Paul. He had come from Palestine to Philippi with his friend Luke to tell people about another rabbi, Jesus of Nazareth, and about the new group of people who were following what Jesus taught.

Lydia listened to all that Paul taught about Jesus and told him that she wanted to become a follower of Jesus, too. Paul welcomed her into this group of people who followed Jesus by baptizing her and everyone who lived in her home. In Baptism women were welcomed into the Church the same way men were. Finally Lydia knew she belonged. Then Lydia welcomed Paul and Luke into *her* home. "If you think that I am faithful to the Lord," she told Paul, "come and stay at my house." Paul and Luke stayed in Lydia's home and ate there. Together they started a Church in her house, the very first Christian Church in all of Europe. And through her Church many other people heard about Jesus.

In today's Bible reading Jesus tells his followers that they will be his witnesses, telling people about him all the way from Jerusalem to the ends of the earth. That's what Paul did when he traveled to Philippi and told Lydia about Jesus. That's what Lydia did when she started a Church in her home. And maybe someday you will be witnesses for Jesus.

Seventh Sunday of Easter (A)

1 Peter 4:12-14; 5:6-11

Today's Bible lesson warns us that there will be times when people will mistreat us because we are doing what God wants us to do. It tells us that even when this happens we should still trust God. Do you know what trust means? Whom do you trust to take care of you?

Once there was a famous tightrope walker named Blondell. He had walked the tightrope in circuses for years and many people thought he was the greatest tightrope walker who had ever lived.

One day Blondell announced that he would do something no one had never done before: He would walk on a rope stretched all the way across the Niagara River between America and Canada. In fact, the rope would be stretched right over Niagara Falls, one of the biggest waterfalls in the whole world. If he fell off the rope, he would certainly be killed.

A huge crowd gathered to watch Blondell try to cross Niagara Falls. Carefully, Blondell checked the rope. Could he *really* do it? Everyone wondered. Slowly, he climbed up onto the tightrope. So much water was tumbling over the waterfall that a cloud of mist rose in the air. Slowly, the famous man walked across the rope toward the middle of the falls. The rope became wet and slippery. All the people held their breath as they watched Blondell. Slowly, cautiously, Blondell kept on going above the roaring waterfall.

The crowd roared with applause when Blondell reached the other side and jumped down. They cheered like crazy. A man pushed through the crowd and called out, "I just *knew* you could do it, Mr. Blondell! You're the greatest!"

"Tell me," Blondell said to the man. "Do you really think I'm the greatest?"

"Oh, yes!" the man said. "You could do anything on the tightrope!"

"Do you think I could walk back across this rope *carrying someone on my back*?" Blondell asked. The crowd gasped. Surely, no one could do that, they thought.

"Yes, Mr. Blondell. I think *you* could do it," the man answered.

"Tell me," Blondell asked the man, "will *you* be the person I carry?"

The man gasped this time, and so did the crowd, but then he agreed. He trusted Blondell with his life.

Blondell picked the man up, stepped back onto the tightrope and slowly carried him all the way back—above the roaring waterfall—to the other side.

Trusting God when it is dangerous means trusting God the way that man trusted the tightrope walker.

Pentecost (A)

Acts 2:1-21

Have you ever noticed how confusing it is when people don't understand each other? People in the country of Haiti tell this story about a misunderstanding:

Once upon a time the people of Haiti elected a new president to lead their country. The new president went to his new palace with his family, and there was a big parade and marching bands to welcome them to their new home. That night the President strolled through the palace and through the beautiful gardens outside. "Ah, what a fine palace we have," he thought to himself.

But very early the next morning, just after the sun came up, the President was suddenly awakened by the ear-splitting sound of metal pounding against metal. Bang! Bang! Clang! Clang!

"Who is making that terrible noise, Daddy?" the President's little girl asked as she ran into his bedroom.

"I don't know, Simone," he told his daughter. "But it's got to stop right away! Run outside and see who is making that racket."

A few minutes later his daughter returned. "Those are the two blacksmiths who live next door, Daddy," she explained. "They used to work for the president who lived here before us."

"But why are they still here making all this noise right next to our house?" the President wanted to know.

"When the old president left, he gave the blacksmiths the two houses right on the other side of our garden wall so they would have a place to make things from metal and fix things for the people from town," Simone reported. "Wasn't that nice of him to give the blacksmiths those houses, Daddy?"

"Yes, yes, I'm sure it was," he answered, "but this noise is going to drive me crazy." And the noise really was terrible. All day long the hammering continued: Bang! Bang! Clang! Clang!

After several days of this, the President, his daughter and all their family thought they really would go crazy. The noise made their ears ring. It gave them headaches. It woke them up at the crack of dawn. They couldn't hear each other talk. They couldn't even think. Finally, when they thought they couldn't stand it any longer, the President had an idea. "I know how I'll get rid of those blacksmiths," he said.

The President went to the home of the first blacksmith and said, "What a pity that you have to live in such a broken-down house. After all your years of hard work, you deserve a better home."

"You are kind to say that, Mr. President, but it's not such a bad place to live," the blacksmith answered.

"No," said the President, "you must have a new home and a new shop to work in, too. I will give you the money."

"Oh, I don't need that, Mr. President. I like the people in this neighborhood, and my best friend lives next door. I'm happy enough here," the blacksmith said.

"No, you must have a new home and a new shop," the President insisted. "Here is the money. Buy a new home anywhere you like. Don't wait, now. Move tonight!"

Then the President went next door to the other blacksmith's home and told him, too, that he deserved a new home. "But I wouldn't want to move away from my friend next door," the second blacksmith objected.

"Ah, but I happen to know that he is moving himself. Tonight, in fact. Now I insist—you really must have a new home. Here is the money. Buy one anywhere you want and get a new shop for yourself, too. Now don't delay. Move tonight!"

The President was very proud of his idea. All night long he dreamed about how wonderful his palace would be when he could have some peace and quiet, when he could hear the birds sing.

But the next morning it was not the sound of birds he heard. Once again he was awakened by the blacksmiths: Bang! Bang! Clang! Clang!

The President jumped out of bed and raced next door. "What is going on?" he shouted at the first blacksmith. "Why are you still here? I gave you money to move!"

"But Mr. President," the blacksmith protested. "I *did* move. I used to live next door. I bought this house from my friend, the other blacksmith. And he bought my house from me. Each of us has a new home and new shop and we are still near each other. Thank you for giving us the money to move!"

And with that the President threw his hands up in the air and started crying. They had not understood him! Sadly he walked back to his palace. And as he walked the hammering continued: Bang! Bang! Clang! Clang!

And that's the sort of thing that happens when people don't understand each other. Today's lesson from the Book of Acts tells us about a marvelous time when the Holy Spirit helped all the followers of Jesus understand each other. That is one of the things the Holy Spirit can do: help us understand each other.

Trinity Sunday (A)

2 Corinthians 13:5-14

In today's Scripture reading Paul writes a letter to his friends in the Church in Corinth. At the end of the letter Paul says to greet one another with a "holy kiss." One of the special things Christians do sometimes when we worship God is called the Holy Kiss, the Kiss of Peace or the Sign of Peace. We shake hands or hug each other or kiss. And we say to each other, "May the peace of Christ be with you." This is one of my favorite parts of worship. It reminds me that Christ has made us friends. When I give people the Kiss of Peace, I remember how much I want people all around the world to be friends, to be at peace and not fight each other.

Once a priest from the Cathedral of St. John the Divine in New York City went halfway around the world to make friends with people in Japan. Some people in Japan who didn't know anything about how Christians worshiped asked him to come and show them a Christian worship service. "Well," the priest said, "could you first show me how you worship in the Shinto religion here in Japan?"

So the Japanese people showed him a Shinto tea ceremony. Everyone sat very, very still and very, very quiet for a long time. Then someone brought out a beautiful bowl and fixed some special tea. Then they all drank tea from the special bowl.

Then the priest showed them a Christian worship service. It was not at all like the Shinto tea ceremony. People prayed out loud to God, people spoke out loud, people sang songs to God out loud.

But what surprised the Japanese most of all was the Kiss of Peace. Hugging and kissing while worshiping God! They had never seen anything like this in Shinto worship! But they were not just shocked by the Kiss of Peace—they also liked it.

A woman named Naohi Oeguchi picked up one of their very special tea bowls for their tea ceremony. "I want you to take this back to New York to your cathedral," she told the priest. "From now on we will call it Kiss of Peace."

See if the Kiss of Peace doesn't make you feel good inside. Could you help me share with everyone here today? You can shake hands with people, hug them, or give them a kiss—whichever you want to do. Then say, "May the peace of Christ be with you."

Sunday After Trinity Sunday (A)

The Body and Blood of Christ

1 Corinthians 10:16-17

Today's Bible lesson says that when Christians share the Eucharist, "we who are many are one body." Sometimes it seems, however, that Christians forget that they are part of the same Body of Christ, the Church.

Once there were two men who both belonged to the Mennonite Church. They had started arguing about something and had become bitter enemies. Each thought that he was right and the other was wrong. They were so angry that they would not even speak to each other.

Both men came to worship one day and, as usual, they did not even say hello to one another as they passed each other. Each pretended not to even *see* the other man, and they sat on opposite sides of the sanctuary, both looking mad.

"What am I going to do with these two people?" the pastor wondered. Then he saw that their stubbornness had to be broken, just the way the bread was broken during the Eucharist, just as the body of Jesus was broken to save us from our sin. When it was time for the foot-washing, which this Mennonite congregation always had before the Eucharist, the pastor said to the two men, "I think you should wash each other's feet."

Neither man liked this idea very much, but finally they agreed to do it. And do you know what happened? As soon as they started to wash each other's feet, they couldn't stay enemies any longer. Their feud was over in an instant. They shook hands, they embraced and they were friends once again. As they received the Eucharist together, and shared in the same loaf, they became united in the one Body of Christ once more.

This story could also be used on Maundy Thursday, particularly if you wash feet then. For more on foot-washing with children, see my article "A Place for Children at the Basin," *Service* (Paulist Press), No. 1, January-March 1986, pp. 41-42.

Sunday Between May 29 and June 4 (A)

Proper 4/Ninth Sunday of the Year/Second Sunday After Pentecost

Matthew 7:21-29

Use this story only after Trinity Sunday. If the Sunday following Trinity Sunday falls between May 24 and May 28, use Proper 3 (the Eighth Sunday After the Epiphany) that day. The date of Easter determines the number of Sunday Propers after Pentecost. In addition, Roman Catholics delay the return to Ordinary Time by celebrating the Feast of the Body and Blood of Christ on the Sunday after Trinity Sunday.

In the country of China, people say, there once was a little bird who was very beautiful and was very proud of how good he looked. The other birds laughed at him and said, "What good is it to be handsome if you don't know how to do anything?"

"Why, I can learn how to do anything I want!" the little bird answered. The very next day the little bird saw an eagle soaring through the sky. "If only I could fly like an eagle," the little bird sighed. "Please, teach me to fly," he called out to the eagle soaring overhead. "Then I can fly for miles and miles and find food to eat. Then I can soar like a hero!"

The eagle came down and showed him how to flap his wings. She patiently encouraged him to practice. For the next two days the little bird practiced flapping his wings, with the eagle helping him again and again. After two days he was able to get off the ground a little bit. But on the third day the little bird was sore all over from flapping his wings hard, and he gave up the flying lessons. "Flying is too hard!" he said.

Another day the little bird saw some ducks swimming through the water, diving under water and pulling up food to eat from the bottom of the pond. He asked the ducks to show him how to swim. The ducks began his first swimming lesson, but after a few strokes he swallowed some water. "Help!" shouted the little bird. "I'm drowning!"

"It's OK," the ducks told him calmly. "You're not drowning; you just swallowed some water. We all swallow a little water while we are learning to swim. Try again," they said. The little bird came back the next day for a second swimming lesson, but once again he swallowed a little water. Sputtering and gasping for air, he crawled out of the water and walked away. "Swimming is too hard," he said.

Later the beautiful little bird saw a robin poking her beak in the ground to find worms. "Oh, now, this is an easy way to get food," the bird thought. So he asked the robin to teach him how to find worms. "Certainly," she told him, "but you'll have to meet me early tomorrow morning to find the most worms."

The next morning the beautiful little bird got up early and met the robin. She showed him where to look for food and how to poke his beak into the ground and pull up worms. "Ugh!" he said, "This is dirty work!" But with the robin's help he found many worms that morning. The next day he got up early once again and learned even more from the robin about how to dig up food. But the third morning the little bird slept in late, and when the robin came looking for him he told her, "I don't want to learn any more digging. You get too dirty and you have to get up too early."

As fall came, the other birds built nests and stored food for the winter or traveled far away to places where they could find food for the winter. But the beautiful little bird had not learned how to build nests or how to find food. When winter came, the little bird was still beautiful, but he was also cold and hungry.

The other birds couldn't bear to see the little bird starve or freeze to death, so they all went together to see him. "Are you ready to learn now?" they asked.

"Brrr," he shivered, "Yes, there's nothing else I *can* do." So the other birds helped him build a nest and find food, and the little bird was finally able to learn from others. He not only listened to what they said, he *did* what they said.

In today's Bible lesson Jesus tells us something very much like this: It is important to not only *hear* what he tells us, but to *do* what he says.

Sunday Between June 5 and 11 (A)

Proper 5/Tenth Sunday of the Year/Third Sunday After Pentecost

Romans 4:13-18

Use this story only after Trinity Sunday.

There was once an old man in Japan who loved to drink tea. He was very fussy about how he liked to have his tea fixed and had to have just the right teakettle. One day in an old secondhand store he found a beautiful iron kettle which was used to boil water when making tea. It was very old and rusty, but he could see that underneath the rust it was beautiful. So he bought the teakettle and took it home. He cleaned and polished it until all the rust was gone and then showed his grandchildren the beautiful teakettle he had found.

His granddaughter put the kettle over a charcoal fire and they sat around waiting for the water to boil. But as the kettle grew hotter and hotter, something strange happened: The spout of the kettle became a badger head and the handle became a bushy badger tail and four little badger feet sprang out of the bottom of the kettle.

"Ouch!" it said. "It's too hot! Too hot!" And the kettle jumped off the fire and began running away on its little badger feet. The little girl raced after it, but when she caught it, it had turned back into a kettle.

"It must be a magic teakettle," the old man said. "We don't want anything like that here. We must get rid of it."

So the old man sold the magic teakettle to a junk man for a very cheap price. That night while the junk man was sleeping, he heard a voice. "Mr. Junk Man. Mr. Junk Man."

The junk man opened his eyes. He saw the teakettle with a badger head and a badger tail and four little badger feet. "Aren't you the teakettle I bought today?" the junk man asked.

"Yes, that's me," the kettle said. "I am not an ordinary kettle. That mean old man put me over a fire, so I ran away. But if you treat me kindly, I will help you so that you and your family will no longer be poor. Just don't put me over the fire again."

"How could *you* help me?" asked the junk man.

"I can do all sorts of wonderful tricks," suggested the kettle.

So the junk man built a little theater and put up a big sign which said, "See the magic teakettle and his extraordinary tricks." Every day more and more people came to see the kettle. The junk man's children sold tickets at the door. The junk man beat a drum. The kettle would sprout a badger's head and legs and tail. He would dance and do all sorts of tricks. But his very best trick came last. The kettle would walk across a tightrope holding a paper fan in one hand and an umbrella in the other. The people cheered and cheered. And after every show, the junk man gave the kettle some delicious rice cakes to eat.

The junk man's family sold so many tickets that they were no longer poor. The junk man said to his wife and children, "We have all the money we need. Why don't we let the teakettle rest?"

So he took the kettle back to the old man he had bought it from, along with some of the kettle's favorite rice cakes. The junk man gave the old man some money to take care of the teakettle and made him promise never to put it over a fire and to give it rice cakes to eat.

The old man took good care of the kettle and once in a while the junk man went to see the magic teakettle. It looked like an ordinary teakettle once again, but he thought that if he looked closely enough the shine of the kettle looked like the shine in a badger's eyes.

The junk man trusted the teakettle when it said, "I will help you if you don't put me over the fire." Today's lesson tells us to keep on trusting God, even when it's hard to trust.

Sunday Between June 12 and 18 (A)

Proper 6/Eleventh Sunday of the Year/Fourth Sunday After Pentecost

Romans 5:6-11

Use this story only after Trinity Sunday.

Today's reading tells us something that is hard to understand. It says that God became a human being—Jesus—to die for us. Why would God want to do that? Once I heard a story that helped me understand why God would do something like that.

Long ago in Hawaii there was a place on the island of Molokai where people were sent if they had a disease called Hansen's disease or leprosy. In those days doctors didn't know how to help people who had this disease. It was a terrible disease. It attacked your feet and hands and skin. First you couldn't feel anything in some part of your body. Next you got sores there. Soon the skin was rotting and ugly. Worst of all, the disease scared other people so much that no one wanted to be near you. So all the lepers—the people who had Hansen's disease—were taken to the island of Molokai and left there.

Then a Catholic priest from the country of Belgium went to Molokai to be with the lepers. His name was Father Joseph Damien de Veuster. Other people told Father Damien he was crazy to go there. "You'll catch their disease!" people warned him. "They need me," is all Father Damien said. He couldn't do much about their sickness, but at least he could stay with the people and be their friend. He came to love them very much.

Then one morning Father Damien was pouring some water into a pan. The water had been boiling on his stove and it was very hot. As Father Damien poured the hot water, some of it splashed on his bare foot. But he didn't feel any pain! He was very surprised. Then he realized what had happened. He had caught Hansen's disease. But in a very strange way, Father Damien was happy. He ran to the church sanctuary and rang the church bell. People came into the sanctuary. He leaped up into the pulpit. He spread his arms out toward the people and said, "Fellow lepers—fellow lepers."

You see, Father Damien loved the poor people who had Hansen's disease so much that he was happy to suffer and die from the sickness himself so that he could help them. I guess God loved us so much that God was willing to become a person to suffer and die to help us. God must love us very much.

Sunday Between June 19 and 25 (A)

Proper 7/Twelfth Sunday of the Year/Fifth Sunday After Pentecost

Matthew 10:24-33

Use this story only after Trinity Sunday.

In today's Bible lesson Jesus tells his followers not to be afraid because God is watching out for them. Of course, the reason he had to tell them *not* to be afraid was that they already *were* afraid. And all of us are afraid sometimes. It is easier to be brave, though, if we remember that God is watching out for us. This is the story of a frightened little girl who managed to be brave.

Sarah Winnemucca was a Native American girl who was born more than a hundred years ago, back in the days when there was still fighting between the U.S. cavalry and many tribes of Native Americans, whom the white people called "Indians." Sarah grew up in what is now part of the state of Nevada, and her family were members of the Southern Paiute tribe.

Like the other children in her tribe, Sarah was afraid of white people because she knew that whites had killed many of the people in her tribe. When Sarah became very sick, though, it was a white woman who nursed her back to health. Then Sarah was no longer so afraid of whites. Sarah became a Christian and her grandfather, who was chief of the Southern Paiutes, decided that Sarah should go to a Christian school.

It must have taken a lot of courage to leave her family, leave her tribe and make the long journey to the school, the first school she had ever seen. But Sarah eagerly went off to the Christian school. When she got there, she learned that not all whites were as kind as the woman who had helped her when she was sick. Many of the white children at the school hated Native Americans, and some of the parents said, "I don't want my child to go to school with an Indian!" You can imagine how much this hurt Sarah's feelings. Sadly, the little girl left the school and went back to her family and her tribe, who were now living on a government reservation—a place where the cavalry said her tribe had to live.

Sarah was happy to see her family and friends again, but sad to see how they were being treated on the reservation. The government agent, a man who worked for the government, was being so unfair to the tribes that lived on this reservation that two tribes had already gone to war against the U.S. cavalry. Sarah didn't want her people to go to war, so she bravely marched into a cavalry fort and told the government officials about the rotten things this government agent was doing. But the government officials wouldn't listen to Sarah. "She's just a troublemaker," they told each other, and they ordered Sarah to leave the reservation and never come back, never to see her family or friends again!

Because the government wouldn't replace their agent, the rebel tribes continued to fight against the whites. Then in 1878 the rebels from the Bannock tribe kidnapped some Southern Paiutes, including Sarah's brother and her father, and carried them away. The rebels said they would force the Southern Paiutes to join them in fighting the U.S. cavalry. Sarah was worried. Her brother and father might be killed in the fighting. Soon all the tribes for hundreds of miles around might get caught up in the warfare.

Sarah went near the Bannock camp as a scout for the cavalry, something no other cavalry scout—white or Native American, man or woman—was willing to risk. Then General Oliver Howard of the U.S. cavalry asked for Sarah's help. He needed her for an even more dangerous mission. He asked Sarah to sneak into the Bannock town, tell the Paiutes that the cavalry knew they wanted peace and help the Paiutes escape from the rebel camp to safety. And, as if this itself was not dangerous enough, the only way she could sneak into the Bannock town without being seen was to cross hundreds of miles of sharp, slippery lava from an old volcano. That was something the rebels would not expect *anyone* to be able to do. Sarah was scared, but she tried to be as brave as she was frightened. She decided to risk her life to save her tribe from war.

Sarah climbed onto a horse and rode toward the Bannock town. She rode 223 miles all by herself over the treacherous lava—three days and two nights without sleep.

The night was dark and stormy when Sarah arrived near the Bannock town. Quickly she slipped off her Paiute clothes and put on some Bannock clothing to disguise herself as one of the rebels. She had heard along the way that the rebels had made her brother a sentry, someone who protected the town from enemy attacks at night. How could she find him in the dark? How could she let him know that she was here without giving herself away and being captured by the rebels?

Then Sarah remembered a special sound that she and her brother had used when they were little children to signal each other. She prayed that her brother would remember their signal after all these years. Sarah crept toward the town, hid in a thicket of bushes and trees and called out with their old signal. But there was no answer. "*Please*, dear God," she prayed, "let him hear me. Let him remember our signal." Over and over she made the signal, hiding first behind one bush and then behind another. She repeated the signal again and again. Finally she heard an answering call: Her brother had recognized her signal!

So Sarah sneaked into the Bannock town and met her brother and her father. She told the Paiutes that the cavalry knew they didn't want to go to war. She persuaded them to follow her. Then she did what may have been the bravest thing of all: She led the captives to freedom, right out from the middle of the town where they were surrounded by 325 Bannock homes!

Maybe God was watching out for Sarah. She was able to lead her family and friends to safety and keep her tribe out of war. Later, as chief of her tribe, she struggled for six years to get farmland from the government so her tribe could grow their own food. Her courage and her stubbornness paid off: Her people were finally able to feed themselves, to be free and to live in peace.

Sunday Between June 26 and July 2 (A)

Proper 8/Thirteenth Sunday of the Year/Sixth Sunday After Pentecost

Genesis 32:22-32

When I was ten years old, my best friend Jerry and I used to wrestle every day. One day as we went outside for recess, Jerry noticed that I was looking sad. "What's wrong?" Jerry asked.

"Nothing," I said.

"Come on, what's bothering you?" Jerry asked again.

"Nothing," I said again.

"Look," Jerry said, "I can tell something is bugging you. What is it?" But I still wouldn't tell him. "All right," Jerry said. "Do I have to pull it out of you?"

Then Jerry jumped on my back and wrestled and wrestled with me until he finally forced me to say what was bothering me. And do you know what? By the time the bell rang for us to go back inside for class, I was feeling a lot better.

In today's story from the Book of Genesis, Jacob is really worried. He is going to go see his brother, hoping to settle an old argument between them, but he is afraid they will end up having an awful fight. On his way to see his brother, Jacob camps out by a stream. During the night, someone jumps on him. Jacob wrestles all night long, and just before dawn the stranger cries out, "Let me go!"

Jacob answers, "I'll let you go only if you bless me."

The stranger agrees and says, "Now you have a new name, *Israel*—which means 'he who strives with God'—because that is what you've been doing tonight!" And just the way I felt better after wrestling with Jerry, Jacob goes on his way feeling much better after wrestling with God.

Sunday Between July 3 and 9 (A)

Proper 9/Fourteenth Sunday of the Year/
Seventh Sunday After Pentecost

Romans 7:14-25a

Once upon a time there was a young princess who was very sad. She never laughed. She never even smiled. She sat the whole day staring out of the window with a sad look on her face. Her father and mother, the king and queen, brought clowns and jesters to the castle to try to make her laugh. "If you make her laugh, we'll give you a whole bag of gold," they said.

One clown made funny faces at the princess. One dressed up in silly costumes. One tried to tickle her nose with a feather. Still the princess didn't laugh. She didn't even smile.

Near the castle a poor woman lived with her son. They were so poor that there was very little food for them to eat. "Go to the castle and see if they will give you a job," the poor woman told her son.

"Don't worry, Mom," he said, "I'll find a job and bring home some food for us."

The boy was very strong, but he wasn't very smart. He found a job that day at the royal chicken coop. He gathered eggs all day. When he was done, the royal chicken keeper gave him some fresh eggs to take home. He tried to carry them home in his hands, but he didn't watch where he was going. He tripped on a rock and started to fall. His feet went one way. His hands went another way. The eggs flew into the air. He tried to catch the eggs, but they fell on the ground, they fell on his feet and they fell on his head. The princess saw him standing there with egg all over his face, but she didn't laugh.

When he got home, his mother said, "Why did you carry the eggs in your hands? If you had put them in your hat, you could have carried them without dropping them. Go back to the castle tomorrow and look for another job. See if you can get some food for us."

The next day, they let the boy work in the castle's dairy. He milked cows all day and when he was finished the royal cow keeper gave him a pail of fresh milk to take home. He started running home with the pail of milk, but some of it started to spill. He remembered what his mother said about the eggs, so do you know what he did? He poured the milk into his hat! Do you think the milk stayed in his hat? The princess saw the boy holding his hat with milk leaking out of it, but she didn't even laugh.

"Why did you pour it in your hat?" his mother yelled when he got home. "You should have carried the pail in your hands!"

The next day the boy went to the castle again hoping to find a job. The royal swineherd needed help feeding the royal pigs, so the boy worked all day feeding pigs. When he was done, the royal swineherd gave the boy a squirmy little pig to take home.

The princess looked out of her window, and do you know what she saw? There was the silly boy trying to carry a pig in his hands, saying to himself, "My mother told me to carry it in my hands." Well, the pig squirmed and wiggled right out of his hands and ran away. The princess saw the silly boy chasing the pig, but she still didn't laugh.

"Don't you have any brains at all?" his mother shouted when he got home. "You should have pulled the pig home with a rope tied around its neck!"

So the next day the boy went to the castle again to find work. He worked all day in the royal kitchen washing the royal dishes. When he was done, the royal cook gave him a great big fish to take home to his mother.

"I know what to do," he said to himself. "I'll tie a rope around it, just like Momma said." So that silly boy tied a rope around the fish and pulled it home! The cats from the castle saw the fish on the rope and, by the time the boy got home, they had eaten up almost the whole fish. The princess saw all this from her window, but she still didn't smile.

"How could you be so dumb!" his mother said. "You should have carried the fish on your shoulder. We have nothing left to eat. You have *got* to bring us some food tomorrow."

So the next day the boy went to the castle and got a job cleaning the royal barn. He worked so hard that the royal cow keeper gave him a cow to take home. "Yippee!" the boy hollered. "Now we'll have milk every day!" But he remembered what his mother said about how to carry the fish, so do you know what he did? He got down on his hands and knees and crawled under the cow. He huffed and he puffed and he tried with all his might to pick up that cow and put it on his shoulder.

Well, when the princess saw a boy trying to carry a cow, she couldn't keep from laughing. She laughed and laughed. The king and the queen heard her and ran to her room. They were so happy to see her laughing that they asked the boy and his mother to come and live in the castle with them so he could keep the princess laughing. And they were never poor again.

Today's reading from the Book of Romans tells us that we are all a lot like the poor boy in this story. We try to do things right, but often we fail. You know what, though? God loves us anyway. I sometimes think that God must be like the princess in this story. When she saw someone trying to do things right but failing, she laughed and laughed. Maybe God laughs at us, too. I know that God forgives us. As Paul writes to the Church in Rome in today's Bible lesson, "Thanks be to God who saves us through Jesus Christ our Lord!"

Sunday Between July 10 and 16 (A)

Proper 10/Fifteenth Sunday of the Year/Eighth Sunday After Pentecost

Matthew 13:1-9, 18-23

Once a young man was taking a load of Bible-story books to a town in Italy. As he was passing through a forest at night, a robber jumped on him from a tree and knocked him down. The robber pointed a gun at him and shouted, "Give me everything you've got or I'll kill you." The young man gave the robber his money. He didn't have very much and that made the robber angry. "Well, then," the robber sneered, "I will burn your precious books. Build me a great big fire."

It hurt the young man to think of burning the books with the Bible stories he loved so much. "Can I at least read a little from each book before I drop it into the fire?" the young man asked.

"Oh, all right!" the robber grumbled. "*Read.* Then burn."

The young man opened one book and read the beginning of Psalm 23. "The LORD is my shepherd," he began. "I shall not want" (Psalm 23:1).

"Well, that's not such a bad poem," the robber said. "I'll keep that one."

Next the young man opened another book and read the story of the Good Samaritan. When he had finished, the robber said, "Well, that's a pretty good story. Maybe we won't burn that book either."

When the young man had finished reading a Bible story from each of his books, the robber had decided not to burn any of them at all but to keep every single one. The robber left the young man and went off into the dark woods with all the books.

Several years later the young man was traveling through that part of Italy again, and as he passed through the same woods he recognized the face of the man coming toward him. It was the man who had robbed him several years earlier. The young man turned and started to run, but he couldn't run fast enough to get away. "Wait!" he heard as the other man caught up with him. "I want to thank you."

"Thank me?" the young man asked. "I thought you wanted to rob me again."

"No, I don't steal anymore," the man said. "I have become a Christian. I am even a clergyman now."

"But how did you change so much?" the young man asked. "What turned you from a robber into a minister?"

"Ah," the man answered with a big smile, "I read your books."

The stories from the Bible had changed a robber into a Christian minister. Today's lesson from Matthew's Gospel tells us that when we spread God's word, wonderful things will happen in all kinds of places we don't expect.

Sunday Between July 17 and 23 (A)

Proper 11/Sixteenth Sunday of the Year/Ninth Sunday After Pentecost

Romans 8:18-25

Once upon a time there were a man and a woman who loved each other very much. Not only did they love each other, the two of them wanted to have a baby whom they could love together. When they found out that the woman was going to have a baby, they were scared because they knew it could be hard sometimes to be good parents. But they were also very happy. You should have seen the smiles on their faces when they felt this new life growing inside the woman's body! You should have seen how excited they were the first time the baby kicked inside her. It felt funny, but it was OK because it told her that her baby was alive and healthy.

When it was time for the baby to be born—to come out of the woman's body—there was pain but also more excitement. It's not easy for a baby to leave a mother's body. Sometimes it hurts very much. But this mother wanted very much to have a baby and she already loved her baby very much. Then, finally, after all the waiting and groaning and hoping and loving, the baby was born.

And the baby was *you*.

Today's lesson tells us that the whole universe is groaning the way your mother did when you were born. We who believe in Christ are waiting and hoping for the wonderful future God is preparing for us, just the way mommies and daddies wait and hope for their babies to be born. Today's lesson says that the hurt we feel now isn't anything compared to the glory that will be shown to us.

Sunday Between July 24 and 30 (A)

Proper 12/Seventeenth Sunday of the Year/
Tenth Sunday After Pentecost

Exodus 3:13-20

Teach the children the chorus of "Go Down, Moses" before beginning the story. Invite them to sing it with you and shake their fingers with you on the line "Let my people go!"

Today's Bible lesson is about an argument God has with Moses. God wants Moses to do something very dangerous: return to the land he had escaped from and tell the emperor, the pharaoh, to let the slaves go and be free. God says to Moses (*sing*):

> Go down, Moses,
> Way down, in Egypt's land.
> Tell old Pharaoh
> Let my people go!

Moses objects, "Who am I to do something like this?" God answers (*sing chorus again*) and adds, "I will go with you." Moses objects that he doesn't even know God's name, and God tells him, "I am who I am. Tell them I AM sent you. Now..." (*sing chorus*).

Moses objects, "But they won't listen to me!" God answers (*sing, a little more forcefully*).

Moses protests, "But I-I can't make speeches. I d-d-don't talk so good."

God answers (*sing with more edge*). "And I will teach you what to speak."

Finally, Moses begs God: "Oh, my Lord, send, I pray, someone else."

Well, God must have been getting pretty fed up with Moses by now. God told Moses, "Enough already! Take your brother Aaron along with you and let *him* make the speeches. But I am telling you for the last time..." (*sing the chorus fiercely*).

And that's what Moses finally did.

Sunday Between July 31 and August 6 (A)

Proper 13/Eighteenth Sunday of the Year/
Eleventh Sunday After Pentecost

Romans 8:31-39

Long ago the people of Hawaii were ruled by kings and queens. The last ruler of Hawaii was a woman named Queen Liliuokalani. During her reign, many people came to the Hawaiian Islands from other countries.

Some of the newcomers did good things and some did bad things. Most worked hard and were kind to others, but a few were greedy. A group of greedy men wanted to take over the government, get rid of the Queen and run Hawaii themselves.

These greedy men got some guns, took over all the big buildings in Honolulu—the biggest town in Hawaii—and overthrew the Queen's government. Not only did these men overthrow Queen Liliuokalani, but a year later they also made her a prisoner in her own home. Guards with guns kept her in her bedroom for nine months, not letting her go out and not letting her see anyone. The shutters of her windows were even closed so that she couldn't see outside for almost a whole year. All night long, soldiers marched outside her room, keeping her from sleeping.

Some people seem to just give up when things go badly, but Liliuokalani was very strong inside. She knew that even though she was suffering, she had not done anything wrong. She knew, too, that God still loved her very much. She asked the guards to bring her a pen, some paper and her ukulele, which is a musical instrument much like a tiny guitar. Locked up as a prisoner in her own palace, Liliuokalani wrote some of the most beautiful songs in all the world. One of the songs is called "The Queen's Prayer." It says:

> O Lord, your loving mercy
> Is as wide as the skies.
> So let us look at ourselves and others
> The way you do—with love and truth.

Even while a prisoner, Liliuokalani sang about God's mercy. She knew what the Bible lesson for today tells us: Even when bad things happen, we can count on God's love and mercy, because nothing can ever separate us from God's love.

Sunday Between August 7 and 13 (A)

Proper 14/Nineteenth Sunday of the Year/
Twelfth Sunday After Pentecost

Exodus 14:19-31

Begin by teaching the children the chorus of "Wade in the Water" and inviting them to sing it with you.

Jewish people celebrate a special holiday called Passover, and so did Jesus and his friends. Every year at Passover, Jewish families have a dinner and a child asks, "Why is tonight different from all other nights?" And the child hears the story of Passover, which includes these words, "Because on this night the Lord led us out of slavery with a mighty arm and an outstretched hand." Today's Bible lesson is part of the story which is told every Passover, the story of how the Jews escaped from slavery.

As the Hebrews were escaping from Egypt where they had been slaves, they came to the Sea of Reeds. Then they saw the army of Pharaoh, ruler of Egypt, coming after them. What were they going to do? How could they get away? God told Moses to tell the Hebrews: [sing]

Wade in the water;
Wade in the water, children.

Wade in the water;
God's gonna trouble the water.

Well, the Hebrews were afraid. The Egyptian army was getting closer. So Moses did what God said to do. Moses told them (*repeat chorus*).

Then Moses stretched out his hand over the water and a strong wind came and blew back the water. Moses told them again (*sing chorus*).

So the slaves started through the Sea of Reeds. They were scared, but Moses kept telling them (*chorus*).

Pharaoh's army came into the sea after them, with swords and spears and chariots and horses. But the wheels of the chariots got stuck in the mud. Then the wind stopped blowing and the water rushed back in. The whole army was trapped in the sea. And the slaves escaped.

That's how much God wants people to be free.

Sunday Between August 14 and 20 (A)

*Proper 15/Twentieth Sunday of the Year/
Thirteenth Sunday After Pentecost*

Matthew 15:21-28

One night a farmer milked her cows before she went to bed and left a tall milk can, filled with fresh milk, standing in the barn without covering the top of the can. Two frogs came hopping by and discovered that the can was open at the top. Quick as a wink the two of them hopped right into the milk can.

But once they were inside, swimming around in all that fresh milk, they found that they couldn't get out of the can. They swam and swam and thrashed around, but still they couldn't get out. Finally, after thrashing around a little more, one tired frog said to the other frog, "It's no use trying anymore. I give up." He stopped kicking, sank to the bottom of the can and drowned. The other frog wouldn't give up, though, and kept kicking and kicking to stay afloat.

The next morning when the farmer came out to the barn to get her milk can, what do you think she found? Inside she saw one frog, tired but still alive, sitting on top of a big cake of butter that it had made by churning the milk. You see, sometimes it pays to keep kicking.

In today's Bible lesson a woman doesn't give up when Jesus and his followers try to send her away. Like the frog who kept kicking, this woman wouldn't give up until Jesus helped her daughter. The frog stayed alive, and so did this woman's daughter.

Sunday Between August 21 and 27 (A)

Proper 16/Twenty-First Sunday of the Year/ Fourteenth Sunday After Pentecost

Romans 11:33-36

Once there was a man named Squanto. He was a Native American who lived in what is now Massachusetts. He was kidnapped by the captain of an English sailing ship and taken across the wide Atlantic Ocean, far from his home. Squanto got back to America by helping another English sea captain, but this man sold Squanto as a slave—just the way a farmer might sell a cow! When Squanto finally managed to get home, after being away for fifteen years, he found that his whole tribe had caught a disease from the English people. His family, his friends and everyone he loved had died.

About this time some people came to Massachusetts from England. They were called Pilgrims. The King of England had been throwing in jail Pilgrims and Catholics and everyone else who would not worship in the King's Church. So these Pilgrims came all the way across the wide Atlantic Ocean to America in the sailing ship Mayflower to be able to worship God their own way.

The Pilgrims had very little food left by the time they reached Massachusetts. They didn't know how to hunt or fish, how to grow food in this new land or how to find wild plants. The Pilgrims were starving.

Now whom do you think God chose to save the Pilgrims? Squanto! Squanto had every reason to hate people from England, but when he saw how hungry they were, he felt sorry for them.

So Squanto welcomed these starving, frightened Pilgrims to his land. He helped them buy corn and beans from nearby tribes. He showed them how to hunt deer and turkey with a bow and arrow, how to find eels and scallops to eat, how to dig clams out of the mud, how to find the best places to fish and how to build traps to catch fish. He taught them to use big seashells from the beach as hoes. And he taught them how to grow corn, which the English had never seen before, by putting small fish in the ground with corn seeds so that the rotting fish would help the corn plants grow.

The Pilgrims had never seen most of the plants that grew in Massachusetts, so they needed Squanto to teach them which plants were good to eat and which were poisonous and which ones could be used to make medicine. Squanto also taught them how to cook fish over a fire, how to bake corn bread, and how to make popcorn and maple syrup. Even more importantly, Squanto helped them make peace with the Native American tribes that lived nearby. The natives and the Pilgrims lived in peace for a very long time, more than fifty-five years.

The Pilgrims knew that they had much to thank God for: their food, peace with their neighbors and their freedom to worship God the way they wanted. The Pilgrims had a big feast of Thanksgiving, a party that went on for three days and nights. More than ninety Native Americans came to the feast and shared food and games and songs and dancing with the Pilgrims. And the Pilgrims thanked God for their friend Squanto, whom their leader William Bradford said was "a special instrument sent by God to help us."

Certainly the Pilgrims never could have guessed that a Native American mistreated by the English would save them. Today's Bible lesson tells us that we cannot know God's ways. We can never know what amazing thing God may do next.

Sunday Between August 28 and September 3 (A)

Proper 17/Twenty-Second Sunday of the Year/
Fifteenth Sunday After Pentecost

Matthew 16:21-28

Once, long ago, there was a girl named Joan of Arc who learned how hard it was to do what God wanted.

Joan grew up in an ordinary family in a little village in France. She helped her family by harvesting crops, growing vegetables in their garden, guarding their sheep and spinning wool. Her family was poor and Joan never had a chance to go to school or to learn to read and write. But Joan's mother took her to church and Joan grew up to be an unselfish girl who had a strong sense of fairness.

Not far from Joan's village a war was going on and people were starving. English soldiers had invaded France and captured half the country. One summer day Joan saw a bright light in her garden and heard voices. She was alone in the garden. Who could be talking to her? The voices told her that she—a thirteen-year-old girl—was going to rescue the King of France! Well, would you believe a message like that? Over and over again for four years the voices returned to her and told her the same thing. Finally, she decided that the voices had to come from *God* and that she had better do what they said.

The English soldiers had already begun to surround the city of Orleans. They were trying to starve the people of Orleans into surrendering. If Orleans surrendered, the English soldiers could take over all of France. The voices told her to go and save the people of Orleans. Filled with courage and faith in God, this teenage girl marched to Orleans. When others saw that she wasn't afraid, they joined her. They marched right past all the English forts and right into the city of Orleans.

Though she was only seventeen years old, Joan went on to lead the people of France in revolt against the foreign soldiers. Led by the voices she heard, Joan and her followers drove the invaders out of most of France.

The Bible lesson for today reminds us it is very important but sometimes very hard to do what God wants us to do. It was certainly not easy for Joan of Arc to be God's messenger and to do what the voices told her to do. But when she followed God's directions, her people regained their country and she helped bring to an end a long war that soldiers and diplomats could not end.

Sunday Between September 4 and 10 (A)

Proper 18/Twenty-Third Sunday of the Year/ Sixteenth Sunday After Pentecost

Psalm 115:1-11

The Psalm for today tells us to trust God, to look to God for help and protection. The Jews of Czechoslovakia tell this old story about how God helped and protected them.

Once, long ago, great danger came to the Jewish community in Prague, a city in what is now the land of Czechoslovakia. One spring night, just before Passover, Rabbi Judah Loew had a terrible dream. In his dream he saw a little girl killed by an evil man named Thaddeus, who threw her body into a sack. Thaddeus was planning to accuse the Jews of Prague of killing this poor little girl. Then in his dream Rabbi Loew heard birds flying overhead in lines that spelled the secret name of God. In his dream the rabbi wrote down this name on a slip of paper and put it between the pages of his Bible. Next he saw a huge man of clay rising out of the ground. On his forehead was the word *emit*, which means "truth." Then the rabbi woke up.

Rabbi Loew shook with fear. Thaddeus must be planning to tell terrible lies, saying that Jews were murdering little boys and girls so that people would turn against the Jews of Prague and kill them. How could he stop evil Thaddeus?

Maybe the Bible could give him a clue, he thought. And as soon as he opened the Bible he found the slip of paper with the secret name of God. Somehow the paper had passed from his dream to his real Bible! It must be magic, he realized. Suddenly he knew that it must be possible to bring the giant to life, too.

Rabbi Loew ran to the home of his student Jacob and woke him up. Then they raced to the home of his daughter's husband, Isaac. Then they hurried to the river Moldau, where the rabbi told Isaac and Jacob to dig out enough clay to equal the weight of three people. The rabbi shaped the clay into the form of a giant. When they finished, he wrote the word *emit* on its forehead. Then he put the paper with the secret name of God in its mouth. They marched around the clay giant in a circle seven times one way and then seven times the other way.

Then the clay giant began to glow in the dark! Then it opened its eyes! Then it sat up and looked right at Rabbi Loew and nodded its head! The rabbi told Jacob and Isaac that they had made a Golem, a silent giant sent by God to protect them from evil.

Slowly, the huge Golem stood up. "Help us find where Thaddeus has hidden the body of the girl he murdered," the rabbi told the Golem. The Golem started walking back toward town, with Jacob, Isaac and Rabbi Loew following close behind. It walked right to the home of a Jewish woman. "Do you have a basement?" the rabbi asked her.

"Yes," she answered, "but I haven't used it in years." She showed them down a steep staircase to the basement, and sure enough, there was the sack!

Just then they heard voices upstairs: "Open up! Police!" Thaddeus must have told the police to look here for the murdered girl! How could they escape?

The Golem picked up the sack which held the girl's body, pulled back a rug in the corner of the basement and opened a secret door under the rug. The rabbi, Jacob and Isaac followed the Golem down a secret staircase, then closed the door behind them. They went through a dark tunnel, following the silent giant for miles. At last they came to another secret door. And where do you think they were when they went through *that* door? In the home of Thaddeus! They heard him laughing upstairs, "I've got them now! The Jews will be killed this very day!" The Golem set the body of the murdered girl down and they hurried away through the secret tunnel.

Rabbi Loew went to the police and told them they should search the house of Thaddeus. Which is exactly what they did, finding the body of the girl he had murdered. And so it came to pass that the police arrested the real killer, Thaddeus, and the Jews of Prague were protected by God.

Sunday Between September 11 and 17 (A)

Proper 19/Twenty-Fourth Sunday of the Year/
Seventeenth Sunday After Pentecost

Matthew 18:21-35

Once upon a time a mother was sitting in the living room reading the newspaper when she heard a loud crash in the kitchen. She ran to the kitchen and found the cookie jar on the floor next to her son, smashed to pieces.

"What are you doing?" she yelled at her son.

"I'm sorry, Mommy," he said. "It was an accident. I didn't mean to do it."

"OK, OK," his mother said, "I'm not going to punish you. Let's see if we can clean up this mess."

But only a few minutes after this, the boy went outside to play. His little sister was outside playing with his toy airplane and she had broken it.

"You little brat!" he shouted at his little sister. "Why did you break my plane? I'm going to beat you up!"

"I'm sorry! I'm sorry!" the little girl said. "I broke it by accident."

"I don't care if it was an accident! I'm going to beat you up!" he shouted, and he started slugging.

Their mother came running outside when she heard the little girl crying. She asked them what had happened. Then she said to her son, "You have been very mean to your sister. I forgave you when you broke the cookie jar, but you wouldn't forgive your sister when she broke the plane. That's unfair and that makes me very mad. Go to your room!"

In today's Bible lesson Jesus tells us that, if we want God to forgive us when we do something wrong, we had better forgive each other.

Sunday Between September 18 and 24 (A)

Proper 20/Twenty-Fifth Sunday of the Year/
Eighteenth Sunday After Pentecost

Matthew 20:1-16

Once upon a time long ago in China there was a poor old woman who lived with her only son. One night their only horse wandered away. All the neighbors came to them and said they were sorry that this terrible thing happened to them. "How do you know it's terrible?" the old woman replied.

Well, a week later the horse returned with a whole herd of wild horses. The neighbors helped them put the horses into a corral and congratulated them at their good luck. But a week later the boy tried to ride one of the wild horses and it threw him off, breaking his leg. "What bad luck!" the neighbors said. "How do you know it's bad luck?" the old woman replied.

Well, soon after that a Chinese warlord rode into town with his army to grab every man and boy in town to fight in his private little war. But when he saw that the old woman's son had a broken leg, the warlord left him in the town and rode away. And once again, the neighbors came and rejoiced in his good luck.

Things that seem unfair when they happen to us sometimes turn out to help us. And in today's Bible lesson Jesus reminds us that God often helps us in ways we human beings wouldn't imagine. We can never tell what amazing thing God may do next.

Sunday Between September 25 and October 1 (A)

Proper 21/Twenty-Sixth Sunday of the Year/
Nineteenth Sunday After Pentecost

Matthew 21:28-32

Once there was a woman who had a son and a daughter. She asked them both to clean up their rooms. The little girl said, "I won't do it!" Later she changed her mind and cleaned up her room. The little boy said, "Yes, Mommy, I'll do it right away," but he never did clean up his room.

Which one of these children did what their mother wanted?

In today's Bible lesson Jesus tells a story like this. A man has two sons. He tells his first son, "Go and work in the vineyard today. We need your help with the vines where our family grows grapes."

"I don't want to," his first son answers, but later he changes his mind and goes and works in the vineyard.

Then the father goes to his other son and tells him to go work in the vineyard. "Yes, sir," this son answers, but he never goes out to the vineyard to work.

Which one of these two sons did what their father wanted? Jesus says that the kingdom of God is like this family. Some people say they love God but never do anything God wants. They are not really God's people. Other people refuse at first to do what God wants. They may seem like bad people, but then they change. It is the people who do what God wants, Jesus says, even if they have refused at first or have done bad things at first, who become God's people.

Sunday Between October 2 and 8 (A)

Proper 22/Twenty-Seventh Sunday of the Year/
Twentieth Sunday After Pentecost

Philippians 3:12-21

Did anyone ever ask you to do anything that was wrong?

Octavio Paz was from Mexico and loved his country very much. He wrote beautiful poems about Mexico that people have read all around the world. Many think that he is his country's greatest writer.

Octavio Paz became a diplomat, someone who tries to help the governments of two different countries get along. Eventually the government of Mexico made him Ambassador to India, the top diplomat to one of the biggest nations in the world. He was paid a lot of money to be an ambassador. He got to live in a huge house and was driven around in a great big limousine.

Then in 1968 the government of Mexico did something very bad. The government arrested thousands of students who were demanding freedom for their universities. Soldiers shot and killed 500 students in Mexico City. People around the world were horrified by what the government of Mexico had done, but the government wanted Octavio Paz to try to convince the people of India that his government had done the right thing when it arrested and killed the students.

Many people would have been afraid to tell the truth. They might have been afraid of losing a nice job and a fancy home and an elegant limousine, but Octavio Paz was not like that. He quit his job as Mexico's ambassador and told the world, "I cannot represent a government which shoots innocent people." He was brave enough to do this even though he knew that it meant he would not be allowed to return home to the country he loved so much. Octavio Paz came to the United States and got a job teaching at Harvard University and continued working for freedom for the people of Mexico.

Today's reading from St. Paul's letter to the Church in Philippi says that Christians are "citizens of heaven." Octavio Paz knew that, in order really to be a citizen of heaven, he had to do what God wanted him to do—even if his government told him to do something else. When you and I do what is right—no matter what anyone else tells us—we are citizens of heaven.

Sunday Between October 9 and 15 (A)

Proper 23/Twenty-Eighth Sunday of the Year/ Twenty-First Sunday After Pentecost

Matthew 22:1-14

Once there was a little girl who was going to have a birthday party. She invited all her friends from school to come to her party, but no one wanted to come. "I'm sorry, but I have to go shopping that day," one boy said. "I can't come," a girl said. "My daddy is taking me to the zoo that day."

"But we've already made a birthday cake and bought balloons and planned games," said the little girl. But none of her friends would come. This made the little girl mad. "If you won't come to my party," she said, "I won't be your friend!"

And do you know what? She went out and invited all kinds of boys and girls to her party: rich children and poor children, children who had no one to play with, children who were blind and crippled, children who were good and children who were bad.

In today's lesson Jesus tells us that God is like this little girl: If some people decide not to be God's friends, God will find other friends.

Sunday Between October 16 and 22 (A)

Proper 24/Twenty-Ninth Sunday of the Year/
Twenty-Second Sunday After Pentecost

Psalm 146

Once there was a pastor named the Reverend Ben Chavis who was working hard for civil rights, trying to make sure that black people were treated fairly. Some people, though, did not like the way Reverend Chavis and his friends were stirring things up and trying to change things, so they managed to get him and nine of his friends arrested and sent to prison.

Chavis was sent to a prison where black and white and Hispanic and Native American prisoners had often fought against one another. A small group of convicts, though, had been studying the Bible together, and Chavis offered to teach the group.

Soon more and more prisoners were coming to his Bible study group. It grew from 30 prisoners to 630 prisoners, and even many guards started coming. Chavis told them, "Even though you are behind bars, you are still a child of God. You still have rights that no government can take away from you." As they studied together, the prisoners stopped fighting with each other and started working together to demand that the superintendent, the boss of the prison, treat all the convicts fairly.

This made the superintendent mad. He told Reverend Chavis, "Chavis, I'm giving you an order! Don't say anything that's not in the Bible!"

Ben Chavis was worried about what the superintendent might do to him, but when a bunch of guards came to him and asked, "Ben, you'll be back to teach us, won't you?" he knew he had to go on teaching no matter what.

At the next Bible study, the room was packed with prisoners and guards. The superintendent himself sat right behind Ben Chavis. "Well," thought Reverend Chavis, "he told me to stick to the Bible," so Chavis opened the Bible and began to read:

> The LORD is my light and my salvation;
> whom shall I fear? (Psalm 27:1a)

The superintendent squirmed in his chair. Chavis read on:

> The LORD is the stronghold of my life;
> of whom shall I be afraid? (Psalm 27:1b)

The superintendent wasn't liking this at all! Chavis kept reading,

> When evildoers assail me...

they shall stumble and fall. (Psalm 27:2a, d)

The superintendent leaped out of his chair, grabbed the Bible from Reverend Chavis and ordered the guards to take him away in chains. The superintendent figured this would scare the other prisoners, but it only made them even more determined to change things.

Finally the superintendent decided to get rid of Chavis by sending him to another prison. He told the guards to march Chavis out through the middle of the prison and to put the handcuffs on him so tight that they would hurt, hoping that this would make Reverend Chavis ashamed.

As they led Chavis away, though, the handcuff on his right wrist fell off. Ben Chavis raised his fist high, which is a way of saying that you will struggle for justice. The other prisoners saw this, rushed to the doors of their cells and raised their fists through the bars with him. Young men and old men, black prisoners and white prisoners, Hispanics and Native Americans all raised their fists to show that they were united. Even the guards who were taking Chavis away lifted their fists. The superintendent who wanted to hurt and humiliate Reverend Chavis turned out to be the one who was embarrassed!

Soon people all over the world were writing letters to the governor demanding that he let Ben Chavis out of prison, and Reverend Chavis was set free. Later a judge said that Chavis and his nine friends should never have been sent to prison in the first place. Their trial had not been fair, the judge said, and they were not guilty of breaking the law.

Today's Psalm says "God sets prisoners free." That's what God did for Ben Chavis and his friends.

Sunday Between October 23 and 29 (A)

Proper 25/Thirtieth Sunday of the Year/
Twenty-Third Sunday After Pentecost

Psalm 128

Once, not long after Jesus' time, there was a powerful king whose name was Asoka. His grandfather was the first ruler of the huge Mauryan Empire in India. Asoka's father had made the empire even bigger. Asoka wanted to make his empire bigger still: He wanted all of India to belong to him. There were only two parts of India that did not belong to him—Kalinga in the east and a little area in the south. Asoka ordered his army to attack Kalinga.

The people in Kalinga had no idea they were in danger. People were taking care of their farms, growing good things to eat. Boys and girls played games and helped their mommies and daddies. Then, suddenly, Asoka's army marched into their land and attacked them. The people of Kalinga fought hard to defend their homes, but Asoka's army was big and powerful.

Soon a boy came running into Asoka's palace with a message. "O great king," the boy said, "your army is winning." Asoka smiled.

Later another boy came with a second message: "O great king, your soldiers have killed many of the enemy. One hundred thousand people of Kalinga are dead on the battlefield." All those people killed, Asoka thought.

Soon a third messenger ran into the palace with this message: "O great king, your army has won. Kalinga is defeated. It is a great victory!"

But all Asoka could think about was all those people dying! All those fathers who would never again play with their little girls! All those mothers and boys crying and dying!

Soon the generals of his army had returned to Asoka's palace. "Your dream is coming true, O great Asoka," the generals said. "We have conquered Kalinga. We are ready now to invade the last part of India which is still not part of your great empire. We are ready to march, O king. Give the command and we will fight!"

Asoka jumped up from his throne. "No!" he said. "We will not invade the south. I feel terrible about all the people who have been hurt and killed by my war. From now on, my empire will be an empire of peace. I will never go to war again!"

Asoka was the first ruler to give up warfare when he was winning. He was also one of the first rulers who tried to teach his people how to live right.

Asoka had put up all over his empire tall stone pillars which had messages carved on them that said, "Tell the truth. Share what you have with the poor. Don't get drunk. Be kind to animals. Be fair. Be kind to travelers."

Instead of continuing to make war, Asoka's government dug wells for water, planted trees along the roads, built resthouses for travelers, built hospitals to help sick people, planted public gardens where herbs to make medicine were grown and set up parks where everyone could go to play and enjoy the trees and flowers. He also made it possible for girls and women to go to school, something they had never been allowed to do in India before this.

Instead of getting ready for war, the people of India planted orchards of fruit trees, made beautiful pictures and wrote wonderful stories. Today's Psalm tells us that God will bless with peace and good things those who do what God wants. Under the wise leadership of Asoka, the people of India did what God wanted, and they were blessed with peace and many good things.

Sunday Between October 30 and November 5 (A)

Proper 26/Thirty-First Sunday of the Year/
Twenty-Fourth Sunday After Pentecost

Matthew 23:1-12

In today's Bible lesson Jesus tells us that we shouldn't act like we're better than other people. Once there was a mouse who learned that lesson the hard way.

Once upon a time in the land of India there was a hermit—a man who lived all by himself in the forest and spent most of his time thinking and praying to God. One day the old man was sitting in the forest thinking when suddenly a tiny little mouse ran by him. A big crow came swooping down after the little mouse. The bird's claws were stretched out. The crow was just about ready to grab the mouse and gobble him up.

Quickly the old man jumped up and chased after the crow. Just in time he pulled the tiny little mouse out of the bird's claws. The kind old hermit took the mouse to his little hut in the forest. The hermit gave the mouse some rice to eat and some milk to drink. "Don't worry, little mouse," the hermit said, "I will take care of you."

Just then the hermit saw a hungry cat creeping toward the hut, wanting to eat the tiny mouse. Now this hermit knew how to work magic as well as how to pray, so he turned the tiny mouse into a great big cat.

That night, though, a big dog came through the forest and chased the cat. The hermit woke up, saw the snarling dog and turned the cat into an even bigger dog.

Not long after that a hungry tiger came prowling through the forest and was ready to pounce on the dog. Fortunately, though, the old hermit was praying nearby. With a nod of his head and a few magic words the hermit turned the dog into a tiger.

Well, you can imagine how proud this animal was now! No one would attack him now. All day long he pranced through the forest, bragging about how big he was, lording it over all the other animals and ordering them around as if he could boss everyone.

"There's no need for you to act better than others!" the hermit scolded him. "Remember, you were once just a tiny little mouse. You wouldn't even be alive if I hadn't saved you!"

"I don't have to listen to this!" the tiger muttered to himself. "I'm bigger than that old man. I'll kill him!"

So the next day, as the kind old hermit was sitting praying, the huge tiger crept up behind him. He crouched, stuck out the long, sharp claws on his front paws and started to jump down on the man.

But the hermit saw the tiger coming down on him. With a wave of his hand he turned the tiger back into a tiny little mouse. "You ungrateful beast!" the hermit cried. "So you thought you were better than everyone else, did you? Now you will be a mouse again!"

And the tiny, weak, frightened mouse ran off into the forest and was never seen again.

Sunday Between November 6 and 12 (A)

Proper 27/Thirty-Second Sunday of the Year/
Twenty-Fifth Sunday After Pentecost

Amos 5:18-24

Once, long ago, there was a British sailing ship called Her Majesty's Ship Bounty. It had huge sails and could travel all the way around the world. But the captain of the Bounty was a cruel man, and one day while sailing across the wide Pacific Ocean, the sailors revolted against their captain. The rebel sailors—or mutineers as they were called—tied up the captain and put him off the ship on a little rowboat. Then they sailed away to the island of Tahiti.

When the mutineers got to Tahiti, though, they realized that the British Navy would try to hunt them down for rebelling against their captain, so they had to sail away to someplace where even the mighty British Navy could not find them. Nine mutineers and nineteen Tahitians sailed far across the Pacific Ocean on the Bounty. Finally they reached just the sort of place they needed: a little island where no one lived called Pitcairn Island.

Once they were on Pitcairn Island, though, the British mutineers were just as cruel toward the Tahitian men and women as their captain had been to them. The British took all the land on the island for themselves and one of them took a Tahitian man's wife away from him. Another British sailor got drunk and killed himself. Then fights broke out between the British and the Tahitians which killed all the men from Tahiti and all but four of the British mutineers. Two of the four British who were left started getting drunk nearly every day: One was executed for trying to kill another sailor so he could take his Tahitian wife, and the other died from drinking too much.

The two mutineers who were left, Alexander Smith and Edward Young, felt so awful about the things they and their friends had done that they repented completely. They decided to stop doing bad things and change the way they lived.

Smith and Young started having worship services twice every Sunday, once in the morning and once in the afternoon. They began praying every morning and every evening with their families. They taught each other and the women and children on Pitcairn everything they could remember from the Bible about how God wanted them to live.

Then Smith found the Bible which had been on the Bounty and the prayer book from the ship. Alexander Smith, who later changed his name to John Adams to show that he had become a new man, had never been to school much. He could not write anything but his name and could not read very well, but he was so happy to find the Bible that he read as much of it as he could every day and told everyone what he had read.

Eighteen years later an American sailing ship stopped at Pitcairn Island. The American sailors could not believe what they found there. There were no hospitals or doctors, but everyone was healthy. There was no place for crazy people, because no one was crazy. There was no jail, because no one committed crimes. Nowhere on earth was there a place where people were safer or healthier or better than they were on Pitcairn Island.

They did exactly what today's Bible reading says: They made things fair and right. And they were happy because they did.

Sunday Between November 13 and 19 (A)

Proper 28/Thirty-Third Sunday of the Year/ Twenty-Sixth Sunday After Pentecost

Psalm 76

In the year 1982 there was a war going on in the country of Afghanistan. Few people wanted to fight in the army of Afghanistan, since it was controlled by soldiers from the Soviet Union who had invaded their country. The government of Afghanistan started drafting men and teenage boys, forcing them to be in the army. The police even started grabbing young men off the streets of Kabul, the capital city of Afghanistan, and dragging them off to the army.

Now there was a tribe of people who lived in Paktia Province in Afghanistan. For fifty years, no one from their tribe had been drafted. When these people in Paktia heard that boys and men from their tribe were being forced into the army, they were really angry.

There was a law in Afghanistan against any big gatherings of people, but the people of Paktia were too angry to sit around and do nothing. Two thousand people marched all the way from Paktia to Kabul to protest the way their brothers, fathers, husbands, uncles and friends were being drafted.

Soldiers surrounded the 2,000 people from Paktia as soon as they marched into the city, but the people would not budge. An important official from the government went to the crowd and said, "You are breaking the law! Go home right now!"

Surrounded by the government soldiers, the people from Paktia bravely stood their ground. "We will *not* leave," they told the government official. "It is wrong for the government to draft our men and boys. We are staying until you let them out of the army. Now *you* leave!"

The government official warned the people from Paktia and threatened them and had his troops point their guns at the crowd, but the people from Paktia still stood their ground. For two more days they peacefully demonstrated in Kabul, surrounded by soldiers, demanding that the government let their men and boys go.

Finally the government realized that these people were not going to give up. The government announced that no more young men from Paktia would be drafted! Soon the men and boys from Paktia were flown to Kabul and told they could go home. Without hurting a single person, the brave people of Paktia got them out of the war.

In today's lesson we hear that God breaks the weapons of war and saves the oppressed. That is what God did through the people of Paktia.

11/21/99

Sunday Between November 20 and 26 (A)

Proper 29/Christ the King/Christ the King

Matthew 25:31-46

Once upon a time in Japan there was a tiny bird, a little brown sparrow. One day this little sparrow was out playing in a garden with his friends. They were hopping merrily about, chirping and singing. Just then some mean boys and girls saw the little birds in the garden. "Let's scare those birds away!" said one child.

"Yeah, let's throw rocks at them!" said another child. So they all found rocks and threw them at the birds.

An old woman was sitting in her house listening to the beautiful songs of the birds. Suddenly she heard a flutter of wings. She turned and saw the flock of birds flying away as rocks zinged through the air. She went outside and chased the mean boys and girls away. But there in the garden was a little brown sparrow, lying on the ground with a broken leg. One of the rocks had hit his leg, and now he couldn't fly away with his friends.

"Oh, you poor bird!" cried the old woman. She picked him up and carried him into her home. For many days she cared for the little bird, giving him water to drink and rice to eat and talking to him. Each day his leg grew stronger and stronger. Finally his leg was all better. The kind old woman carried the tiny sparrow outside and said, "Good-bye, little bird. You are strong enough to fly now."

The bird happily flew in circles around her. He chirped and sang and soared high into the sky. The old woman stood outside watching him fly away. "Well, I never knew such a little bird could fly so high," she said. She watched him soar higher and higher until she couldn't see him anymore. "I'm going to miss that little bird," she said to herself.

Just then, who should come flying down to her, but the little sparrow! In his beak he carried a gourd seed. He flew around the old woman and dropped the seed at her feet. "My, my, what a polite bird you are," said the old woman. "You brought me a thank-you gift." The bird chirped to her and flew away once more.

The old woman planted the gourd seed in her garden. Soon a vine sprouted up out of the ground. Before long the vine had the biggest gourds on it that the old woman had ever seen. That summer, when the gourds had grown ripe, the old woman picked out the most beautiful gourd and took it into her house to cook. But as she set it down in her kitchen she heard a funny sound inside the gourd. "That's odd," said the old woman. She shook the big gourd, and it sounded like a rattle! She cut a hole into the top of it with a knife and turned the gourd upside down. Much to her surprise, rice poured out of the hole—lots of rice, a whole pile of rice.

This must be a magic gourd!

Well, the old woman cooked some of the rice for her dinner. There was more than she could eat all by herself, so she gave some of the rice to poor people in her neighborhood who didn't have enough food to eat. And when she got home, her gourd was filled with *more* rice. Every day she shared rice with the poor people of her neighborhood, and every day the magic gourd filled up with rice again. So now everyone in her village had plenty of rice to eat—all because an old woman was kind to a tiny little bird.

Today's Scripture reading says that God will judge us by whether or not we are kind to other people. Jesus says that whatever we do to one of the least members of his family—the poor, the hungry, strangers, prisoners—we do for him.

People in Japan say that God sent that old woman a magic gourd to thank her for being kind to the poorest of her neighbors and the smallest of birds.

Year B

Sunday Between November 27 and December 3 (B)

First Sunday of Advent

Isaiah 63:16-64:8

One day a few weeks before Christmas, a kindergarten class was playing with *dreidels*, little tops that Jewish children spin on Hanukkah, a Jewish holiday that is celebrated in December. The boys and girls had been spinning the little tops to see how long they could make them spin. Their teacher had taught them a song that said,

> Dreidel, dreidel, dreidel!
> I made it out of clay,
> and when it's baked and ready,
> the dreidel I will play.

One little girl thought about this and asked her teacher, "Can you really make a dreidel out of clay? Would it really spin?"

"Sure," he answered. "That's exactly how children did it long ago."

The little girl got up quietly and went over to the clay bucket in the classroom. She took out a ball of clay and covered up the bucket again. She picked up a pounding board and set it on a table. Then she started pounding the clay on the board to make it easier to shape. Over and over again, she picked up the clay in her hands, made it into a ball and whacked it on the board.

Finally the clay was nice and soft. The little girl pinched the clay between her fingers and shaped it into a little top. She carefully lifted it off the pounding board and took it to a sunny window to dry out. When it was all dried out, her teacher put it in an oven to bake. And when it was baked and ready, she spun it and sang the dreidel song again. She treasured that little top so much that when she saw her teacher at worship many years later she told him with a great big smile, "Do you know what? I still have the dreidel I made. And I can still sing the song you taught me."

Today's reading from the Book of Isaiah is a prayer that says that we are like clay and God is like a potter. We are all the work of God's hands. God made you and me and treasures us the way that little girl worked the clay and treasured what her hands had made.

Sunday Between December 4 and 10 (B)

Second Sunday of Advent

Psalm 85:8-13

Once there was a kindergarten class where there were lots of fights. Whenever two children became angry with each other, they would immediately haul off and clobber one another. Every time there was an argument, someone got hurt. It was awful: You never knew who might hit you next. The teacher told the children, "Don't fight," but the fights kept happening day after day.

One girl named Erika was bigger than the other children and a lot stronger. She was always raising her fist over her head and threatening to hit other kids. The teacher made Erika sit by herself whenever she started a fight, but she kept starting them. And Erika kept getting in trouble.

Then one day on the playground, something remarkable happened. A girl stepped on Erika's foot by accident. The other girl got ready to fight, but this time Erika yelled, "Ow! That hurts! *I don't like that*!"

Suddenly everyone was quiet. "She didn't hit her!" the teacher said in amazement. "I'm so glad you told her that," he said to Erika. "I'm so proud of you!"

The girl who stepped on Erika's foot was amazed, too. "I'm sorry," she said, surprised that she hadn't been clobbered. "I didn't mean to."

And do you know what? The next time two children got mad at each other, they remembered what Erika had done. "I don't like that!" a boy yelled. "Well, I didn't like what you did either," another boy answered. But they didn't hit each other. And pretty soon they were talking about it instead of fighting about it. And before long that kindergarten became a much nicer place to be.

Today's Psalm tells us that someday nations will learn what these children learned. It says that God promises peace to us if we do not go back to our foolish ways.

> Steadfast love and faithfulness will meet;
>   righteousness and peace will kiss each other. (Psalm 85:10)

Sunday Between December 11 and 17 (B)

Third Sunday of Advent

Luke 1:46b-55

Early one morning long ago, on December 9 in the year 1531, ten years after Spain had conquered Mexico, an old man named Juan Diego was walking near Mexico City. Juan was a poor Aztec Indian who worked as a weaver and a farmer. He had converted to Christianity and was on his way to church to worship.

As he was climbing a little hill, Juan Diego saw a girl about fifteen years old. She was dressed in blue-green, the Aztec royal color, and she spoke to Juan in his language—Nahuatl, the language of the Aztecs. She said to Juan, "I am Mary, the mother of the true God, through whom there is life." Then she told him to go to the bishop of Mexico City—the leader of all the Christians in that area—and ask him to build her a temple where people could worship on that hillside.

Juan went to see the bishop, but the bishop refused to listen. He went again, but still the bishop thought Juan was just a foolish old man.

Juan Diego was feeling discouraged, but the girl on the hillside asked him to go a third time and to take the bishop a gift and a message. Juan agreed, so the girl filled Juan's cape, his *tilde*, with roses that were blooming in the middle of a freezing winter! She asked Juan not to give the roses to anyone but the bishop of Mexico City.

The bishop reluctantly agreed to see the poor Aztec once again and to accept the gift from the girl, but do you know what happened when he opened Juan's *tilde*? He found not only the roses Juan brought but also a beautiful picture of the girl Juan had met, printed right on Juan's cape!

Finally the bishop was ready to hear her message. So Juan repeated what she had told him:

> I deeply desire that a temple be built for me here, so that I may show and bestow all my love, compassion, aid and protection, for I am indeed your merciful Mother: yours, your fellow-dwellers in this land and my other lovers who plead with me and confide in me; that I may hear in it their griefs and mend all their miseries, pains and afflictions.

So the bishop built a church on the hillside where Juan Diego met Mary and called it Guadalupe. Juan's *tilde* is there for everyone to see. Each year, millions of people go to Guadalupe to worship and to have a look at it. In Mary's song today, the Magnificat, Mary, the mother of Jesus, says that God, her Savior, puts poor people in places of power and gives the hungry good things to eat. And ever since

Juan Diego met Mary on that hillside, the people of Mexico have remembered Mary and believed that God helps the poor.

This story can also be used for the Feast of Our Lady of Guadalupe, December 12.

Sunday Between December 18 and 24 (B)

Fourth Sunday of Advent

Luke 1:26-38

In today's Bible story an angel, a messenger from God, tells Mary (who is probably only about fourteen years old) that she will have a baby who will save her people. But how could a teenage girl be brave enough to bring salvation to her people? Well, listen to what another girl named Harriet Tubman did.

Long ago there was a terrible thing called slavery. Black people were kidnapped in Africa and taken away from their kingdoms, from their families and from their friends. They were taken in chains to the Caribbean and to the southern states in America and sold like cattle. They were forced to work all day, six days a week and could be beaten and whipped by their masters.

Some slave owners eventually let their slaves be free, but for most slaves the only way to get their freedom was to run away from their masters and escape north to someplace where there was no slavery.

When Harriet Tubman was born on a farm in Maryland, her mother and father were slaves. That made her a slave, too, who belonged to the man who owned them. As a little girl, Harriet saw children taken away from their mothers and fathers and sold to work on other farms. When she was only six years old she herself was taken away from her family for a long time and forced to work for another master. One master of hers whipped her so badly that she had scars on her neck for the rest of her life.

Another time, when Harriet was still just a teenage girl, her owner told her to hold a runaway slave so her owner could whip him. Harriet shook her head no and the other slave took off running. When her master started to chase him, Harriet quickly blocked the doorway. Her owner was so angry about this that he hurled an iron weight at her and almost killed her. From that day, Harriet knew she would someday run away herself.

Then one night she had a dream about running away. She saw a land with a line running through it, with slavery on one side and liberty on the other. White women reached across the line to welcome Harriet. Harriet knew that God was telling her something in this dream, that if she escaped, other people would help her reach a place where she could be free.

Before long Harriet heard that her master was going to sell her and her family to an owner who lived much further south. If she was ever going to get away, now was the time. Late at night, when it was very dark, Harriet and her brother sneaked away from their master's farm and started walking north. Her brother became frightened and turned around and went back, but Harriet wouldn't give up. She prayed to God, "I'm going to hold steady onto you, and you've got to see me through."

As Harriet walked north all alone, she met both white and black women and men who helped her, just as she had dreamed. These people were part of something called the Underground Railroad, and they risked their lives to help slaves escape. They hid Harriet in their homes and barns each day. Then every night, when it was dark, she walked closer and closer to freedom. Finally she reached a free state—a state where no one was allowed to own slaves. She was free at last! "There was such a glory over everything," she said. "The sun came like gold through the trees and over the fields, and I felt like I was in heaven."

But Harriet Tubman wanted other slaves to be free, too. So in the middle of winter, she went back south and led her sister, her sister's husband and their two children through miles and miles of snow to freedom. And she went back south again and again to help other people escape. They called her "a conductor on the Underground Railroad," guiding runaway slaves to freedom.

The slaves called Harriet "Moses" because she led them to freedom the way Moses led the Israelites out of slavery to freedom. When she sneaked onto a plantation or farm, the slaves would let one another know she was there by singing,

> Go down, Moses,
> Way down in Egypt's land.
> Tell old Pharaoh
> Let my people go.

Then, late at night when it was time to meet Harriet in the woods, they sang,

> Steal away, steal away,
> Steal away to Jesus.
> Steal away, steal away home.
> I ain't got long to stay here.

Then Harriet would lead the runaway slaves through woods and swamps, across rivers and fields for miles and miles to a free state. When the slaves were no longer safe anywhere in the United States, she guided them all the way to Canada.

The slave owners offered a huge reward for anyone who could capture or kill Harriet Tubman. Many people tried, but no one ever succeeded. She led runaway slaves into the water of streams and rivers so the slave-catchers' dogs could not follow their scent. She used disguises that made her look one time like an old woman and another time like a rich young lady.

Once she disguised herself as an old woman and waded right into the middle of a crowd at Troy, New York. The police had captured a runaway slave named Charles Nalle and his owner had come to get him with guards and handcuffs. Hundreds of people who hated slavery surrounded the police and shouted "Let him go! Let him go!"

Harriet Tubman, bent over like a weak old woman, pushed her way through the crowd toward Nalle. "Watch out, granny," a police officer said, "you might get hurt." But Harriet, still bent over, kept on going, pretending she couldn't hear. Suddenly she grabbed Charles Nalle and with her powerful arms yanked him away from his master and all the guards. The guards hit her with their fists and clubs, but Harriet would not let go of Charles Nalle. While her friends blocked the way of the guards, Harriet Tubman dragged him all the way through the crowd to a boat by the river where someone else rowed him across to escape.

Harriet had a dream that someday all slaves would be free. She personally led her brothers and sisters, her mother and father and over three hundred slaves to freedom. And during the Civil War she led three hundred soldiers on a raid far behind enemy lines that freed eighty more slaves.

When all the slaves in the country were free, Harriet helped build schools for them so that they could finally have a chance to learn how to read and write. And she went on helping people. She started a home for old people who were poor and had nowhere to live. She helped start a church in upstate New York, and she spent the last years of her life working for women's rights, so that women would be treated fairly and would be able to vote.

Harriet Tubman had to be awfully brave to lead others to freedom, and she had to trust God to help her. In the same way Mary had to be brave to become the mother of Jesus and she had to trust the message she received from God. Through their faith and their courage, these girls brought salvation to their people.

You might teach the children the choruses of "Go Down, Moses" and "Steal Away to Jesus" and invite them to sing these with you.

December 24/25 (ABC)

Christmas (First Proper)/Mass at Midnight/
The Nativity of Our Lord, Midnight

See page 21

December 25 (ABC)

Christmas (Second Proper)/Mass at Dawn

See page 24

December 24/25 (ABC)

Christmas (Third Proper)/Mass During the Day/
The Nativity of Our Lord, Morning

See page 25

Sunday Between December 26 and January 1 (B)

First Sunday After Christmas/Holy Family/
First Sunday After Christmas

Luke 2:22-40

Once upon a time a tiny, little baby was born. At first this baby could not see or hear or do much of anything. All the baby could do was cry and wiggle around a little and suck milk. But after a few weeks this baby was able to see things and hear things: the face of a mother or father, the voice of a brother or sister.

Then this baby learned how to reach up and grab things, and before long, how to rock back and forth. Eventually the baby learned how to roll over and crawl. Later, this baby managed to stand up and take a step or two.

Next the baby learned how to walk, how to talk, how to listen, how to run, how to climb steps, how to laugh, how to sing, how to dance—all kinds of things. The tiny little baby had grown into a child who was bigger and stronger and smarter every day. And do you know who that child is? You! And you! And you and you and you...(*point to every child*).

That is how Jesus grew up, too. Today's reading from the Gospel according to St. Luke tells us that the child Jesus grew and became strong and very wise, and God's blessing was on him.

Sunday Between January 2 and 5 (ABC)

Second Sunday After Christmas

See page 28

January 6 or First Sunday in January (ABC)

Epiphany

See page 29

Sunday Between January 7 and 13 (B)

Baptism of the Lord/Baptism of Our Lord/
First Sunday After the Epiphany

Psalm 29

Once there was a man who was hated by millions of people. Anwar el-Sadat was born in a little village in the country of Egypt in Africa. His father was an Arab from Egypt and his mother was a black woman from the Sudan. His family was very poor and Sadat did whatever he could to survive. Sometimes he did terrible things: He was put in a British prison for helping to murder someone.

Sadat became a soldier when he got out of prison and later the vice president of Egypt. When the president of Egypt died in 1970, Sadat became the new president of his nation—and he continued to do the same awful things. He often threw people in jail if they simply disagreed with him. He even sent his army to invade the country of Israel while the people there were celebrating their holiest holy day, Yom Kippur.

But then Anwar el-Sadat did something very brave. This man who hated Israel and had started a war with Israel decided to make peace with his enemy. He did this even though he knew that Israel's other enemies would be so angry at him that they would want to kill him.

Anwar el-Sadat did what no other leader of a nation which was a neighbor of Israel had ever done. He got on a jet and flew to Israel, the nation he had fought against. He hugged the prime minister of Israel—his old enemy—and he sat down with him to talk. They talked and talked for days. And finally, these enemies became friends. With many more talks, and with the help of the president of the United States, Jimmy Carter, peace was made between Israel and Egypt.

Today's Psalm says, "May the LORD bless his people with peace!" (29:11b). Because of Sadat's courage, two nations found peace. God used an enemy of Israel to give Israel a chance for peace.

Sunday Between January 14 and 20 (B)

Second Sunday After the Epiphany/Second Sunday of the Year/ Second Sunday After the Epiphany

1 Corinthians 6:12-20

Once there were three friends named Tanya, Erica and Lisa. One morning on the playground at school, they asked their teacher, "Can you tell us a new game to play? We're tired of playing all the games we know."

Their teacher thought about this, and then he said, "I know! You could have a race. You haven't done that for a long time."

"But that wouldn't be fair!" Tanya objected. "I'm the littlest. I'll lose!"

"There you go, you spoilsport Tanya!" Lisa said.

"Yeah, what a baby you are!" Erica said. "Who wants to race with you anyway?"

"Hey, wait a minute," their teacher said. "How do you know you'll lose, Tanya?"

"I just know it!" she answered. "I'm the littlest. I'll lose!"

"Well, you can't be sure until you try a few times," she suggested.

"All right," Tanya agreed, pouting. "I'll race once."

"OK," their teacher said. "To the wall and back. Here's the finish line. On your marks! Get set! Go!"

Off they ran! Tanya barely tried at first, since she was sure she would lose, but then she noticed that she was keeping up with the other two girls. They all reached the wall at the same time. The other children on the playground started yelling, "Go, Lisa!" "Run, Erica!" and "Go, Tanya!"

The closer they got to the finish line, the farther ahead Tanya was. "Yay!" the other children cheered as Tanya crossed the finish line first.

"It's not fair!" Lisa protested angrily. "I should have won. Let's do it over!" Tanya had discovered she liked racing after all, so she agreed to run again.

And do you know who won the second race? Tanya. And do you know who won the third and fourth races? Tanya!

"I quit," Lisa finally said, gasping for breath.

"Me, too," said Erica. "I don't get it. How come Tanya beat us?" she asked the teacher.

"I don't know," he shrugged.

"Well, I'm going to win tomorrow!" Erica said.

When Erica got out of bed the next morning, the very first thing she thought about was racing at school. "I'm going to win today," she told herself. "I'm going to wear my running shoes and win that race!"

"Erica," her father called. "It's almost time to go to school. Aren't you going to have some breakfast?"

"I haven't got time," she answered, grabbing her gym shoes from the closet.

Meanwhile, at her house, Lisa was thinking about the race as she hurried to the breakfast table. She gobbled down a doughnut, took a sip of her mother's coffee and ran off to school.

At her home, though, Tanya wasn't in such a hurry. She took the time for a big bowl of oatmeal. She poured some milk into the bowl. She sliced a banana onto the oatmeal, and then she put raisins on top of it, because she liked her cereal that way. She also poured herself a big glass of orange juice to drink.

Which of these girls do you think ate the best breakfast? And which one do you think won the race at school that day?

The Bible lesson for today says to take good care of your body so you can "glorify God with your body" (1 Corinthians 6:20). Tanya did just that—and Tanya won the race.

Sunday Between January 21 and 27 (B)

Third Sunday After the Epiphany/Third Sunday of the Year/ Third Sunday After the Epiphany

Jonah 3:1-5, 10

Once there was a pilot whale named Bimbo who lived in a big tank with some dolphins at Marineland of the Pacific in California. Bimbo was one of the first pilot whales to live in a tank instead of the ocean, and for many months he lived happily with the dolphins. But suddenly he started picking on them, particularly the baby dolphins. Bimbo, who was much bigger than the dolphins, weighed as much as a car. You can image how he must have frightened the dolphins, especially the babies.

The people who worked at Marineland were worried. How could they protect the dolphins? Would they have to get rid of Bimbo? Then the director of Marineland had an idea. He had the Marineland workers let water out of Bimbo's tank until there was only about three feet of water in the bottom of it. (That's about as high as you are.) The smaller dolphins could swim around in that much water, but Bimbo couldn't move at all. Half of him was in the water and half was out.

Bimbo was stuck and he was scared. He started making a high, sharp whistle that means, "Help! Help!"

The dolphins had every reason to be mad at this big bully (and I bet they were), but when they heard his frightened whistles, they felt sorry for him, too. They swam over to Bimbo and made soft, gentle whistles that said, "You'll be OK. We're right here with you." Bimbo listened to the dolphins and calmed down. He still didn't like being stuck at the bottom of the tank, but at least he wasn't so afraid anymore.

Then the Marineland workers filled the tank up so Bimbo could swim once more. He must have remembered how scared he had been and how kind the dolphins were to him, because he changed completely. He stopped being a bully and never picked on the dolphins again. And the director of Marineland knew that Bimbo could stay.

In today's Bible lesson from the Book of Jonah God sends a prophet named Jonah to the city of Nineveh in the country we now call Iraq to warn the people there that God is going to punish them for doing bad things. But then God sees the people of Nineveh repent. They stop doing evil, just the way Bimbo stopped being a bully. And just the way the director of Marineland decided not to get rid of Bimbo, God decided not to punish the people of Nineveh.

Sunday Between January 28 and February 3 (B)

Fourth Sunday After the Epiphany/Fourth Sunday of the Year/ Fourth Sunday After the Epiphany

Deuteronomy 18:15-20

Long ago in Denmark, a man named Hans Christian Anderson told this story about an emperor who liked beautiful clothes more than anything else in the whole world:

One day two swindlers came into the land. They pretended to be weavers and said they would weave the finest cloth ever made. Not only were the colors and patterns extraordinary, but clothing made from this cloth also had a remarkable quality, they claimed: Anyone who was stupid could not see it!

"How wonderful!" thought the emperor. "If I wore clothes like that, I could tell which of the people who work for me are smart and which are stupid. I could wear it at my next parade and know which people were fit for their jobs and which ones I should get rid of."

So he gave the swindlers some money and told them to make him a new outfit immediately.

The scoundrels set up two looms in the royal palace and pretended to be hard at work—but really they had nothing on their looms at all. They demanded money to buy the finest silk and the finest gold thread, but kept the money instead. All day and late into the night they pretended to weave, but actually they were weaving nothing at all.

The emperor sent his prime minister to find out how their work was coming. "Surely he is a good one to judge the cloth," the emperor thought, "since he is very smart. No one does his job better than the prime minister."

"Bless my soul!" thought the prime minister when he looked at the empty looms. "I can't see a thing!"

"How do you like it?" one of the rogues asked him.

"Oh, dear me," thought the prime minister. "If anyone discovers I cannot see the material, I'll lose my job for sure." So he replied, "Why, it is absolutely stunning!" And that is exactly what he told the emperor, too. The swindlers asked for more money and went right on weaving nothing at all.

When the day of the parade drew near, the emperor sent the general who would lead the parade to inspect the cloth. When he looked at the looms, of course, he could not see a thing at all. "Isn't it lovely?" asked one of the scoundrels.

"No one must know how stupid I am!" thought the general. So he praised the fabric he could not see and rushed to tell the emperor how beautiful it was.

One official after another did the same thing, each afraid to appear unfit, as the swindlers pretended to take the cloth off their looms, cut the air with scissors and sew with unthreaded needles.

On the morning of the parade they went to the Emperor with their arms stretched out as if they were carrying something. "Here are your new pants, your majesty," they said. "Here is your shirt and jacket. And here is your robe. See—they are light as a feather. It will feel as if they are hardly on you at all."

The emperor was horrified that he could not see anything, but he did not want anyone to know that he could not see the clothes. So he knighted the weavers on the spot and gave them each the title "royal weaver." Then he stepped up to the mirror and took off his clothes. The weavers told him to lift one leg and then the other as he carefully stepped into the pants. They asked him to raise his arms and pulled the new shirt over his head. They buttoned the jacket and lifted the long train of his robe and handed it to two servants. As he stepped out of the palace, everyone clapped their hands in applause for the emperor's new clothes. With great dignity the emperor, the prime minister, the general and the other officials marched through the streets of the city.

"How marvelous the emperor's new clothes are!" everyone said, afraid their neighbors would think them stupid. Then one little boy saw the emperor pass by. "But he doesn't have anything on!" he laughed. "Look! The king is naked!" Soon the whole crowd was laughing and shouting, "The king is naked!"

The emperor, however, held his head up even higher and continued on his way with his servants carrying the train of a robe that wasn't there at all.

Today's Bible lesson tells us that God will send prophets to say things people may not want to hear. Like the little boy in this tale, the prophets may say that our rulers are foolish and that we have been silly to go along with their nonsense. The prophets will say the truth God wants us to hear.

Sunday Between February 4 and 10 (B)

Fifth Sunday After the Epiphany/Fifth Sunday of the Year/ Fifth Sunday After the Epiphany

1 Corinthians 9:16-23

Easter can occur as early as March 22 and as late as April 25. When Easter is early, the number of Sundays after Epiphany is reduced as necessary, from as many as nine to as few as four. In addition, the Protestant lectionaries observe the Transfiguration of the Lord on the Last Sunday After Epiphany.

A long time ago there was a prince named Harun al-Rashid. He lived in a beautiful palace in a faraway city called Baghdad. One day while he was riding his horse through the city with his family, he heard someone on the street grumbling to another person near her as she nodded toward the caliph—the king. He could not tell what the woman was saying, but he knew that she was unhappy about something.

"Why would our people be unhappy?" he asked his father when they got back to the palace.

"Why, I have no idea," the caliph said. "Everything seems to be just fine in our land. Now don't you worry about it. Just go along and play."

He was a curious little boy, though. He kept asking others if there was something wrong that might be making people unhappy, but no one who lived in the palace had any idea what it might be.

Still, he wondered what might be troubling people—and this prince was wise as well as curious. Late one night, after his family had gone to sleep, the prince crept quietly out of his room and out of the castle. He dressed himself in rags and pretended to be a poor traveler. Going from house to house, he asked for a drink or a bite of food or just a chance to warm himself by the fire. Most people welcomed him into their homes and shared what they could with him, never guessing who this poor traveler really was.

In every home the prince listened carefully to what the people talked about. He learned so much that first night about what was really happening in the land that he decided to sneak out of the castle again. Over and over again, the prince disguised himself, slipped out of the castle and wandered among the ordinary people.

He heard people say that they could not find jobs. He heard parents say that they did not have enough money to feed their children well. He heard people grumbling about how high taxes were.

"The caliph takes our money and wastes it on his army!" one man complained.

"Yes, and they also spend our taxes on all those fancy clothes the caliph's family wears!" a woman said.

"The caliph and his family live in luxury while we do not even have enough food to eat!" another person said.

After many years the prince became the caliph of Baghdad. And do you know what he did? He lowered taxes and spent less money on himself. He gave less to the army and did not buy so many fancy clothes. He made sure that everyone in his land had a job and enough food to eat. And every so often he crept out of the castle at night in disguise to see how things really were among his subjects.

Now he saw only smiles as he rode his horse through the streets of Baghdad. And what he heard from the people when he huddled in disguise with them beside the fire was that he was the wisest ruler they had ever had. Harun al-Rashid led his people well because he was willing to learn something from them. They loved him so much that someone even wrote about him in a book you may have read: *The Arabian Nights*.

We can only teach somebody something, it seems, if we become enough like them that we can learn from them. In today's Bible lesson St. Paul says that he became like other people so that he could teach them about Jesus.

Sunday Between February 11 and 17 (B)

Proper 1/Sixth Sunday of the Year/Sixth Sunday After the Epiphany

Mark 1:40-45

Long ago many people had a disease they called leprosy. (Today we call it Hansen's disease.) It wasn't really the worst way in the world to get sick, and it wasn't very easy to catch, but it frightened people terribly because of the ugly spots it made on people's skin when they caught it.

For thousands of years, nobody knew how to help lepers (that's what they called people who had leprosy) get better. And nearly everyone was so afraid of catching it that they forced the lepers to go away and live by themselves, leaving their family and friends, as soon as the spots appeared on their skin. In Hawaii, those who got leprosy could not even stay on the same island they had lived on. Lepers were forced to live on a little piece of land, a peninsula from which they could not escape, on the island of Molokai.

A young Hawaiian princess named Liliuokalani knew that she would some day lead her people as their queen. To prepare herself to rule Hawaii, she set out on a long voyage to visit the Hawaiian people, to learn more about the people she would lead. She traveled around the big island of Hawaii and met people. She sailed to Maui and talked with Hawaiians there. She visited the islands of Lanai and Oahu and Kauai and even tiny little Niihau.

And then Princess Liliuokalani decided to do something very brave: She would go to Molokai and visit the lepers.

Her friends begged her not to go. "Liliuokalani," they pleaded, "you might catch leprosy from them yourself! You could get sick and die!"

But Princess Liliuokalani went anyway. She met the lepers and gave them gifts of food and clothing and books—things they needed very badly in their poor community. She met Father Damien de Veuster, a Roman Catholic priest from Belgium who had come to Molokai to live with the lepers and show them that God still loved them, even if they were sick.

Liliuokalani later became the most beloved queen the Hawaiians ever had. They never forgot how she had showed them that, sick or well, they were all her people. In today's Bible lesson Jesus reaches out and touches a leper to make him well. He loved the leper enough to do what no one else would do: to reach out and touch.

Sunday Between February 18 and 24 (B)

Proper 2/Seventh Sunday of the Year/
Seventh Sunday After the Epiphany

Mark 2:1-12

To understand today's Gospel, I need to tell you two things about how people lived in the time of Jesus. First I need to tell you something about their houses. Most people in Palestine back then had homes made out of sticks and baked mud. The roof was flat and there was a staircase outside that went up to the roof.

The second thing I need to tell you is how people felt when they got sick. It was even worse back then to be sick than it is today. Not only did doctors not know very much about how to make you well, when people got sick in the time of Jesus they thought it was because they had done something wrong and God was punishing them. Maybe that sounds pretty silly to you, but that's what people believed back then. And if you think you're really bad, that will often make you sicker. Sometimes it will even make you so sick that you cannot move.

In today's Gospel there is a man who is paralyzed—he cannot move. And he feels he is being punished by God for his sin, for the things he has done wrong. I don't know whether he felt he was bad because he got sick or got sick because he felt he was bad, but either way, he was paralyzed and must have felt that he was very bad.

Jesus was in a house and lots of people had crowded into the house to see him and to listen to what he had to say. While he was preaching, four people came up to the house carrying the paralyzed man on a stretcher—sort of like a mat with poles along the side of it.

They couldn't even get in the door because there were so many people in the house. But they were desperate. They really wanted to get their sick friend to Jesus. They really hoped to make him well. And they really did not want to have to carry him all the way back home.

So do you know what these four men did? They carried the paralyzed man up the stairs onto the roof. Then they took the poles from his stretcher and pounded them on the roof with all their might. They smashed right through the mud roof and clawed at the pieces furiously with their hands and lowered their friend down on the mat.

Well, you can imagine how scared the people down below inside the house must have been as the roof was ripped apart. And they must have been glad they didn't invite Jesus to their house!

But Jesus saw how desperate these men were to help their friend. And he could tell that they trusted him to make him better. Jesus said to the paralyzed man, "Your sins are forgiven. Get up! Pick up your mat and go on home."

And suddenly the man was no longer paralyzed. He got up, picked up his mat and went home! And everyone in the house was amazed—and frightened—by what Jesus had done.

Sunday Between February 25 and 29 (B)

Proper 3/Eighth Sunday of the Year/Eighth Sunday After Epiphany

Hosea 2:14-20

Long ago there was a man named Thomas E. Lawrence who was trying to help Arab people win their freedom. He wanted them to have their own country, to live their own way. He became known as Lawrence of Arabia.

Once Lawrence led a group of Arabs across the desert on camels. They had almost run out of food and water. The wind started blowing hard as they rode along on their camels. Soon they were in the middle of a terrible sandstorm. They pulled the hoods of their coats over their heads to keep the stinging sand and scorching hot wind away from their faces.

After they had traveled a while through the sandstorm, someone noticed that there was a camel with no one riding it. "Whose camel is that?" Lawrence asked.

"It's Jasmin's camel," said another man.

"Who is he?" the first man asked.

"He's that guy who killed the Turkish tax collector and fled out into the desert. That's why he joined our army."

"Good riddance!" a third man said.

"Yes," said the second man, "he's weak and stupid. He probably fell off his camel."

"Well, it doesn't matter. He's no good anyway."

They rode on, but Lawrence turned around and rode back through the sandstorm for an hour and a half. All by himself, in the blazing heat and stinging sand, Lawrence looked for Jasmin. Finally Lawrence found him lying on the sand, nearly dead. Lawrence gave Jasmin the last water he had, lifted Jasmin up onto his camel and slowly rode back to his other men.

His men couldn't believe it. Their leader had risked his life to save someone like Jasmin, even if Jasmin didn't deserve it.

In today's Bible lesson God promises to give the people of Israel another chance even though they have not been faithful to God. That is the way God is: God loves us even though we don't deserve it.

Sunday Before Ash Wednesday (B)

Last Sunday After the Epiphany/Transfiguration of Our Lord

2 Corinthians 4:3-6

One day a pastor was walking down a street in Scotland when he saw a little girl he knew with a small mirror in her hand. She was catching the sunlight on her mirror and reflecting it into an upstairs window of her home on the shady side of the street.

"Hi," the pastor said. "What are you doing?"

"My brother is in that room," the little girl explained. "He's sick and can't get out of bed. He's feeling sad and miserable and doesn't even get any sunlight in his room. So I'm sending him some sunlight with my mirror."

Today's Bible lesson tells us that God shone a light into our hearts: We can see God's glory shining in the face of Jesus. When we are sad or sick or lonely, God shines light into our hearts, just the way that Scottish girl sent sunlight to her brother.

Ash Wednesday (ABC)

See page 47

First Sunday in Lent (B)

Mark 1:9-15

In today's Bible reading Jesus tells people, "Repent! Turn away from your sins." It is hard to understand what that means, isn't it? Let me tell you about someone who repented, someone who turned away from his sins.

There is a little town in Vermont that is far from any city. There was only one doctor and one nurse in this town. Everyone in town loved this doctor and this nurse. Late one night a woman was ready to have a baby and her husband called the doctor. The doctor got up, put on his clothes and drove to her house. After helping her give birth to the new baby, the doctor got in his car and headed home.

Coming the other way down that country road was another driver—someone that nobody in town liked very much, a young man who was smart but lazy. He had gone away to college but then quit school and returned to this town. He loafed around all day and raced his car at night while everyone else was trying to sleep. This night he was racing his car as usual—only this time he was drunk and could not control his car.

As the doctor neared home, the young man swerved right in front of him, lost control of his steering wheel and smashed right into the doctor's car.

A farmer heard the terrible crash, rushed to the accident and then called the nurse. She could see at once that both the young man and the doctor were hurt very badly and there was not much time to save either one of them. She rushed to the doctor as soon as she could, but he said, gasping for breath, "No. Help that young man first."

"That drunk?" she asked. "But this town needs you! You're the only doctor we've got!"

With his last bit of strength the doctor insisted, "I'm an old man who has had a long and good life. His is just beginning. Help him first."

So the nurse did as he had asked. The next morning, the young man was alive—and the doctor was dead. "See what you've done?" she screamed at the young man. "You killed the best person in this whole town, you lousy drunk! You should be dead—not him! He died so you could live! And now we have no doctor! What are you going to do about *that*?"

That day the young man's life changed. He went back to school and studied medicine. Then he returned to that little town in Vermont and he became their new doctor. And the people of that town came to love him as much as they had loved the man who gave up his life so that the young man could live.

That is what it means to *repent*: to turn your life around, to change direction, to head a new way, just as that young man did.

Second Sunday in Lent (B)

Psalm 105:1-11
Mark 8:31-38

Today's Psalm tells us to sing praise to God, and today's lesson from the Gospel tells us how important it is that we not be ashamed to follow Jesus.

In the Old West, right after the Civil War, there was a man who wasn't ashamed to follow Jesus. Willie Van Orsdell went all the way from the eastern part of America to the Montana territory to be a missionary to the Blackfoot tribe. Along the way he stopped at the frontier town of Fort Benton and walked into a saloon. Before him at the long bar were all the Sunday morning customers, and they were a pretty tough crowd. The bartenders had to wear pistols in holsters strapped over their white aprons.

Willie was thinking of leaving when a cowboy grabbed his elbow and said, "This ain't no place for preachin'! You better leave before it's too late!"

"No," Willie replied. "I came to Montana to preach and I might as well start here." He went to the owner of the saloon and said, "I want to have a worship service here this morning."

"Worship?" the owner laughed. "This here is a saloon."

Other men at the bar laughed, too. Some started talking about "initiating" this stranger: tarring and feathering him and throwing him in the river!

The cowboy who had grabbed Willie's elbow spoke up and said, "Hey! This man's traveled all the way from back East to preach here. You forget that we were all strangers here once." Other customers started arguing with the cowboy, and some got up and left.

Then the saloon owner whistled as loud as he could and shouted, "I'm telling this man he can preach here. And any of you that don't want to stay is a coward! We're all sinners and anything this man has to say won't hurt us none."

Willie didn't know what to say next, but the words of a hymn came to his mind, so he just sang it. And soon the saloon's piano player was playing along with him, the stub of a cigar still in his mouth. After the hymn he started to say something, but a man called out, "Don't talk. Just sing. I ain't heard singing like that since my mother sang me lullabies."

So Willie Van Orsdell sang another hymn and a few men sang along with him. They sang it through three times before Willie said anything at all. By then the people in the saloon were ready to listen to him—and eager for him to lead them in worship the next time he was in town.

That is how the very first Christian worship service ever happened in Montana: One man who wasn't ashamed to follow Jesus sang praise to God in a saloon.

Third Sunday in Lent (B)

Exodus 20:1-17

In today's Bible lesson God gives the Israelites the Ten Commandments. In the very first commandment God says to "worship no god but me. Do not bow down and worship any picture or statue, because I am your God and I want all your love."

People keep trying, though, to get us to worship someone or something besides God. Pontius Pilate, the Roman governor who condemned Jesus to be executed, tried a few years earlier to get the Jews to worship someone besides God. And this is what happened:

In the year A.D. 26, when Jesus was a young man but before he had done anything anyone heard about, Pontius Pilate was sent by the Roman Emperor Tiberias to rule Palestine as the procurator or governor. Pilate wanted to do something to please the emperor and to force the Jews to obey him, and he thought he knew just what would do it. He sent the Roman army from his headquarters in Caesarea into the holy city Jerusalem and ordered them to fly their military flag, with a picture of Tiberias on it, on the fortress that overlooked the sacred Temple in Jerusalem. "I'll show them who is boss!" Pilate said.

The commander of the army, who had been in Palestine a long time, warned Pilate that the Jewish people would be outraged if they did this. "You see, they do not worship the emperor the way we do," he explained. "They believe there is only one God. We have never brought our flags or statues of the emperor near the Jewish Temple for fear of provoking a revolt."

"Just let them try it!" Pilate roared. "We'll kill them! Surround the city at once and put up the flag!"

So the Roman legions surrounded Jerusalem during the night and raised their flag, with its picture of the emperor, high above the Temple. The next morning the city was in an uproar. The Jewish people were wild with rage, but what could they do with fully armed soldiers surrounding them? Any revolt would end in a terrible slaughter.

That very day a huge group of Jews began walking to Pilate's palace in Caesarea. They gathered under his balcony and shouted, "We beg you: Please remove the picture of the emperor from Jerusalem!"

"Go home!" Pilate coldly answered. "The flag will stay where it is. Tiberias is your lord!" With that he went back into his house—but continued to watch them secretly through a window, ready to order his soldiers to kill them all at the first sign of rebellion.

But the Jews did not revolt—and they did not leave. To Pilate's amazement, they all knelt where they were and started to pray.

The next morning they were still there. They shouted one more time, "Remove the picture of the emperor!" Pilate did not even answer them this time, but they still would not leave. For five days they remained in front of his house, praying that he would remove the flag that offended them so much.

Finally, on the sixth day he sent word that he would meet with them in the center of Caesarea, where he had his throne. Then he told his soldiers to hide nearby.

As the Jews assembled before him, Pilate asked, "Now, what is it you want?"

They shouted together again, "Remove the picture of the emperor!" At a signal from Pilate, the soldiers came out of hiding and surrounded the Jews. "If anyone says another word about the emperor's picture," Pilate yelled, "they will be killed at once!"

A silence fell over the crowd.

Then a young Jew walked up, knelt down before Pilate's throne, pulled his coat back to expose his neck and said, "Kill me, then, for I would rather die than see the emperor's picture defile the holy Temple of my Creator."

And in an instant, all the other Jews knelt silently and bared their necks, too.

Pilate knew then that their faith in God was more mighty than his army. "The flag with the emperor's picture will be removed from Jerusalem," he said.

The soldiers left and the Jews got up silently and returned to Jerusalem, giving thanks to God, the only one they would worship.

Fourth Sunday in Lent (B)

2 Chronicles 36:14-23

Long ago, in the seventh century, there was a woman named Baiko-san who lived in Japan. Like most people in Japan, she was not a Christian. In fact, she had never heard of Jesus or Christianity; she worshiped the Shinto gods and goddesses.

Baiko-san's husband was a priest in the Shinto religion. They lived at a little shrine among tall pine trees, overlooking a river, in a little village called Makido. They never turned away anyone who needed help. After being a priest for only a year, though, Baiko-san's husband died, and Baiko-san moved far away.

One priest after another came to work in Makido, but the villagers did not like any of them very much. Finally, two villagers were sent to find Baiko-san. They walked over a hundred miles on foot. And when they found her they begged her to return to their village to be their priest.

"But how can I be your priest?" she asked, for there were still no women priests in the Shinto religion in those days.

"You are the only priest we want," the villagers answered.

"I think about your village every day," she admitted. "I really do miss it. Nothing would make me happier than to return to your shrine!"

So Baiko-san happily returned to the little shrine in Makido. She cared for the villagers when they were sick and helped those who did not know how to read. She loved to tell stories to the children of the village and to answer their questions. When families had problems they often went to Baiko-san to talk about things with her.

One night, though, Baiko-san woke up suddenly and saw something that nearly frightened her to death. A robber was standing over her and holding a sword right over her head!

"Get up, you old hag!" he shouted at her. "Get up and show me where the money is!"

"What money?" she asked.

"People came to this shrine last night," the thief said. "They must have left an offering. Give it to me or I'll stab you like this!" And he slashed his sword through the mat right next to her.

"Young man," Baiko-san calmly replied, "you could certainly kill me with your sword, but what will happen to you then? I am ready to die, but what will happen to your soul? As for money, I have saved a little. It is in a jar by the altar. Help yourself to what little is there, but there isn't any more. Good night." Saying that, Baiko-san rolled over and went back to sleep! Can you imagine going to sleep with a robber holding a sword over you?

When Baiko-san woke up the next morning, it all seemed like a dream. When she saw the hole beside her in the mat, though, she knew a thief really had been there. But do you know what? All her money was still in the jar near the altar! The robber had not robbed her! Perhaps by offering to give the money to him and by asking him to think about what would happen to his soul, this Shinto priest had helped him—and then he could not steal from her.

Today's Bible lesson tells us that God used King Cyrus of Persia (which is called Iran today) to build a great temple for God in Jerusalem, even though Cyrus did not believe in God. Just as God used a woman like Baiko-san who was not a Christian to do something good, God can use people who do not even believe in God to do good things.

For further information, see Allan Hunter, *Courage in Both Hands*, and Michi Kawaii, *My Lantern* (Tokyo: Kyo Bun Kiwan, 1939), pp. 1-11.

Fifth Sunday in Lent (B)

Jeremiah 31:31-34

Did you ever find it hard to remember to do something you were supposed to do? Once there was a little boy who wanted to have a goldfish. His mother bought him a tiny fish and a fishbowl but told him, "You will have to feed this just a little food every day."

The little boy *wanted* to take care of his fish, but he kept forgetting to feed it. He had a hard time waking up in the morning and often forgot to feed the goldfish before he went to school. And when he came home from school in the afternoon, there were so many other things to do that he often forgot again. Some days he did not feed the goldfish at all. On other days he tried to make up for it by giving the tiny fish twice as much food as it should have. Pretty soon the little goldfish died.

The little boy wanted another goldfish, but his mother thought for a long time about whether or not to give the boy another one. She was afraid that he would still forget to feed it each day. She did not want another goldfish to die. Then she thought of something.

She went to the pet shop and bought another fish for her son. Then she drew a picture of a goldfish and wrote on her drawing the word *remember*. Then she put the picture in the bathroom, right next to the boy's toothbrush.

Now the boy could not possibly forget. Every morning and every evening when he brushed his teeth, there was the picture to remind him what he needed to do. The boy took very good care of the second goldfish and remembered to feed it every day.

In today's Scripture lesson the prophet Jeremiah tells us that God, like that little boy's mother, knows how easily we forget the things we are supposed to do. Jeremiah says that God will write in our hearts what we should do, just the way this little boy's mother wrote "remember" on the picture of the goldfish.

Passion Sunday or Palm Sunday (B)

Mark 14:1—15:47

Once there was a painter whose life was both wonderful and painful. Her name was Mary Cassatt, and she was born in America in Pittsburgh in 1844. Very few women were artists when Mary was a little girl, but both she and her family could see how much she loved to paint and how good she was at it. So when Mary was a teenager, only seventeen years old, she went to the Pennsylvania Academy of Fine Arts to learn more about painting. Four years later she moved to Paris in France to continue her study of art.

When she was still just a young woman, Mary began showing her work with a group of artists called the Impressionists, who are my favorite painters in the whole world. She wanted to show people what life seemed like from a woman's point of view and that she did, with beautiful paintings that showed the happiness of a woman reading a book she loved, the quiet joy of taking your child for a ride in a rowboat, the pleasure of driving a horse and buggy.

Mary Cassatt, who had learned so much from the artists of another country, France, wanted the people of France and America to learn more about art from Japan, so she worked on a series of aquatints—printed pictures—that are probably the finest colored prints anyone has ever created. Mary Cassatt was soon recognized both in France and America as the best American artist of her time.

There was much sadness in Mary Cassatt's life, too, but she used the pain she felt to do wonderful things. She had felt how women were often kept from expressing themselves, so she sold some of her paintings to raise money for women in America who were struggling to get the right to vote in elections. Mary loved children but never had a child herself. This must have hurt sometimes, but do you know what she did? She spent the later part of her life painting many pictures of mothers and their children, showing them the way they really were and showing more of their feelings than nearly anyone before her had ever done.

The most painful thing that happened to her was losing her eyesight. But, as it got harder for her to see, she decided to try a whole new kind of art, using pastel paints that were easier for her to use with little vision. And even when she became completely blind, she continued to be an important advocate for the Impressionist painters, telling people about their work.

I used to have a hard time understanding today's Bible lesson. Why did Jesus have to suffer? How could God let terrible things happen to a good person like Jesus or Mary Cassatt? But now I see that some people like Mary Cassatt can use their suffering to do beautiful things. In much the same way, God uses the pain that Jesus felt to help us, to make us better and to show us how much God loves us.

Passion Sunday or Palm Sunday (B)

Mark 11:1-11

Today's Bible story tells us how Jesus came into Jerusalem on the very first Palm Sunday. Crowds of people waved palm branches as Jesus entered the city. But he did not ride into the holy city on a big tall horse or in a war chariot the way most kings did. To show that he was the Prince of Peace, he rode on the back of a little donkey. People did not understand this, of course, since they wanted a warrior king who would lead an army against their enemies. Ever since then, it seems, people keep forgetting what kind of a ruler Jesus is: one who wants not to conquer others but to save everyone. This is the story of how one man was reminded who Jesus really is.

Long ago in the country of France there was a bishop—the leader of many Christians—who was also a poet and a teacher: Theodulph. King Louis I got very mad at Theodulph because he thought Theodulph was his enemy. The king had the bishop taken to the city of Angers and thrown in prison.

Some time after this King Louis proudly led a Palm Sunday parade through the streets of Angers. As he passed by the prison he heard a voice singing out loud and clear from a tower *(sing)*:

> All glory, laud and honor
> To thee, Redeemer King!

"Stop the parade!" King Louis ordered with a big smile. "I want to hear this wonderful new song from one of my loyal subjects!"

The parade stopped and everyone listened, trying to figure out where the singing was coming from. Soon the king was surprised to see people pointing to the prison tower. "Who is that who is singing?" Louis asked. Everyone listened some more.

"I know that voice!" a little girl shouted out. "I used to hear it in church! It's the bishop—Bishop Theodulph!"

"Bishop Theodulph?" the king sputtered. "Perhaps he is not my enemy after all if he sings such a greeting to me."

As everyone listened, Theodulph kept singing *(sing)*:

> ...To whom the lips of children
> Made sweet hosannas ring.

You know how children like to learn new songs, especially songs about children, so soon the children of Angers were singing *(sing)*:

> All glory, laud and honor

To thee, Redeemer King!
To whom the lips of children
Made sweet hosannas ring.

Slowly King Louis realized that no children had sung hosannas to him when he came into Angers. This wasn't a song about Louis's Palm Sunday parade; this was a song about the *first* Palm Sunday. It was a song about how the little children welcomed Jesus into Jerusalem with shouts of "Hosanna!"

And then King Louis realized that Theodulph was not his enemy but was only trying to be faithful to Jesus, the Prince of Peace whom the parade was supposed to honor. "Let him out of prison!" the king called to the guards.

As the children of Angers kept singing "All Glory Laud and Honor," King Louis started the parade again, a little more humbly than before. And this time he remembered what Theodulph's song taught him: that the Palm Sunday parade was really for Jesus, the Prince of Peace.

Monday in Holy Week (ABC)

See page 55

Tuesday in Holy Week (ABC)

See page 56

Wednesday in Holy Week (ABC)

See page 57

Maundy Thursday or Holy Thursday (B)

Mark 14:12-26

One of the hardest things to understand in this morning's Bible lesson is what Jesus tells his friends: that he loves them enough to let his body be broken for them. Can you imagine loving people enough to do that?

In Japan there is a railroad train which goes up a steep mountainside. One day, as usual, hundreds of people piled into the train on their way home from work, including a teenage boy who worked in a factory and who climbed into the last car. We don't know what he was doing as the train pulled out of the station. Maybe he was talking to friends or reading the newspaper. Maybe he was tired and was trying to nap. He was a Christian, so maybe he was reading the Bible. Slowly the train started up the mountain.

Then something terrible happened. A little piece of metal broke in the coupling, the part that held the last car to the rest of the train. The engine and the other cars kept chugging up the hillside, but the last car stopped—and then started to roll back down the mountain. It crept slowly at first, but then picked up speed, rolling down faster and faster. Suddenly, everyone in the car realized what was happening and panicked. They started screaming and crying, knowing that soon their car would be barreling down the mountain so fast that it would fly off the tracks at the first curve. They all might be killed.

No one knew what to do, but the boy knew he had to do something. He climbed outside the car and found the big brake. He pulled and pulled on it, but it did not slow down the train very much. If only they could slow down enough to roll off the tracks in a safe place where they wouldn't be hurt!

The boy pulled on the brake with all his strength until he couldn't pull anymore. Then he saw that there was only one way to stop the train car. He lowered himself between the wheels of the train. The wheels crushed his body and killed him, but the car came to a stop. Everyone on the train car was saved.

The boy did not even know most of the people on that car, but he gave up his own life to save them. And that is how much Jesus loves me and you and the whole world. When Christians share the Eucharist (Communion, the Lord's Supper), we remember that he loved us enough to let his body be broken for us.

I must warn you that you cannot tell some stories, true though they may be, without offending some parents. In one parish where I told this children's sermon, outraged parents protested that this was simply too gruesome for their children to hear. Reminding them that the crucifixion itself was gory but taking their criticism seriously, I visited each Sunday School class and asked the children which stories they liked best and which least—and what they remembered about them. Guess which was the favorite of the gentlest, meekest, most sensitive girl in the first- through third-grade class? This one! Parents heard only death and horror; she heard a tale of immense courage and sacrificial love. I urge you to preach the Good News as best you can—but be prepared to duck!

Good Friday (ABC)

See page 59

Easter Vigil (ABC)

See page 61

Easter Day (B)

Mark 16:1-8

It is hard for many people to believe that there can be such a place as heaven, that there can be life after death, but I know someone who returned from dying and told me what she discovered.

Her name is Kim Kelly and she is a wonderful young woman who lives at Bayview Nursing Home down the road, where I lead worship services twice a month. Kim has cerebral palsy, a disease that keeps her from going anywhere without a wheelchair, and she is slowly going blind, but she is still one of the most joyful people you could ever meet. Not long ago, Kim got very sick and had to be taken to the hospital for operations. When she came out of the hospital, this is what she told me and the other people at a worship service:

> I want to thank all of you for praying for me while I was in the hospital. And I have to tell you something. I had to have an operation and three different times I died on the operating table. Three times my heart stopped and I stopped breathing. And the third time, I saw God. I felt I was drifting away from my body where the doctors and nurses were trying to bring me back to life, and I really didn't want to come back to this world.
>
> I have been afraid of death and afraid of God all my life, and I can tell you we have nothing to fear in death and nothing to fear in God. It is a far better place that we are going to after death. And do you know what? There are no wheelchairs there! There are no handicaps there! We will all be whole!

Well, the doctors and nurses did get Kim's heart going again and she did start breathing again and she did come back to this life, but she came back no longer afraid of dying and certain that God loves her. And people all around the world who have come close to death and been saved say that it was the same for them as it was for Kim Kelly. They caught a glimpse of heaven, of life after death, and they can now live without fear of death.

In today's Bible lesson the women who have followed Jesus discover that he has been raised from the dead. They go to the tomb where his body was buried, but they find that the tomb is empty! They thought that death had defeated Jesus, but they learn that God is more powerful than death.

Told by Kim Kelly at UCP/Bayview, Island Park, New York, and used with her permission.

Easter Evening (ABC)

See page 64

Second Sunday of Easter (B)

John 20:19-31

The little boy looked up from his play to ask his mother, "Why does water flow downhill?"

"There is something called gravity that pulls things down," she explained. "Gravity pulls you back to the ground when you jump up and it makes the water come down, too."

"But why does it pull down instead of up?" her son asked.

"I guess because the earth has more gravity than the sky," she answered.

"But why is there more gravity in the earth?"

"Maybe the ground has more gravity than the air," she replied.

"But why does it?" he persisted.

"Because it was made that way, that's all," she replied.

"But why was it made that way?" he asked.

"Because God wanted it that way!" she said firmly, nearing the end of her patience.

"Oh," her son said, thinking a moment. "But why did God want it to be that way?"

"I don't know!" his mother answered, nearly shouting. "You ask so many questions!"

The boy thought about this only a second or two before asking his last question: "Why do I do that?"

In today's Bible lesson we hear about a friend of Jesus named Thomas. Thomas is someone who asked lots of questions. People sometimes get mad at questions—the way this mother finally did—but Jesus doesn't. Instead, Jesus tells Thomas, "Here! Look! Here's your answer! Touch me and know that I have risen from the dead!"

Third Sunday of Easter (B)

Luke 24:35-48

In today's Scripture reading Jesus tells his disciples that repentance and forgiveness of sins will be preached in his name to all nations and adds, "You are witnesses of these things." Why would Jesus need witnesses?

There's an old story which says that when Jesus arrived in heaven, all the angels gathered around him and looked at the scars on his body from the nails and thorns, the spear and death on the cross. "You must have suffered terribly for humanity," Joseph said.

"I did," Jesus replied.

"And do they all know how much you loved them and what you did for them?" Joseph asked.

"No," Jesus said, "not yet."

"What have you done to make sure everyone knows?" Joseph asked.

"Well," Jesus answered, "I have asked Peter and James and Mary and a few others to tell about it and to ask those whom they tell to pass the word along to others still, until everyone everywhere knows."

"But what if Peter and James and Mary don't do it?" Joseph asked. "What if they grow tired of trying to tell others? What if people who come after them forget? What if people who hear much later won't tell others what you have done? Have you made any other plans?"

"No, I haven't made other plans," Jesus said. "I'm counting on them."

Jesus counted on his first disciples to be witnesses—to tell others what they had seen and heard Jesus do. And so it is today. Jesus is counting on you and me to be witnesses, too, telling what we know about him.

Fourth Sunday of Easter (B)

John 10:11-18

Long ago, in the fourth century, there was a slave in Egypt who was so mean that his owner sent him away without even trying to sell him. This slave was a strong black man from Nubia (the Sudan) named Moses, just like the man who led the Hebrews out of slavery. This Moses, though, became a thief and the leader of a gang of bandits, and he was so strong that he once swam across the Nile River carrying four sheep he had stolen. He became famous and was called Moses the Robber or Moses the Black. After being a thief for a while, Moses went to Scetis, a place in the desert in Egypt where Christian monks lived together and spent most of their time praying. While living there, Moses changed from a robber into a Christian and gained the respect of the other monks, who called him *Abba* Moses: Father Moses.

The Patriarch of Alexandria in Egypt, one of the most important Christian leaders in the world, ordained Moses as a priest, an honor that was seldom given to the monks who lived in the desert. Later, the Church called him St. Moses, "the Desert Father."

Moses taught the other monks many things that they wrote down in a book called *The Sayings of the Desert Fathers*. But what St. Moses is most remembered for is what he taught them about forgiveness and how he helped keep people within the community at Scetis. He said that because he had been a sinner himself, he could not condemn others.

Once there was a monk at Scetis who had done something bad. A meeting was called to decide whether or not to throw the monk out of the community and make him leave Scetis. Moses was invited to the meeting but refused to go. Finally a priest sent someone to his room with the message, "Come. Everyone is waiting for you."

Moses got up and went to the meeting, but he took with him a water jug that leaked. He filled the jug with water and carried it to the meeting, dripping a trail of water behind him. "Why are you doing this, Father Moses?" they asked.

"My sins run out behind me," Moses answered, "just like this water. I do not even see them, but you have brought me here to judge the mistakes made by another man."

When they heard this, the other monks at once forgave the man who had done wrong and agreed he should stay in their community.

In today's Bible lesson Jesus calls himself the Good Shepherd and says he cares for all the sheep in his flock. St. Moses the Robber reminds Christians that we should care for all the others in Jesus' flock, too. When we remember how God loves us even though we have made mistakes, we will want to forgive other people and keep them in our flock, too.

For more information, see Benedicta Ward, *The Desert Christian* (New York: Macmillan, 1975).

Fifth Sunday of Easter (B)

1 John 4:7-12

Today's Bible passage is from a letter written by a man named John. John says that because God loves us, we should love each other.

There is a very old story about this man. When John was quite old and weak, he was asked to preach a sermon to a group of Christians. He was too weak to walk, so he had to be carried into the worship service on a chair. A hush fell over the room as the famous old man was carried in. Everyone wanted to hear what John had to say.

For a long time, he did not say a word. Then, with a shaky voice, he mumbled to the group (most of whom were grown-ups), "Little children, love one another." He was quiet again for a while, then he repeated, slowly but a little louder, "Little children, love one another." He was silent again, then repeated louder still, "Little children, love one another." And that was all he said, over and over again: "Little children, love one another."

Some people thought that the old man had finally lost his mind, but other people said that it was the best sermon they had ever heard. They said to each other, "John told us exactly what we needed to hear."

Sixth Sunday of Easter (B)

John 15:9-17

Once there were a boy and a girl who lived in Hawaii on the island of Oahu. They liked to slide down the muddy hillsides along the Nuuanu Stream. One day they climbed way up the hillside, higher than they had ever climbed before. They found some ti plants with big flat leaves growing there. Suddenly the little girl had an idea: She pulled a big leaf off of a ti plant, and said, "Maybe I could slide all the way down the hill on this leaf!"

"That's a great idea!" her brother said. But then do you know what happened? The boy grabbed one end of the big ti leaf and shouted, "Let me go first!"

His sister pulled on the other end. "It's mine!" she said. "It was my idea!" They both tugged and pulled. Finally the leaf split right in half and they both fell down in the mud.

They were mad, but then they saw the mud on each other's faces. "You look silly," the boy said.

"You look silly, too," his sister said. "We both look silly," she added. They both laughed and laughed.

Finally the little boy said, "Do you know what we could do? We could take turns."

"Good idea!" his sister agreed. "Maybe we could give each other a little push, too, to help us slide further."

So they found another big ti leaf and took turns and helped push each other instead of fighting, and they slid further down the muddy hillside than ever before. And they had more fun than they had ever had before.

In today's Bible passage Jesus tells his friends, "Love one another the way I have loved you." This boy and girl learned that when we love one another, life is much more fun.

Ascension Day (ABC)

See page 73

Seventh Sunday of Easter (B)

Psalm 1

One day an old woman named Louise Degrafinried was in her home in Tennessee talking on the telephone with a friend when she heard a sound in her backyard. She looked up and saw a young man in prison clothes pointing a shotgun right at her husband Nathan! Nathan was nearly scared to death by this, but Louise stayed calm.

She knew at once that the man must be one of the murderers the police had been searching for all week. Five convicts had escaped from prison. They had already killed one man who had seen them and had raced into his house to get a gun. Louise quickly told her friend to call the police. But how could she protect her husband? And how she could prevent a shoot-out between this convict and the police?

The young convict, whose name was Riley Arzeneaux, ordered Nathan Degrafinried, who was seventy-one-years old, to go back into the house. Riley followed him in, still pointing the shotgun at Nathan. Louise, who was seventy-three-years old herself, still stayed calm.

"Young man, I am a Christian lady," she told Riley. "I don't believe in violence. Put that gun down and you sit down. I don't allow no violence here."

Riley lowered the gun barrel and said, "Lady, I'm so hungry. I haven't had nothing to eat for three days."

"Young man," Louise said, "you just sit down here, and I'll fix you breakfast." She cooked scrambled eggs and bacon and gave him some bread and a whole quart of milk. Then she said, "Young man, let's give thanks that you came here and that you are safe," and led them in prayer.

After Riley finished eating, Louise prayed again and then told Riley, "Young man, I love you and God loves you. God loves us all, every one of us, especially you. Jesus died for you because he loves you so much." Then she asked Riley to give himself up to the police and go back to prison peacefully, so nobody would get hurt.

Soon the Tennessee Highway Patrol arrived. Worried that there was a dangerous criminal inside with a gun, they got out of their police cars at the end of the driveway and pointed their guns toward the house. Riley was scared and said, "Oh, they're going to get me now!"

"Don't you move out of that chair," Louise ordered. "I'm going to talk to them."

The police could not have been more startled by what happened next. Here they were braced for a shoot-out with an escaped murderer, and what should they see but an elderly black woman walking out the door and shouting, "Y'all put those guns away. I don't allow no violence here. Put them away! This man wants to go back."

So Riley left the shotgun on the sofa and walked quietly out the door to surrender.

Today's Psalm says that those who find pleasure in the law of God will be blessed; they will be happy. Louise Degrafinried showed kindness to a murderer, prayed with him and made sure that no one got hurt. With faith and courage, she delighted in doing what God wanted. And she and her husband and a scared young man were blessed.

For more information, see *The New York Times*, February 22, 1984; *Christian Century*, March 14, 1984.

Pentecost (B)

Acts 2:1-21

Have any of you ever seen the wind? How do you know it's there?

Once there were a boy and a girl who lived by the edge of a little pond. When they were very little, they couldn't go into the pond alone; they were only allowed to wade into the water up to their knees and their mother or father had to be near them. As they grew up, though, they learned how to swim and eventually they were both strong enough to swim all the way across the pond.

They decided to make a raft for themselves and found some old boards and scrap wood that they hammered together. The girl made a mast out of a big pole and the boy tied an old sheet to it. Then they paddled their little boat out into the pond.

They had never paid much attention to the wind before, but when they got out toward the middle of the pond they learned all sorts of things about the wind right away. It was really hard to paddle against the wind, they discovered. It was much easier to open up their sheet like a sail and let the wind blow them across the pond.

The wind did not always go where they were planning to head, though, and it didn't always blow in the same direction. The wind blew wherever it wanted, they soon found out, and there was no way that they could guess where it would blow next. They could not control the wind but could only go in the same general direction the wind was blowing. They could never see the wind, but they could feel it and see how it moved things around. Sometimes it felt as gentle as someone's breath and other times it was strong and powerful.

Today's Scripture reading tells how the Holy Spirit blew on the followers of Jesus on the day of Pentecost like a mighty wind from heaven. I have learned some of the things about the Holy Spirit that this boy and girl learned about the wind. It is a lot easier to go where the Spirit wants than to go in the opposite direction. The Spirit does not always blow in the same direction, and I can't ever be sure where it will blow next. I can't control the Spirit; I can only try to move with it. I can't see the Holy Spirit, but I can feel it and see how it changes things. Sometimes the Holy Spirit feels soft and gentle like a breeze, and other times it is fierce and powerful like a mighty wind. On the day of Pentecost, the Holy Spirit blew so powerfully that it sent the followers of Jesus all over the world to tell people about him.

Trinity Sunday (B)

Isaiah 6:1-8

Today's Bible lesson tells us how Isaiah became a prophet. Isaiah has a vision in which he hears God ask, "Whom shall I send? Who will be my messenger?" and Isaiah answers, "Here I am! Send me!" Some parts of today's reading seem to happen every time God calls someone to be a prophet, such as the way the person at first does not feel worthy to be God's messenger. Other parts of today's lesson, though, like the seraphs with six wings who touch Isaiah's lips with a burning coal, may seem pretty strange to us, since you and I have never seen anything like this.

I believe that God really does call prophets, though, and sends these messengers to tell us things we may not want to hear. Listen to how God used St. Anthony of Padua as a messenger:

Anthony was born in Lisbon, Portugal, and as a young man he studied with the Augustinian Order to become a priest. While he was studying in Coimbra, the capital of Portugal, he heard about the Franciscans, the new order started by St. Francis of Assisi. St. Francis had sent brave missionaries to Morocco in North Africa and they had died trying to preach to people there. Anthony decided to join the Franciscans himself.

The very same year, 1221, Anthony went to Morocco, convinced that God wanted him to be a missionary. But soon after he arrived he became very sick and had to spend the whole winter in bed. When he failed to get better, he was sent home on a sailing ship. The ship was blown off course by a big storm at sea, though, and instead of arriving in Portugal, Anthony ended up in Sicily, in southern Italy. He had no idea where to go next and spent a year at a small convent in Tuscany, living in a little cave, praying, saying Mass, sweeping the floor of the convent and washing dishes. People thought Anthony was a very good man, but no one thought of him as being very smart.

Then one evening Anthony was asked to speak at a meeting of Franciscans and Dominicans. They all agreed it was the best speech they had ever heard. St. Francis himself chose Anthony to teach the Franciscans. For nine years, Anthony not only taught but also preached throughout France and Italy. Everywhere he went, crowds flocked to him. People closed their shops and offices to hear him preach. Women got up early in the morning or stayed in the church overnight just to be sure they would have a place to hear him. Criminals confessed the bad things they had done and returned to church. Often more people came to hear Anthony than could fit in the church. Then he would preach outdoors in the town square or the marketplace.

But like the prophets, Anthony sometimes told people things they did not want to hear. He became famous as one of the greatest preachers of all time, but he also told people how important it was to help the poor. He worked to abolish the debtors' prisons. In those days people just took it for granted that if you owed someone money you should be thrown in jail, but Anthony said that this was wrong and unfair, that God wanted the poor to be treated with justice.

Anthony, who thought God wanted him to go to Africa, learned that God needed him to be a messenger elsewhere instead. Like Isaiah, he was willing to go where God sent him.

Sunday After Trinity Sunday (B)

The Body and Blood of Christ

Mark 14:12-16, 22-26

In today's Gospel reading the followers of Jesus ask him where they should prepare the Passover supper for him. Jesus tells them that they should go out into the city streets of Jerusalem, and when they see a man carrying a water jug they should follow him home.

Did you ever wonder how these disciples could ever possibly find the right man carrying water in a crowded city like Jerusalem? Here's something interesting I learned: In those days carrying water jugs was considered work which only women should do. The disciples won't have a hard time at all knowing which *man* to follow. The right one will be the man who is doing this "women's work." I wonder if Jesus might have been telling us that sometimes we need to follow someone who is doing something totally unexpected.

Giovanni Bosco was a priest in Italy who did the unexpected. During the middle of the last century, many priests lived lonely lives in which they studied hard and prayed a great deal but did not have much contact with ordinary people.

Giovanni—or John Bosco, as he is often called in this country—was different, though. He prayed and studied, but he also worked among ordinary people. He also was not ashamed to do work which others thought of as "women's work," such as taking care of children. In 1859 John Bosco started the Salesian Order of Priests, which worked with working-class poor people, especially young boys.

Doing "women's work," a man carrying a jug of water led the apostles to the Last Supper. And doing work that some other people thought men and priests should not do, John Bosco led the Church into the future.

Sunday Between May 29 and June 4 (B)

Proper 4/Ninth Sunday of the Year/Second Sunday After Pentecost

1 Samuel 16:1-13

Use this story only after Trinity Sunday. If the Sunday following Trinity Sunday falls between May 24 and May 28, use Proper 3 (the Eighth Sunday After Epiphany) that day. The date of Easter determines the number of Sunday Propers after Pentecost. In addition, Roman Catholics delay the return to Ordinary Time by celebrating the Feast of the Body and Blood of Christ on the Sunday after Trinity Sunday.

Once there was a man who lived with his three children in a small cabin on the edge of a forest. One day he asked his oldest child to go into the forest to chop some firewood.

The eldest child took a hatchet and went into the woods. He found an old tree branch on the ground and started to chop it up. He had barely taken a whack at it, though, before he felt a tap on his shoulder. He spun around and saw the biggest, ugliest, meanest-looking troll you can imagine.

"If you chop wood in my forest, I'll break you in pieces!" the troll growled, and the boy ran home as fast as he could.

The next morning the second-oldest child went into the forest with a bigger ax. He tried to be brave, but as soon as he started to chop some firewood, the troll jumped down behind him and yelled, "If you take one more whack, I'll smash you to bits!" He dropped the ax and ran all the way home.

The next day the youngest child said, "Today I will go and get us some firewood."

"You?" her brothers laughed. "You're too small. What could a little girl like you do?"

The girl said not a word but picked up a ball of soft white cheese and the biggest ax in the house and marched into the forest. As soon as she touched the blade of the ax to some wood, the huge troll leaped out at her—and then rolled on the ground laughing.

"So they sent you!" he said. "What could a foolish little girl like you do?"

"I bet you have no idea how strong I really am," she said.

"You!" the troll laughed again. "Why, you're just a little girl!"

"Can you pick up a rock this big?" she asked, holding up the ball of cheese and pretending it was a big stone.

"You silly girl," the troll laughed, "I can pick up boulders as big as you are!"

"That's nothing," she calmly replied. "Are you strong enough to squish a stone?" And with that she squeezed the ball of cheese and squirted its juice right into the troll's eye!

"Oh, don't hurt me!" begged the troll, cowering with fear before her. "You can come into the forest anytime you want. In fact, I'll chop wood for you every day."

And from then on, her family had all the firewood it needed. And no one ever said to her again, "What can a little girl like you do?"

In today's Bible story God sends the prophet Samuel to pick a new king. Samuel chooses one of Jesse's eight sons, but do you think he chooses the oldest son, the one who is biggest and strongest? No. Samuel picks little David, someone Jesse never expected anyone to choose, the youngest of his sons. As God tells Samuel, "I do not see the way people see: I see what is in the heart."

Sometimes other people see only a little boy or a little girl who they think cannot do anything, but God sees someone who can do something wonderful.

Sunday Between June 5 and 11 (B)

Proper 5/Tenth Sunday of the Year/Third Sunday After Pentecost

2 Corinthians 4:13—5:1

Use this story only after Trinity Sunday.

When Benedict XV was elected Pope in 1914, it probably seemed to him the worst possible time to become leader of the Church. Only a month earlier, warfare had broken out and soon almost the entire world was at war. It was such a huge war that it was called the World War. Benedict must have been discouraged at times as he tried to lead Christians who were busy killing each other, but he believed in God—he trusted in God—so he spoke the things he knew God wanted him to say.

Pope Benedict XV said that God was not on either side in this war, and he resisted the efforts nations made to get him to support their side. He put the resources of the Roman Catholic Church to work helping the victims of the war. Church officials from the Vatican arranged for nations to release each other's captured soldiers who were being held as prisoners of war. The Church gave money to help the sick and the wounded. The Church opened orphanages for children whose parents were killed during the war.

Because of what Pope Benedict XV said and what he did, no pope since him has ever taken sides with any warring nation or spoken in favor of any war. No matter how discouraging the war was, Benedict kept living his faith in God and speaking what he believed. He did exactly what today's Bible lesson says: "I spoke because I believed."

Sunday Between June 12 and 18 (B)

Proper 6/Eleventh Sunday of the Year/Fourth Sunday After Pentecost

2 Corinthians 5:6-10, 14-17

Use this story only after Trinity Sunday.

Once there was a fuzzy little caterpillar. She didn't do much but crawl around and eat leaves. This is all she thought she would ever do. Then one day she had the strangest urge to do something she had never done before: She climbed out on a branch and started spinning a cocoon around herself. She spun and she spun, which was very hard work, and by the time she was finished making her cocoon she was so tired she thought she was going to die.

But she didn't die. She slept inside her cocoon and, as she slept, her body began to change. Then one day she woke up, pushed her way out of her cocoon and discovered that she had wings—strong, beautiful wings!

She moved them slowly at first, for it felt very strange to have wings, and then faster and faster and faster until she discovered she could do something brand-new: She could fly. The little caterpillar that could only crawl had turned into a glorious butterfly who could fly.

In today's Bible passage St. Paul says that Jesus can help us change and grow in ways we can never imagine. With Jesus, we can become new creatures, just the way the caterpillars turn into butterflies.

Sunday Between June 19 and 25 (B)

Proper 7/Twelfth Sunday of the Year/Fifth Sunday After Pentecost

Mark 4:35-41

Use this story only after Trinity Sunday.

My grandmother prayed to God every morning. Once, when my grandmother and grandfather were both already quite old, Grandpa was feeling pains in his back and having trouble sleeping. Grandma was really worried about him. Night after night she helped him crawl into bed and get comfortable, but one night it hurt no matter which way he tried to lie down. He was in pain and she was frustrated. Finally she shouted out, "Lord, what are you trying to do to us?"

Grandpa was shocked to hear her talk to Jesus like this, but Grandma wasn't at all sorry she had said it. It was the question she had wanted to ask in her morning prayers but had never gotten up the courage to say. And do you know what? Once she had gotten it out, she was able to relax. She and Grandpa finally got a good night's sleep and felt much better the next morning than they had felt in a long time. Grandma told me that even though she thought she was only shouting—not praying—Jesus heard her prayer anyway.

In today's Bible lesson Jesus is in a boat with his disciples and a big storm comes up on the lake. Water is pouring into the boat, but Jesus sleeps through the storm. Frightened, the disciples wake up Jesus and shout at him, "Don't you care if we die?" Jesus calms the storm and calms their fears, because Jesus loves us even when we are angry.

Sunday Between June 26 and July 2 (B)

Proper 8/Thirteenth Sunday of the Year/Sixth Sunday After Pentecost

2 Corinthians 8:7-15
Mark 5:21-43

Long ago in the twelfth century, there was a girl named Hedwig (or Jadwiga) who grew up in Silesia, which is now a part of Poland. Hedwig went to school at a convent that her sister ran and wanted to be a nun, but she was taken out of the convent when she was only twelve years old and forced to marry Duke Henry of Silesia.

Henry was very wealthy, but Hedwig got him to use his money to build a monastery for Cistercian nuns, the first monastery for women that was ever built in Silesia. Together they started many other hospitals and monasteries, too. When Henry died, Hedwig became a nun and started her own convent, where she trained young women to become nuns themselves.

Hedwig was famous for her medical skill. At her convent she and her nuns cared for poor people who were sick, particularly for those who had leprosy, a disease that scared many other people away. To make it easier for her nuns to work, she urged them to wear plain, simple clothes like those that poor people wore. Hedwig saw how warfare hurt poor people, too, and she negotiated a treaty that ended a war between Silesia and another nation. Hedwig helped others so much, especially poor people, that she became St. Hedwig, the patron saint of Silesia.

In the Gospel lesson Jesus shows that he is not afraid of a woman whose disease scares other people, just as Hedwig was not afraid to care for those with leprosy. And in today's letter, St. Paul asks Christians to help the poor. That is what Christians such as St. Hedwig have been doing ever since.

Sunday Between July 3 and 9 (B)

*Proper 9/Fourteenth Sunday of the Year/
Seventh Sunday After Pentecost*

2 Corinthians 12:1-10

Once there was a young man who decided he would read the Bible and pray every morning. He did this for a whole summer and it was great: He started each day happy, full of energy and closer to God. But in the fall he started traveling a lot and he forgot to read and pray some mornings. Sometimes he remembered but told himself, "I don't have time today." Before long he hardly ever read the Bible or prayed at all.

Another time this young man decided he would do everything he could to take care of the earth. He bicycled everywhere and seldom drove a car in order to make less air pollution. He washed out cans and bottles and recycled them, so there would be less garbage and so glass and metal would not be wasted. At his school he even started a place called Ecology House where students worked together to protect the environment.

Later, though, this young man moved to New York City, where he lived in a small apartment. There wasn't much room to store bottles and cans, so he stopped recycling them. "It's too dangerous riding a bicycle on the busy streets of this city, and it's too much hassle taking the bus or the subway," he told himself, so he started driving a car a lot more.

Do you know who this young man was? Me! I discovered something that Paul writes about in today's Bible lesson: I can't do the right thing all by myself; I need God's help. The only way I can live the way I should is if I ask God to help me. When I think I can do everything without God's help, that is when I am really foolish and weak. But when I know I am weak and need God's help, that is when God's power can help me.

Sunday Between July 10 and 16 (B)

Proper 10/Fifteenth Sunday of the Year/Eighth Sunday After Pentecost

Ephesians 1:1-10

Once there was a little girl who was in kindergarten. Lisa had friends at school she liked to play with, but sometimes they fought, as all children do sometimes, and when they were mad at each other they sometimes called each other names. One day when they were arguing about something on the playground, Lisa said to her friend, "Quit acting like such a baby, Tanya!"

This made Tanya mad—especially because she really was acting like a baby—and she tried to think of the worst thing she could say to Lisa. So she shouted out, loud enough for everyone on the playground to hear, "You know what you are, Lisa? You're adopted!"

Their teacher started toward the two of them, sure that Lisa would soon burst into tears and wondering what he could say to her that would comfort her. He knew that Lisa was adopted, and he thought that was just fine, but he also knew how it can hurt when someone teases you. But as he crossed the playground, do you know what he heard Lisa say? She looked at Tanya and said, "You bet I am! I was chosen! My mommy and daddy picked me out and adopted me."

Today's Bible lesson reminds us that we were all chosen by God, who adopted us as children through Jesus Christ. And we can be as happy about that as Lisa was that her mother and father adopted her.

Sunday Between July 17 and 23 (B)

Proper 11/Sixteenth Sunday of the Year/Ninth Sunday After Pentecost

Ephesians 2:11-22

Long ago, when Hawaii was a kingdom instead of a state, there was something called *kapu*. From the time they were babies, boys and girls were told that all sorts of things were forbidden—kapu. Girls were told they could not eat some food, including bananas and coconuts: These were kapu for women and girls. Some clothing was kapu: Only chiefs could wear it. It was kapu for girls or women to eat with men and boys. If visitors came to her home, it was kapu for a girl or a woman to talk to them. Kapu was bad for everyone in Hawaii, but it was particularly bad for girls, for women and for poor people.

The chiefs said that if anybody did anything that was kapu, the gods would punish them. Then visitors from other nations came to Hawaii in sailing ships. The Hawaiians noticed that these visitors did things that were kapu and nothing bad happened to them. The Hawaiian people started wondering if what the chiefs said was true, and this worried the chiefs. One woman walked into a room where her husband was eating; the chiefs had her put to death. A man wore clothes that only the chiefs were allowed to wear; the chiefs killed him, too. Another man walked into a house that was kapu; the gods did not strike him dead, but the chiefs did.

Then, in the year 1819, the first king of all the Hawaiian Islands, Kamehameha the Great, died. His son Liholiho, a young man only twenty-two-years old, became king. Keopulani, his mother, and Kaahumanu, one of his father's other wives, decided the time had come for them to do something.

Secretly, without telling anyone, they did something brave: They ate food that was kapu for women. And something amazing happened: absolutely nothing. They didn't get sick. They didn't fall down dead. No gods swooped down to punish them.

Then Kaahumanu did another brave thing: As Liholiho was on his way to his new palace to become king, she sent him a message that said, "When you get to the palace, I am going to tell everyone that kapu is wrong."

"Oh, no!" he thought. "Now there is going to be trouble! What am I going to do?"

When Liholiho reached the palace, there was a huge feast to welcome him as the new king. As always, some tables were set up for men and others set up for women. Some food, including all the best things, was cooked for men; other food was for the women.

Then Keopulani did something braver than she had ever done in her whole life. Right in front of everyone, right in front of her son Liholiho, she ate a forbidden banana and drank forbidden coconut milk! And something amazing happened: absolutely nothing. She didn't get sick. She didn't fall down dead. No gods swooped down to punish her.

Then Kaahumanu whispered to the new king, "If you have the courage of your father, this will be a great day for Hawaii." Liholiho finally knew what he had to do. As the feast began, he silently got up from the men's table, walked over to the women's table and sat down next to his mother.

People gasped. They couldn't believe what they had just seen. "How can he do what is kapu?" they asked each other. "The king must be drunk!" some whispered. "Or else he's crazy!" others said. "No matter," they agreed, "the gods will strike him down right now."

And something amazing happened: absolutely nothing. Liholiho and his mother didn't get sick. They didn't fall down dead. No gods swooped down to punish them.

Next, Liholiho ate some of the women's food and ordered the special kapu food to be brought to the women.

Seeing that Liholiho was still alive, the chiefs got up, walked over to the women's tables, and ate with their wives and daughters and mothers and sisters for the first time in their lives.

People began to whisper, "The kapu is broken! The kapu is dead!" Then they said out loud, "The kapu is broken! The kapu is dead!" They started running and shouting, "The kapu is broken! The kapu is dead!"

There were celebrations all over Hawaii. Boys and girls ate together for the first time. Girls and women ate wonderful things they had never tasted before. They spoke with people they had never talked to before. People went places they had never gone before. They discovered how good it was to live together without the kapu.

The next spring, in March 1820, Christian missionaries came from the United States to tell the people of Hawaii about Jesus. They told the Hawaiians how Jesus breaks down the things that keep people apart, things like the terrible kapu. The missionaries told the Hawaiians what St. Paul says in today's Bible lesson: Jesus brings people together—"He is our unity."

Kaahumanu, a recorded and illustrated version of this story for older elementary students, by Paula Brandes and me, is available from the Eclectic Company in its "Women of Courage" record/book series.

Sunday Between July 24 and 30 (B)

Proper 12/Seventeenth Sunday of the Year/
Tenth Sunday After Pentecost

John 6:1-15

In today's Bible reading, a little boy who shares his lunch with others helps Jesus make a miracle, feeding a whole crowd of people. And sometimes things like that still happen.

One Sunday in 1962 the chaplain of Brooklyn Methodist Hospital was preaching in a parish on Long Island at Southampton. He mentioned that the hospital needed $50,000 for a cobalt machine which could be used to help people who have cancer. He told the people in Southampton that he was praying for a miracle.

The next week an eleven-year-old girl named Bonnie Andrews wrote to Chaplain Stacey. She had heard him preach in Southampton, she said, and added "I heard about the $50,000 you need for the cobalt machine. Maybe this dollar I have saved out of my allowance will help."

The chaplain took the dollar to the Board of Managers that ran the hospital and told them, "Bonnie gave all she had." Then he challenged them to do the same thing. And within three months people had given all the money needed to buy the new cobalt machine.

The Board of Managers decided to call it "The Bonnie Machine" and to make Bonnie Andrews the guest of honor at the party that celebrated their getting it. Her generosity, giving all she could in the same way the boy gave Jesus his few loaves and fishes, made a miracle happen.

Sunday Between July 31 and August 6 (B)

Proper 13/Eighteenth Sunday of the Year/
Eleventh Sunday After Pentecost

Ephesians 4:1-6

Toyohiko Kagawa grew up in Japan. When he was in a Christian seminary learning how to be a pastor, he preached every day in Shinkawa, the worst slum of the city of Kobe. There was much hunger and sickness there and Toyohiko himself caught tuberculosis and almost died. His Christian friends prayed for him, though, and much to his doctor's surprise, he got better.

Finally Kagawa moved into Shinkawa. He lived as the poor people did and used the money he earned to help the hungry and the sick. It was not easy being a Christian in Japan, where very few people were Christian, and Kagawa upset a lot of people. Government leaders were angry that Kagawa said the government should help the people in the slums. Landlords were irate that he asked that new homes be built for the poor. Factory owners were upset that he stood up for the rights of workers. Generals were furious at him for preaching that war was wrong.

Eventually, though, people throughout Japan learned about the work he did with the poor. When two cities in Japan, Tokyo and Yokohama, were destroyed by an earthquake and tidal wave, the people who had disliked him before asked him to help plan how Tokyo should be rebuilt. Largely because of his work, the government decided to build new homes for the people who lived in the slums of Japan's six largest cities, and Kagawa was praised for this.

Then World War II broke out and before long Japan attacked the United States. Most Japanese wanted their nation to be powerful and triumphant in the war, but Toyohiko Kagawa continued to preach that war was wrong. For years many people in Japan hated him.

Japan finally lost the war and the prime minister of Japan turned to Toyohiko for help. "We have lost the war and our people are angry. They have been taught to hate Americans and now there will be lots of Americans in Japan. Dr. Kagawa," the prime minister said, "you must teach us how to love our enemies."

And that is what Toyohiko Kagawa did. He spent the rest of his life teaching people how to love their enemies, to love the way Jesus loved. And he is remembered now as one of the greatest Christians in the history of his land. Today's Scripture reading tells us to be gentle and patient with each other and to show our love by being tolerant of one another. Throughout his life, Dr. Kagawa showed his people how to be tolerant and loving, gentle and patient—just what God wants you and me to be.

Sunday Between August 7 and 13 (B)

Proper 14/Nineteenth Sunday of the Year/
Twelfth Sunday After Pentecost

Ephesians 4:25—5:2

Today's Bible lesson tells us to be kind and tenderhearted and forgiving toward one another. Long ago in the land of Greece, a man named Aesop told this tale about why it is good to be that way.

One evening a group of mice were wandering through the jungle when they came upon a sleeping lion. "What a big animal he is!" the youngest mouse said.

"Yes, and it is only because he is asleep that we dare go near him," warned an older mouse. "We had best be careful."

But the youngest mouse got too near the lion. Suddenly the lion awoke and a huge paw bolted out at the little mouse, catching his tail. The other mice ran away, but the youngest one was trapped. "Gr-rr-rr," growled the lion.

"Oh, please," begged the mouse, "Let me go!"

"Why should I?" snarled the lion. "Why, with one swipe of my paw I could crush you."

"Oh, please," the mouse begged. "I'm sorry I woke you. I'll never do it again." The big lion growled some more, and then chuckled. She silently lifted her paw and let the little creature scurry away.

One evening months later the mouse heard a tremendous roar and a terrible thrashing noise. At first he ran and hid, but soon he realized that the roars sounded familiar. He tiptoed quietly in the direction of all the ruckus. And what do you suppose he found? It was the lion who had let him go. She was caught in a net. Hunters had set a trap and caught her. She roared and thrashed because she knew she was trapped, but the more she rolled around, the more tangled up she became.

"Please, do not be afraid," the mouse whispered.

"Don't be afraid?" the lion roared. "The hunters will be coming to get me soon!"

"Perhaps I can help you," the little mouse suggested.

"You! What could a tiny creature like you do?" The lion laughed, but she really wanted to cry.

"Just lie still a few minutes," the mouse said as he began to chew through the net with his sharp teeth. Soon the lion was free.

"Thank you, thank you," she said. "I never would have guessed that my kindness to a little creature like you would bring me such a reward."

When we are kind and tenderhearted and forgiving the way today's Scripture says, you never can tell what wonderful things may happen.

Sunday Between August 14 and 20 (B)

*Proper 15/Twentieth Sunday of the Year/
Thirteenth Sunday After Pentecost*

Ephesians 5:15-20

Once there was a girl named Ayele who lived in a little village in Ghana in West Africa. Ayele and her friends liked to climb the hills near their village and watch the monkeys play. They liked to listen to the birds along the river. Ayele liked to catch little silver fish in her hands and take them home to her mother and father.

One afternoon Ayele and her friends wandered down to the river to play and then decided to climb a hill to gather flowers. Ayele's parents had told her to always tell them where she was going, but this day she forgot.

The boys and girls ran up the hill picking flowers. They saw some tiny *ntay* insects and chased after them, laughing all the way. They had so much fun that they did not notice how late it was. Before long, the sun was going down.

As the sun was setting, Ayele's mother and father went through the village, asking, "Have you seen our daughter?"

"No, I haven't," one man replied, "and I was just wondering where my own daughter was."

"No," said a woman, "I haven't seen Ayele, and I'm getting a little worried about why my son isn't home yet."

As it started to get dark, all the mothers and fathers and aunts and uncles and grandparents and older brothers and sisters went looking for the children. They searched all around the village, but there was not a trace of the boys and girls to be found. They went down to the river—which is where the children had said they would be—but the children were not there.

High up on a hill, Ayele and her friends were getting scared. They had wandered farther from home than ever before. It was dark now and they were completely lost. The boys and girls huddled together and cried. Ayele started singing, hoping this would cheer them up and praying that someone somewhere would hear her.

She made up a song (*make up your own sing-song tune and sing*):

> Little Ayele lost her mother;
> say sorry to Ayele.
> Oh! Oh! Say sorry to Ayele.
> Little Ayele lost her father;
> say sorry to Ayele.

A few of the other boys and girls joined in the song, though some were still crying too hard to sing. Far down below, an old man from the village heard the sound of the singing and told the others, "Listen! Up there!"

Up on the hill all the boys and girls had now joined Ayele in singing her sad song. Far away, Ayele's mother heard, "Little Ayele lost her mother," and started running up the hill. Nearby, Ayele's father heard, "Little Ayele lost her father," and scrambled up the hill as fast as he could.

Soon there were mothers and fathers and aunts and uncles and grandparents and brothers and sisters racing up the hill. They were angry at the boys and girls, of course, and scolded them for not saying where they were going, but mostly they were overjoyed to find them. Everyone hugged and cried and hugged some more. Then they all walked home together, singing the song that had saved Ayele and her friends.

Today's Bible reading tells us to sing hymns and psalms to God with praise in our hearts even when times are hard. If you sing praise to God when you are scared or lost, maybe the songs will help you, just the way Ayele's song helped her and her friends.

Sunday Between August 21 and 27 (B)

Proper 16/Twenty-First Sunday of the Year/
Fourteenth Sunday After Pentecost

2 Samuel 23:1-7

It is said in Ethiopia that once there was a queen whose name was Makeda. She was a beautiful young black woman who ruled a nation in East Africa called Sheba. Her realm included parts of Ethiopia, Egypt and the Sudan.

Queen Makeda sent merchants to trade with lands as far away as India, across the Sea of Arabia. One day a merchant named Tamrin returned from a long voyage to the land of Israel. Tamrin told Makeda about the beautiful city he had seen, Jerusalem. Tamrin told her about the magnificent Temple in Jerusalem, where the people worshiped only one God, and about Israel's king, Solomon.

"Solomon rules his kingdom wisely," Tamrin told the queen, "just as you lead our people with wisdom. He, too, trades with nations far away. He has become friends with those who rule Israel's neighbors and he has made peace with Pharaoh, the mighty ruler of Egypt, by marrying Pharaoh's daughter."

Tamrin was particularly impressed with the way King Solomon treated the people who worked for him. "When Solomon must tell people what to do," Tamrin reported, "he speaks to them kindly. When they have done something wrong, he corrects them gently. He smiles graciously when he sees those who are foolish and sets them on the right way."

When the queen heard this, she wanted to trade with Israel. She also wanted to meet the wise King Solomon. She had told her own people:

> Wisdom is the best of all treasures. I will love her like my mother and she will embrace me like her child. I will follow her footprints and she will protect me forever.... I will seek protection in her, and she shall be my power and strength....
>
> Let us seek Wisdom, and we shall find her; let us love Wisdom and she will not withdraw herself from us.

So the young queen decided to go to Jerusalem herself to meet Solomon. It was a long journey from her home in the royal city of Axum all the way to Jerusalem. Makeda and her attendants traveled 1,200 miles—2,000 kilometers—by horse and camel. The Queen brought gifts of spices, jewels and gold for Solomon—almost five tons of gold and many jewels and more spices than anyone else had ever given the king.

When the Queen saw Solomon's Temple, she was breathless with amazement.

Makeda was not sure that everything she had heard about Solomon's wisdom could be true, so she also brought a special present to test him. She had the most skilled craftspeople of her realm make a bouquet of artificial flowers which looked just like real rose of Sharon and lilies of the valley. When Solomon welcomed the queen with a huge feast, the Queen had the fake flowers brought into the banquet hall along with a bouquet of real rose of Sharon and lilies of the valley.

"Can you tell me which are the real flowers," she asked Solomon, "without getting up to take a closer look?"

A hush fell over the guests. None of them could see any difference. "What a clever test the queen has made up!" they whispered to each other.

King Solomon thought quietly for a moment. "Open a window!" he called out to a servant. The window was opened. And Solomon waited.

After a while a tiny little bee flew into the window and buzzed around the room. The king watched as it buzzed right past one bunch of flowers and landed on the other bunch.

"Those," the king said with a smile, pointing toward the bee, "are the real flowers! The bee can tell which ones are real."

During her visit in Jerusalem, Queen Makeda continued to ask Solomon the hardest questions and riddles she knew. She was impressed with him. "Your wisdom is even greater than I was told in my country," she said to him, and he was impressed with the young queen's wisdom, too. They spent several happy months together and learned many things from each other.

Solomon, for example, taught Queen Makeda that we human beings were placed on earth in order to love others and show them kindness. "What is the use of us," he said, "if we do not exercise kindness and love while we are alive?"

Makeda told Solomon how her people worshiped the sun, so the king told her about the God of Israel. "Praise the Lord your God!" Makeda declared and she promised,

> ...from this moment I will no longer worship the sun but will worship the Creator of the sun, the God of Israel. And the Temple of the God of Israel will be my Lady and that of my children and all my people.

Solomon fell in love with Makeda and wanted her to stay with him in Jerusalem, but she insisted she must return to lead her people. Makeda asked a number of Israelites to come to her royal city of Axum to teach her people about the Jewish religion. The Queen's rule became even more wise and just than it had been before her journey to Jerusalem. She led her nation for another twenty-five years, teaching her people things which they remember to this day. She taught them:

> "Do no scold or oppress each other."

> "When you see someone with a heavy burden, help carry the load."

"Do not take bribes to turn aside from doing what is right, and do not tell lies."

Makeda's people began to worship the God of Israel, and for nearly three thousand years the people of Ethiopia have remembered what they learned from her journey.

Today's Bible lesson tells us that a ruler who is fair and reverent toward God shines like the rising sun. Both Solomon and Makeda, the Queen of Sheba, were rulers like that.

This retelling of the Ethiopian version of Sheba's visit to Solomon is based on the Ethiopian legend *Kebra Nagast*. For an analysis of this Ethiopian legend and theories about the origins of Judaism in the Horn of Africa, see my articles "Origins of Ethiopia's Black Jews" (*Catholic Near East Magazine*, Fall 1986); "The House of Israel in the Horn of Africa" (*Midstream*, January 1988); and "The Queen of Sheba's Children" (*Congress Monthly*, July/August 1991). An earlier, shorter version of this story appeared in *Hadassah's Young Judean*, April 1985.

Sunday Between August 28 and September 3 (B)

*Proper 17/Twenty-Second Sunday of the Year/
Fifteenth Sunday After Pentecost*

Ephesians 6:10-20

An old legend from Iran tells about a boy named Selim, who was a camel-driver. One day his caravan was surrounded by a gang of robbers who shouted to everyone in the caravan, "Give us your money and jewels!" Eventually the thieves made their way down the line of camels to Selim. They searched his pockets but did not find any money. The chief of the robbers asked Selim, "Don't you have any money, boy?"

"I have three gold coins sewn into the corner of my coat," Selim answered.

"But why did you tell me that," the astonished thief said. "I never would have found them there!"

"Because my mother taught me to do three things," Selim replied. "She told me to be kind to everyone, to pray to God every day and always to tell the truth."

This was something the robbers had not seen before: a person who told the truth even if it meant losing money. The gang leader thought for a minute, scratching his chin. "Here," he said to Selim, "instead of taking your money I will *give* you three gold coins. If my mother had taught me what yours taught you, I would not be a robber today."

Today's reading from the Letter to the Ephesians tells us to stand ready with truth wrapped around us like a soldier's belt. It is not always easy to tell the truth, but as Selim learned, it is almost always the best thing to do.

Sunday Between September 4 and 10 (B)

Proper 18/Twenty-Third Sunday of the Year/
Sixteenth Sunday After Pentecost

James 1:17-22

Today's Bible lesson tells us that it is not enough to *hear* God's word; we also have to *do* what God wants us to do. A long time ago in the land of Greece, a man named Aesop told this story about some mice who learned this very thing.

Once upon a time the mice called a meeting to decide what to do about their enemy, Cat. Whenever they went looking for food, Cat chased them and tried to catch them.

"Only yesterday," a big mouse said, "I saw some sugar on the table, but Cat caught me before I could get it. I escaped, but Cat bit my tail off! Oh, woe is me!"

"What can we do?" they asked themselves.

Then a young mouse said, "I know! All we have to do is hang a bell around Cat's neck. Then when we hear the bell, we will know that Cat is coming and we can escape!"

All the mice agreed that this was a wonderful idea. They were all rejoicing about how they would now be safe when a wise old mouse asked, "But *who* will hang the bell around Cat's neck?"

Not one of the mice volunteered. Each one feared that Cat would gobble him up as soon as he got near Cat's neck. No one would try to put the bell on, so to this day, the mice are still chased by their enemy, Cat.

Hearing what you should do is not much help unless you do it.

Sunday Between September 11 and 17 (B)

Proper 19/Twenty-Fourth Sunday of the Year/ Seventeenth Sunday After Pentecost

Proverbs 22:1-2, 8-9

One day Felisa Rincón de Gautier went for a walk that changed her life. Felisa had grown up in the town of Fajardo, which is on the eastern tip of the island of Puerto Rico. Her family had plenty of money and she imagined that other people were all as well-off as she was, living in a big house with nice gardens on a clean street.

Then one day, when Felisa was still just a young girl, she took a walk from her nice home in a pretty neighborhood to the slum where her family's maid lived. There, for the first time in her life, she saw the rickety shacks where the poor people had to live, with mud streets and rats running through a neighborhood full of hungry children who did not have enough food to eat. Felisa ran home sobbing. She never forgot what she saw in the slum that day. Somehow, she told herself, she would change things when she grew up. And change things she did!

When Felisa grew up she moved to San Juan, the biggest city in Puerto Rico. She started her own business, a store where she sold clothes she designed herself. Felisa worked hard and people in San Juan loved the clothes she designed. Soon Felisa earned lots of money.

Felisa used some of this money to start a new political party, a group of people working to build better schools, homes and hospitals for poor people. Soon her friends wanted Felisa to run in the election for mayor of San Juan. Both her father and her husband were against the idea, though. Back in those days hardly any women were mayors anywhere, and both her father and her husband thought that it was wrong for a woman to be mayor. They talked Felisa out of running in the election.

Then in 1945 a terrible storm hit Puerto Rico and destroyed the homes of thousands of people who lived in the slums of San Juan. Felisa did what she could to help these homeless people, but she realized that she could have done much more if she had the power a mayor has. She decided that she wanted to run in the next election no matter what anyone else thought. In 1946 Felisa Rincón de Gautier became the first woman ever to be mayor of San Juan.

As the new mayor, she had streetlights put up in the slums, the old mud roads paved and fresh water piped to the homes of the poor—things which had never been done before. Every Wednesday she opened the door of her office at City Hall and invited everyone, rich and poor, to come in and talk to her. Felisa listened to the problems they told her about and did everything she could to help, finding jobs and homes for thousands of people.

Felisa Rincón de Gautier cared particularly for poor children and tried to make life better for them. She started a child care center for children in San Juan, for example, at a time when there were very few places like this for little children. In 1948, when the people of Puerto Rico elected a friend of Felisa's named Munoz Marín governor of Puerto Rico and he asked Felisa to organize the celebration of his election, do you know what she did? She held a party on January 6, *El Dia de Los Tres Reyes* (Three Kings Day or Epiphany), and she invited *thousands* of poor children of San Juan to the party—and gave every one of them a gift. Just as the three kings brought gifts for a baby born without a place to stay, Felisa Rincón de Gautier brought gifts for thousands of boys and girls who had very little.

The people of San Juan loved Felisa and they elected her their mayor over and over again, four times altogether, for another twenty years. Today's Bible lesson reminds us that God made both the rich and the poor, and that the generous will be blessed for sharing with the poor. Felisa Rincón de Gautier did just that. She shared with the poor people of her city—and she was blessed for doing it.

Sunday Between September 18 and 24 (B)

Proper 20/Twenty-Fifth Sunday of the Year/
Eighteenth Sunday After Pentecost

James 3:13-18

Once, long ago, there was much fighting among the Native American nations of North America. Hardly a year passed without war parties attacking one nation or another. Warriors were wounded and killed, and no one had any idea how to stop the warfare.

Then one night a Huron Indian named Deganawidah dreamed of wonderful things that had never happened before. He woke up wondering how he could make them come true. What if nations who lived near each other promised to stop fighting each other? What if they promised to help each other if anyone should attack one of them?

Deganawidah paddled his canoe to a lodge on the eastern shore of Lake Ontario, where a Seneca woman called Peace Woman lived. Her home was famous as a place where guests left their weapons at the door before entering, for it was a place for rest and refuge, not a place for fighting.

Deganawidah told his dream to Peace Woman. He said that the dream was a gift from the Giver of Life. The Great Creator, Deganawidah insisted, did not intend for human beings to abuse one another. Peace Woman was the first person to share his dream.

Next Deganawidah told his dream to a Mohawk chief—or sachem—named Hiawatha. Every one of Hiawatha's daughters had been killed in warfare, one after another, and he had gone completely crazy with grief. Reeling with rage and depression, Hiawatha had left his village and walked off into the forest alone.

Deganawidah found Hiawatha wandering in the woods and taught him rituals which relieved his sorrow and restored his mind. Then he told Hiawatha about his dream of peace in which war and retaliation raids would become unnecessary. "When people accept this message of peace," Deganawidah said, "they will stop killing, and bloodshed will cease from the land."

Deganawidah and Peace Woman traveled with Hiawatha in a white canoe, a symbol that Deganawidah was sent by the Creator. They paddled hundreds of miles to tell other nations about Deganawidah's dream.

Soon five nations wanted to make peace, but the chief of the Onondagas, a man named Tododaho, refused—and just looking at him could strike fear in your heart. He wore his hair braided to look like snakes. Some people even said there were *real* snakes tied into his hair.

Tododaho feared that if the nations united in peace, he would no longer seem so important as the chief of his nation. Tododaho opposed Deganawidah's dream—and no one was able to change his mind.

Then Peace Woman had an idea: "Why don't we tell Tododaho," she said, "that if our nations unite we will call him 'the Grand Chief of the Five Nations.' " Of course, the women could still get rid of him if he was not a good chief and pick a new sachem—for the women of these nations had long had this power. And the women could change any bad laws that Tododaho or the other chiefs made—for they had long had that power, too. And they still would have the right to stop him or any other chief from making war—for that was their right, also. But being Grand Chief *sounded* important, at least, so Tododaho began working to bring the nations together.

Soon fifty chiefs from five nations—the Mohawks, the Oneidas, the Onondagas, the Cayugas and the Senecas—met together along the shore of Onondaga Lake and created the League of Five Nations. Peace Woman planted a beautiful pine tree beside the lake and called it "Tree of Peace." Beneath this tree the Five Nations buried weapons of war, and the Great Peace began.

The League of Five Nations, which was also called the League for Peace or the Iroquois Confederacy, offered peace to every nation that wished to unite with them. Peace Woman proclaimed, "If any nation shall show a desire to obey the laws of the Great Peace, they shall be welcomed to take shelter beneath the tree." The Tuscaroras joined them and the Confederacy became the League of Six Nations. Then the Lenapes joined. Eventually so many of the native tribes and nations joined the League that warfare was stopped in almost all the northeastern United States and much of eastern Canada. As the League grew, the Iroquois people prospered.

Eventually other people came to America from across the wide Atlantic Ocean. These settlers had to find a way to work together in peace. An Onondaga named Canassatego suggested to these newcomers that they unite as a new nation, just as the Iroquois had done. The newcomers, particularly a man named Benjamin Franklin, thought about all the good things they had seen in the League for Peace. People should be free to say what they thought, some of the settlers said, just as it was among the Iroquois. People should be able to pick their leaders. No leader should be able to make war or make laws unless others agreed, just as it was among the Iroquois. Learning from the Great Peace, these newcomers discovered how to make a new nation—and they called it the United States of America.

Peace Woman and Hiawatha had turned a beautiful dream into something real—and they showed other people how to do the same thing. The Iroquois people were so happy with their League and with the Great Peace that they gave Peace Woman a new name—Jikonsaseh, or "Mother of Nations"—and made up a story about what she had done:

> The Five Nations dug a big hole in the ground. Then they buried all their weapons of war in it. Above the weapons they planted a Tree of Peace. They put an eagle on top of the Tree to watch in all directions and to warn them if any enemy came to cut down the Tree.
>
> The Tree of Peace grew and grew. The Five Nations sat below its branches in its pleasant shade. When they saw that there was still room under the tree, they invited other nations to join them under the spreading branches of the Tree of Peace. And the Tree of Peace kept growing.

Today's letter from James says that goodness is the harvest grown from the seeds peacemakers sow. Peace Woman and the other Iroquois sowed a great idea in peace and their people reaped a wonderful harvest.

This, of course, is legend, not history, but there is a great deal of truth in it.

The Iroquois came as close to a true matriarchy as has any society, ancient or modern. Women owned the fields, the crops and the houses. Descent was traced through women; all titles, rights and property passed through the female line. Iroquois women not only chose the sachem of each clan but also decided if he was doing a good job. Among the Shawnee of Kentucky, a relative of the principal chief was always appointed Peace Woman to argue against unnecessary spilling of blood, and powerful women among the Iroquois played a similar role.

Most historians believe the Iroquois League was founded around A.D. 1450, but some Iroquois poems date its origins to around A.D. 1000. Iroquois culture flourished after the founding of the League of Five Nations, reaching its peak from 1450 to 1600. The Iroquois Confederacy was so successful that by the seventeenth century its influence extended from Tennessee to eastern Canada much further than that of any of the European colonies in North America.

The framers of the U.S. Constitution were indeed influenced by the League. At the Albany Congress of 1754, for example, Iroquois and colonial representatives heard Benjamin Franklin champion the League as the model for the plan of union he proposed for the colonies. Iroquois traditionalists, who call themselves *Haudenosaunee* or "People of the Longhouse," continue to live under the constitution and government of the League of Six Nations in upstate New York.

Sunday Between September 25 and October 1 (B)

Proper 21/Twenty-Sixth Sunday of the Year/
Nineteenth Sunday After Pentecost

James 4:13-17; 5:7-11

Today's lesson from the Letter of James tells us not to brag or complain about each other. Often, it seems, God has a way of making people look silly when they brag and complain. In the Middle East people tell this story about one man who bragged and boasted and who complained about others.

Once there was a mullah, a Muslim teacher, who appeared to be a simple, uneducated man. His name was Nasrudin. Nasrudin used to make money by carrying people on his boat.

One day a scholar from the university came to Nasrudin and hired Nasrudin to take him across a very wide river. As they pushed away from shore, the scholar asked, "Will it be a rough crossing?"

"I don't know nothing about it," replied Nasrudin as he rowed.

"Listen to the way you talk!" complained the scholar. "Have you never studied grammar? Have you never learned to speak correctly?"

"Nope. Don't know nothing about grammar," Nasrudin answered as he kept rowing.

"Well, if you have not learned how to speak correctly, you've wasted half of your life," the scholar complained. "I, on the other hand," he bragged, "have studied grammar for years at the university!"

Nasrudin kept on rowing without saying a thing. Before long a fierce storm came and water started pouring into the boat. Nasrudin leaned over toward the scholar and asked, "Have you ever learned how to swim?"

"No," said the scholar.

"Well, then," Nasrudin said with a smile, "you have wasted all those years you spent studying grammar, for our boat is sinking!"

Sunday Between October 2 and 8 (B)

*Proper 22/Twenty-Seventh Sunday of the Year/
Twentieth Sunday After Pentecost*

Hebrews 1:1-4; 2:9-11

Before telling this tale invite children to sing its song with you. Children also love making hand movements to music. You might take a moment to ask them how they might use gestures to represent such words as me, you, sun *and* apple seed. *Then encourage them to follow you in using these movements when you sing the "Johnny Appleseed Grace" as you tell the story. You can find the melody in* Table Graces for the Family *(Broadman Press).*

Once there was a man whose name was John Chapman. You may know him by his nickname, "Johnny Appleseed." John Chapman grew up in Massachusetts in the eastern part of the United States but soon set off for the forests of Pennsylvania, Ohio and Indiana. Perhaps you have heard his song (*sing*):

> Oh, the Lord is good to me,
> and so I thank the Lord
> for giving me the things I need:
> the sun, the rain and the apple seed.
> The Lord is good to me!
>
> And every seed I sow
> will grow into a tree,
> and someday there'll be apples there
> for you and me and the world to share.
> The Lord is good to me!

Johnny Appleseed was a pioneer who traveled ahead of the first settlers. He knew how hard it would be for the men and women and boys and girls who followed him. He wanted to make life a little sweeter for them, so he bought apple seeds and little apple tree seedlings and planted them in clearings he found in the woods. When the settlers came along years later to build homes and farm, they found trees loaded with apples. Not only did they have apples to eat because of what Johnny Appleseed had left them, they could make apple juice and apple cider, apple bread and apple butter, applesauce and apple cakes.

Johnny Appleseed was a Christian who believed he should live a very simple life. He usually had only roasted potatoes and cornmeal mush to eat. He never ate meat, because he loved the rabbits and deer and other wild things too much to kill them. When he found horses being mistreated by their owners, he used the little money he had to buy the horses and pay someone else to take good care of them. He owned almost nothing except his Bible. He had few clothes and wore a shirt made out of an old food sack. He wore a simple, beat-up hat; for a while he even wore a cooking pot on his head—the only pot he owned to cook in.

Johnny Appleseed got along well with the Native Americans he met, and tried to help the white settlers become their friends, too. He shared his beliefs about God with everyone he met, reading them stories out of his Bible. He never had a wife or children of his own, but loved playing with the children he met and telling them stories. Johnny Appleseed traveled ahead of the settlers, planting apple trees, for almost fifty years. He said that the apple trees give us fruit just the way God gives us things we need, so we should share food with those who need it.

As his song says (*sing)*:

Oh, the Lord is good to me,
and so I thank the Lord
for giving me the things I need:
the sun, the rain and the apple seed.
The Lord is good to me!

And every seed I sow
will grow into a tree,
and someday there'll be apples there
for you and me and the world to share.
The Lord is good to me!

The people who followed John Chapman into Pennsylvania and Ohio and Indiana were grateful for this pioneer who made life so much better for them. Today's Bible lesson tells us that Jesus was a pioneer, too, the pioneer of our salvation. He went ahead of us, just like Johnny Appleseed went ahead of the settlers. He suffered and died for us so that it will be easier for us when we suffer and die. He was raised from the dead for us to lead the way for us into heaven. He is the pioneer of our salvation.

Walt Disney's cartoon *Johnny Appleseed* tells this story well. You might show it to the children instead of telling the story.

Sunday Between October 9 and 15 (B)

Proper 23/Twenty-Eighth Sunday of the Year/
Twenty-First Sunday After Pentecost

Mark 10:17-30

Did you ever wonder what animals are saying when they make sounds? People in Haiti tell this story about what frogs are telling us when they say "ribbit."

Once upon a time there was no rain for weeks and weeks. The animals could not find any water to drink, so they got together and asked God to help them. God said, "I will give you a well in a grove of cool shade trees. It will be for everyone to use, but you will have to take good care of this well. I will make Lizard the caretaker of the well. He will stay near it to make sure nobody kicks dirt into it."

Lizard sat by the well and soon heard the cow coming for a drink. "Who is walking in my grove of trees?" the lizard asked.

"Mooo," said the cow. "It is I, the cow, coming to drink some water."

"Go away," the lizard said. The cow went away very thirsty.

Soon the horse came. "Who is walking in my grove of trees?" the lizard asked.

"Neigh," said the horse. "It is I, the horse, coming to drink some water."

"Go away," the lizard said. The horse went away, very thirsty.

This happened with one animal after another. God saw that the animals were still thirsty and would die if they did not get something to drink soon.

Soon the lizard heard a noise and demanded, "Who is walking in my grove of trees?"

"It is I, God, coming to drink some water."

"Go away," the lizard started to say, and this made God very angry. God called all the animals to the well and said, "I gave you a well. I made Lizard the caretaker, but he started to act as if the water belonged to him alone. From now on, Lizard can drink only the water he finds in puddles when the rain falls. I am making Frog the new caretaker. Frog will remind all of you to share the water."

The frog hopped over to the well. All night long, Frog called out to the other animals in a deep voice (*say this as closely as you can to your "ribbit"*):

> "This is God's well!
> This is God's well!
> This is God's well!"

In today's Bible lesson a rich man goes away very sad because he couldn't be one of Jesus's disciples. Jesus tells him that to be a disciple he must share his money with others but, like the lizard, this rich man refuses to share.

To this very day the people of Haiti remember the frog and the lizard and they remind themselves to share with this saying: "The hole in your garden may be yours, but the water belongs to God."

Sunday Between October 16 and 22 (B)

Proper 24/Twenty-Ninth Sunday of the Year/
Twenty-Second Sunday After Pentecost

Isaiah 53:7-12

Today's Bible lesson tells us about someone special, a "suffering servant" of God who bore the faults of many people, praying all the time for sinners. It can be hard, though, to understand why God would need someone to suffer because other people were doing wrong. Let me tell you about a time long ago when God needed someone like that:

Long ago, when the Roman Empire ruled much of the earth, there was a Christian named Telemachus, who lived in that part of the Roman Empire which is called Turkey today.

Telemachus was very upset about something that other people just took for granted: the gladiator games. Thousands of people would go to watch these "games" which were hardly games at all. Slaves and prisoners were forced to fight each other just to entertain the crowds who watched. For hundreds of years, all over the vast Roman Empire, huge numbers of people loved watching these gladiators fight. Sometimes as many as 700 gladiators would be forced to fight each other in a single day, to kill or be killed.

Telemachus was particularly upset that Emperor Honorius, who was himself a Christian, sponsored these gladiator fights and that many Christians went to watch them. The Church said that the fights should stop, but hardly anyone seemed to pay any attention to what the Church said. Telemachus talked to many people about why he thought these fights were wrong. Finally, he knew it was time for him to *do* something about them.

Telemachus traveled all the way from his home in Turkey to the city of Rome in Italy, the biggest city in the Roman Empire. People were flocking to the Coliseum, the place where the gladiators fought, and Telemachus followed them.

High above the arena was a special throne where the Emperor presided over the fights. Down below, two young slaves were forced out into the arena. Swords were tossed to each of them and they bowed toward the emperor. "Let the games begin!" Honorius shouted and the crowds roared their approval. The two young slaves stepped slowly toward each other. In a few minutes one of them would be on the ground, bleeding.

Telemachus knew what he had to do. He leaped out of his seat, raced down the stairs, vaulted over the wall and ran into the middle of the arena. He threw himself between the two gladiators. "In the name of Christ," he shouted, "stop!"

The two slaves stopped. What was going on? Nothing like this had ever happened before. What were they supposed to do now?

But the crowd was angry! Telemachus was ruining their games! They had come to see a battle! They booed and hissed at him. Some threw things at him. Then they raced down to the arena and hit him with sticks and rocks. Enraged, the mob beat Telemachus to death.

Then the crowd grew quiet. They had become killers themselves, they realized, just as they had forced others to kill for their entertainment. Suddenly, they were deeply ashamed. Emperor Honorius stood up, disgusted with them and with himself. He turned around and left the Coliseum. Everyone followed him. Abruptly, the fights were over.

Honorius made a law that there would be no more gladiator fights. God needed a servant like Telemachus who was willing to suffer because other people were doing wrong. Because Telemachus was willing to suffer and die, the killing of slaves and prisoners stopped.

For more information, see Leslie Weatherhead, *It Happened in Palestine*, 1936. See also *The Christian Pacifist*, April 1942, pp. 68-69.

Sunday Between October 23 and 29 (B)

Proper 25/Thirtieth Sunday of the Year/
Twenty-Third Sunday After Pentecost

Jeremiah 31:7-9

Once upon a time in Germany there was a donkey who had worked hard on a farm for many years until he hurt his leg and became lame. Since he could not work anymore, he feared that the farmer would put an end to him. "I know what I'll do," the donkey told himself, "I'll run away to the town of Bremen. With my fine voice I can be a singer."

As the lame donkey limped down the road to Bremen he met a sad-looking dog lying by the side of the road. "Why are you so sad?" asked the donkey.

"Alas, I can no longer see," replied the old dog. "I am afraid my master will not feed me anymore, now that I am blind, so I have decided to run away—but I cannot see which way to go."

"Come with me," said the donkey. "I will lead the way to Bremen town. I will sing and you can beat the drum with your tail and we will make beautiful music together."

Soon the lame donkey and the blind dog met a cat who was meowing most mournfully. "What is wrong?" they asked the cat.

"Oh, woe is me!" howled the cat. "I am too old and weak to catch mice anymore. I fear my mistress will drown me!"

"Come with us to Bremen," the dog said. "I have heard how beautifully cats serenade at night. We will be musicians together in Bremen."

Soon they passed by a barnyard where a worried old rooster was crowing loudly in the middle of the day, "Cock-a-doodle-do! Cock-a-doodle-do!"

"What's bothering you?" the cat asked.

"I cannot get up early in the morning anymore. I heard my owner say he was going to make rooster soup for dinner tonight!" the old rooster crowed.

"Well, we could use a voice like yours," the other animals agreed. "Come with us to Bremen and make music with us."

The four animals traveled down the road together. When night came they looked for a place to sleep. The rooster flew up and spotted a little cabin not far away. As the animals crept quietly up to the cabin, the donkey, being the tallest, looked in the window. Inside was a band of robbers eating a huge feast.

The donkey told the other animals what to do next. The donkey put his front feet on the windowsill. The dog climbed on his back. The cat jumped on the dog's back. The rooster perched on the cat's head.

"Now!" said the donkey. The donkey brayed as loud as he could, "He-haw, he-haw, he-haw!" The dog barked, "Woof! Woof! Woof!" The cat yowled, "Yeow! Yeow! Yeow!" The rooster crowed loudly, "Cock-a-doodle-do! Cock-a-doodle-do! Cock-a-doodle-do!" Then they all leaped through the window with a crash. The robbers were frightened half out of their wits and ran out of the house, certain they had been attacked by evil spirits.

The animals happily ate the food the robbers had left behind and then went to sleep. The donkey lay down in front of the door. The dog stretched out behind the door. The cat curled up near the fireplace. The rooster perched on the rooftop.

Meanwhile, the gang of thieves gathered in the woods near the cabin. "Maybe the ghosts and goblins have gone away," one robber said. So when the fire and the lamps had burned out, he crawled in through the window. He took a candle out of his pocket and crept up to the fireplace. Then he bent over to light the candle from what he thought were two glowing embers. But what he saw were not glowing coals but the cat's eyes glowing in the dark!

The old cat leapt at the robber's face, spitting and scratching. The frightened thief ran toward the door, but the blind dog heard him coming and bit him on the ankle. In the dark the robber tripped over the lame donkey, who gave him a hard kick. The commotion woke the rooster, who blurted out, "Cock-a-doodle-do!"

That thief ran out the door and into the woods as fast as his feet could carry him. "Run!" he shouted to the other robbers. "Run for your life! There's a witch in there that spat at me and scratched my face! There's a goblin who stabbed me in the ankle! There's an ogre who hit me with a club! And as I ran out the door I heard a ghost shout, 'Let me get him, too! Let me get him, too!' "

The gang of thieves never went near the cabin again. The lame donkey and the old rooster, the blind dog and the old cat lived happily in their new home for many years.

In today's Bible lesson the prophet Jeremiah tells us that someday God will make a home for everyone who is lame and blind and unwanted. What a great day that will be!

Sunday Between October 30 and November 5 (B)

Proper 26/Thirty-First Sunday of the Year/
Twenty-Fourth Sunday After Pentecost

Mark 12:28b-34

Today's Bible lesson tells us that what God wants each of us to do, more than anything else, is to love God and to love others as much as we love ourselves. This is not easy to do, though. In Japan people tell this story about a boy who loved others as much as he loved himself.

Once upon a time there was a boy named Shobei who lived in a little village in Japan. He was poor, but he still shared things with other people—and that made him very happy.

One day on his way home from the fields where he worked, Shobei tripped on a rock and fell to the ground. As he started to get up he found that he had grabbed hold of a straw. "Maybe this straw has been waiting for me to pick it up," Shobei said to himself. "I think I'll take it with me.

As Shobei walked on toward home, a dragonfly came along and began buzzing around his head. "What a pesky dragonfly," Shobei thought, as he tried to brush it away. But the dragonfly kept flying around him in circles, so the boy caught it in his hands and tied its tail to his straw with a little piece of thread. "That will slow him down," Shobei said, and he continued on his way home.

Soon a little girl and her father passed by Shobei on the road. She saw his dragonfly and thought it was the most beautiful dragonfly she had ever seen. "Here," Shobei said to her, handing her the thread, "you may have it." The little girl thanked him, and this made Shobei very happy. The girl's father was so grateful that he gave Shobei three of the oranges he was carrying.

Shobei thanked the man and headed home. Before long he came to a man carrying a huge load of cloth he was going to sell. The man was very tired and about to faint from thirst. Seeing that there was no water nearby to drink, Shobei gave him the oranges and said, "Here, take these and drink the juice you squeeze from them." The man was so grateful that he gave Shobei three big, pretty pieces of cloth.

Shobei continued toward home, but before long a carriage passed by and in it was a princess. She looked out the window and saw the boy and the cloth he was carrying. "What beautiful cloth!" she exclaimed.

"Do you really like it?" Shobei asked the princess. "Here, let me give it to you."

The princess was amazed at the boy's kindness and thanked him over and over again. Then she told Shobei that she would give him a wonderful gift, too: three large fields of very fertile farmland.

Shobei ran the rest of the way home to tell his friends about his good luck. He divided the farmland among all the poor people of his village. They worked hard and built new barns and soon they all had plenty to eat for the first time in their lives. And they all remembered the boy who was happy because he loved others as much as himself.

Sunday Between November 6 and 12 (B)

Proper 27/Thirty-Second Sunday of the Year/
Twenty-Fifth Sunday After Pentecost

Mark 12:38-44

In today's Gospel story Jesus says that a poor woman who gives two pennies gives more than a rich person who gives many dollars. How can that be true? How could she be giving more? Let me tell you why I know that Jesus was right.

In India there was a man named Vinoba Bhave who worked with Mahatma Gandhi, who had helped the people of India win independence without violence. Vinoba Bhave walked from village to village in India asking people to give some of their farmland to poor people who had none.

One day Bhave walked into a village and was immediately surrounded by a crowd of people eager to see this famous man. Bhave sat down and spoke to the crowd: "Here in this village are forty poor families. They cannot find jobs and they have no land on which to grow food. How can they feed their families? Some of you have more land than you need and more food than you can eat."

Bhave sat quietly for a moment, then repeated an idea from the Bible, "The earth and everything in it belongs to God." Again, Bhave sat silently, letting the crowd think about what he had said. Finally he asked, "Is there anybody in this village who will give up some of their land to the poor the way people in other villages have shared theirs?"

Bhave sat quietly. No one said anything. Then he explained how he would use their land to help poor people grow food to feed their families. He waited again for someone to offer some of their land, but no one did. Then Bhave got up slowly and said sadly, "Tomorrow I shall have to leave here and walk on to the next village."

Just then an old man named Mongru, who was very poor, said, "I have only one quarter of an acre of land, but I also have a job in a factory now. I know that there are families here who have neither a job nor a place to farm. Perhaps my small plot of land will help such a family. I give you my land, Bhave, to give to someone else."

Bhave smiled at Mongru but shook his head, "No, I am not asking those as poor as you are to give up their land."

But Mongru insisted, "I want you to take it."

When the others saw how generous poor Mongru had been, they knew that they, too, could share some of what they owned. One after another, people came forward to give a few acres of land. Finally the richest man in the village knew what he had to do, and made a gift of 170 acres of good farmland.

It was just as Jesus had said about the poor widow: Mongru gave only a quarter of an acre, but he gave all that he had. His gift made others give. Poor Mongru, like the widow Jesus talked about, had given the most.

For more information, see Blaise Levai, "The Bhoodan Mission," *Christian Century* (August 28, 1957); Mary Esther McWhirter, *Candles in the Dark* (Philadelphia, Pa.: Philadelphia Yearly Meeting of the Religious Society of Friends, 1964).

Sunday Between November 13 and 19 (B)

Proper 28/Thirty-Third Sunday of the Year/
Twenty-Sixth Sunday After Pentecost

Psalm 145:8-13

When I was eighteen years old I went away to a college five hundred miles from home. I came back home at Thanksgiving, after being away for two months. We had a big dinner at our house and my grandparents—my mother's mom and dad—were there. You might think of Thanksgiving as always being happy, but this dinner was terrible. The food was good, but my grandmother took one look at the mustache I had grown and decided that I must have changed in ways that she did not like. I still do not understand why she thought this way, but she seems to have felt that anyone who grew a beard or a mustache must be a communist and hate America. At one point she burst into tears, saying "It breaks your old grandma's heart to see you don't love your country anymore!"

I went back to school a few days later wondering why I had bothered coming home at all. I wondered, too, if grandpa was also upset with me, even though he hadn't said anything. I worried whether any new idea I had or anything new that I did while I was away from home would scare my mother and father, also.

I went back home again just before Christmas, not sure that things would be any better. And do you know what I found—and what my grandma saw—when we walked into the living room? Sitting right on top of an old marble-topped table that had belonged to my other grandmother, my father's mom, was the beautiful, porcelain mustache cup that had belonged to my father's father, with a special little cover over the top so he wouldn't get coffee in his mustache. Without saying a word to her mother, my mom was reminding everyone that my other grandfather had had a mustache himself!

And do you know what was the best Christmas present I received that year, something I still use nearly every day? Under the Christmas tree, wrapped up in a pretty box, was a gift from my parents to me: my very own mustache cup!

Never again did Grandma give me a hard time about my mustache, for my mother and father had shown me—and had shown Grandma—that whether or not they liked the hair on my face, they still loved me. Today's Psalm assures us that God loves us that way, too, that God is merciful and full of constant love.

I often bring a mustache cup and pull it out to show the children when I get to the part of the story where I reveal what I found on the living room table. After the Children's Sermon, I announce—for the benefit of adults as much as children—that I am setting the mug on the altar as a personal symbol of grace. Perhaps you can think of some time that your parents powerfully reassured you of their acceptance and constant love—and tell the tale.

Sunday Between November 20 and 26 (B)

Proper 29/Christ the King

Jeremiah 23:1-6

Clara Brown was born as a slave in Virginia in the year 1803. Life was hard for slaves, and it was particularly hard for her. Slaves could be taken away from their family and friends, and this is exactly what happened to Clara. When she was thirty-five-years old, her husband, her son and her daughters were all sold to different owners. Clara herself was sold to a new owner who took her to faraway Kentucky. Never again would she ever see most of the family that she loved so much.

Clara worked for her new owner in Kentucky for twenty years. When he finally died, his three daughters helped Clara buy her freedom from slavery, but a law in Kentucky at that time said that as soon as slaves became free they had to leave the state. Once again, Clara was forced to leave everything and everyone she knew.

Clara Brown set out on a long journey. She traveled all the way to St. Louis, Missouri. There she heard people talking about the discovery of gold in distant Colorado, and she headed west one more time. At the age of fifty-five, she joined a covered-wagon train and made an eight-week trip from St. Louis to Denver, Colorado, which was then not a big city, but only a little frontier town. Along the way, she proved her strength and courage during epidemics, battles with natives and the other dangers of the journey.

Finally the covered wagons rolled into Denver. Clara promised herself that she would save her money and that she would gather together as much of her family as she could. She found a job in Denver and saved her money and also helped two Methodist ministers start the first Sunday School classes in Denver.

Soon, though, she followed the miners who were looking for gold into the mountains, where she knew she could earn more money. She set up a laundry business near the miners' campsites in the mountains west of Denver and became a pioneer, the first person to settle permanently in a place that is now called Central City. She worked hard and ran her business well, made lots of money and saved everything she could. The miners came to Clara for help when they were sick or needed a place to stay, and her home became the first hospital and the first hotel in Central City. In her home Clara also started Central City's first Sunday School and the St. James Methodist Church.

The Civil War, or War Between the States, raged between the North and the South for four years. When it finally ended and all the slaves were freed, Clara bought some land in Denver and then went back to Kentucky and Virginia to seek the family she had not seen for many years.

Clara did not find her children, but she did find many cousins and nieces and nephews and other relatives. She brought thirty-four of her relatives all the way to Kansas on a steamboat and then all the rest of the way to Denver in covered wagons, where they settled on the land she had bought for them.

You would think that an old woman like her might have just rested for a good long while, but Clara Brown kept helping other black people move to Colorado, where they could start new lives in freedom. And then one day a neighbor of Clara's found Eliza Jane, Clara's daughter, whom Clara had not seen in years and years. You can imagine the joy with which they hugged each other when they were reunited.

Through her courage and hard work Clara Brown helped to build two cities on the frontier and gathered together again a family that had been scattered across the nation. In today's Bible lesson the prophet Jeremiah says that God will send leaders who will do the same thing that Clara Brown did: They will gather together again all God's people who have been scattered far and wide.

Year C

Sunday Between November 27 and December 3 (C)

First Sunday of Advent

1 Thessalonians 3:9-13

Once there was a mother of a little boy named Walter, whose doctor told her, "Your son has a disease called infantile paralysis. His legs will be weak his whole life. He will never walk again."

But this mother believed her son *would* walk. She rubbed his legs every day and soaked them in hot compresses to make it easier for Walter to move them. She kept this up until he *could* walk—and eventually run.

One day, while watching some boys compete in the high jump at a high school track meet, Walter said to himself, "I want to become the best high jumper in the world!" What an idea! But Walter's mother helped him believe that he would not only walk and run, but jump, too.

As the years passed, Walter competed in high school and college sports. One day at a track meet, Walter jumped over a bar of metal that was set six feet, eleven and a half inches above the ground—much taller than I am. When the officials set the metal bar a little higher, at six feet, eleven and five-eighths inches, the crowd realized that if Walter could jump this high he would set a new world record; he would jump higher than anyone in the whole world had ever jumped before. Walter ran toward the bar and leaped high—but not quite high enough, and he knocked down the bar. He tried a second time and did the same thing. He could try only one more time that day.

Walter stood back and imagined himself sailing high through the air. He ran and leaped with all his might and jumped right over the bar! The boy who had been told he would never walk had grown up to jump higher than anyone else in the world!

His mother's love made Walter stronger, ready not only to walk but to run and to leap. In today's Bible lesson St. Paul prays that Jesus will help us to love one another more and more to strengthen us and to make us ready when the Lord Jesus comes with all his saints. That's what God's love can do: It can make us stronger and make us ready for the coming of Jesus.

Sunday Between December 4 and 10 (C)

Second Sunday of Advent

Luke 3:1-6

Is anyone here three? Anyone five?

Once a father bought his three-year-old son a big toy truck. One day while the little boy was playing with his new toy, it turned over. A piece of sharp metal on the side of the truck cut a deep scratch into the beautiful wooden floor of their living room.

When the father saw the scratch in the floor, he got very angry. "You're not ever going to play with this again!" he yelled, and he took the truck away.

That wasn't fair, was it? It wasn't the boy's fault that the truck had metal pieces sticking out of its sides. His father was probably angry that he'd wasted his money buying a truck that his son was too young to play with. And he may have been ashamed of the fuss he made about one scratch in the floor. It would have been nice if this father could have told his son he was sorry he took the truck away, but people often have a hard time admitting they make mistakes. This father wouldn't say he was sorry, and he wouldn't give the truck back to his son.

Two years went by, and the boy was now five years old. He and his baby sister and his mother and father were eating turkey for dinner one night. The boy found a wishbone in the turkey. "Why don't you make a wish?" his father said.

So the boy held onto one end of the wishbone. His mother grabbed the other end of the wishbone and pulled on it. The wishbone broke and the boy had the biggest piece. "What did you wish for?" his mother asked him.

"I wished I could have my truck," the boy answered quietly. His father didn't say anything, but he must have felt terrible. After two years his son still missed that truck!

Now it's too bad the father couldn't say, "I'm sorry I kept it so long." But I suppose he was still too ashamed of what he had done to talk about it. What his father did instead was this: Late that night, after the boy had gone to sleep, he sneaked into the boy's room and left the toy truck on his bed.

"It's magic!" the boy said when he woke up and saw the truck. He ran around the house shouting, "I got my wish! It's magic!" And the next day when he went to school the first thing he said to his teacher was, "Magic happened in our house last night."

"What happened last night?" his teacher asked his mother.

The mother told the teacher all about the truck. Then she added, "It may not have been magic that put that truck back on the bed, but it must have taken some real magic to make his father let him have it again."

In today's Bible lesson a man named John tells people to turn back to God because they need God's forgiveness. Like this little boy's father, you and I often have a hard time changing and a hard time saying "I'm sorry I did that." That's why we need God's help—and God's forgiveness.

Sunday Between December 11 and 17 (C)

Third Sunday of Advent

Luke 3:7-18

In today's Gospel John the Baptist says that people who have two coats should give one to someone who has none, and those who have food should share it with those who don't.

Once this really happened. America had been in a horrible war. It was called World War II because it was the second time that nearly every nation in the world was involved in a war. Millions of people had been killed in the fighting, and even those who weren't killed often lost their homes, their farms and their jobs. For several years after the war was over, all across the continent of Europe, many people did not have enough food to eat.

Then an American Army general named George Marshall had an idea, one that became known as the Marshall Plan. Wasn't there some way, General Marshall wondered, that the people of the United States could share their food with the people in Europe? And millions of Americans decided to help the Europeans, both those who had been their friends in the war and those who had been their enemies. All across the United States, Americans didn't eat meat one day each week so that there would be more meat—and even more grain—that could be sent to Europe. Millions of Americans tried very hard not to waste food so that they would have more food to share with friends and enemies in Europe. All across the land, little boys and girls like me learned to eat everything on their plates because, as our mommies and daddies reminded us, "Clean your plate and don't waste food, because children are hungry in Europe."

Farmers in the United States fed their cattle grass and hay instead of corn and other grains so that corn could be sent to hungry people in Europe. Many Americans drank less beer and whiskey and other kinds of alcohol that is made from grain or potatoes just so that there would be more food to share with people overseas.

By doing all these things, Americans were able to feed sixty million people in Europe, sharing their food with both their friends and their enemies. They did exactly what John the Baptist tells us to do today: They shared their food with those who didn't have any.

Sunday Between December 18 and 24 (C)

Fourth Sunday of Advent

Luke 1:39-55

Once, long ago, there was a pope named Leo I. Leo lived in Rome, the city from which the Romans had once ruled a huge part of the world. In Leo's time, the fifth century, their empire was falling apart. People from Germany called Huns were invading the Empire, burning cities and taking over the land. The scariest of all of them was a king and general called Attila the Hun. Attila decided to rob and destroy Rome, the very capital of the Empire, and burn it to the ground. His army swept south through Italy, defeating all the soldiers who fought against them.

Leo I did not have an army—in fact, he didn't have any soldiers at all. But as Attila and the Huns marched toward Rome, Leo went right up to Attila and asked him to spare the city and its people. And do you know what happened? Attila agreed. "Why did you agree not to attack?" one of his officers asked Attila in disbelief. "Were you afraid of that old man?"

"No," Attila replied. "It was someone else I saw standing next to Leo who frightened me. I think the person beside him was God!"

In today's Bible story Mary sings about how God brings down the mighty and puts lowly people in places of power. That's what God did with Pope Leo I: God gave Leo the power to stop a mighty general. And that's what God did when a lowly teenage girl named Mary gave birth to Jesus, the Son of God.

December 24/25 (ABC)

Christmas (First Proper)/Mass at Midnight/
The Nativity of Our Lord, Midnight

See page 21

December 25 (ABC)

Christmas (Second Proper)/Mass at Dawn

See page 24

December 24/25 (ABC)

Christmas (Third Proper)/Mass During the Day/
The Nativity of Our Lord, Morning

See page 25

Sunday Between December 26 and January 1 (C)

First Sunday After Christmas/Holy Family/
First Sunday After Christmas

Colossians 3:12-17

Long ago in the land of Greece, more than six hundred years before the birth of Jesus, a slave named Aesop told this tale.

Once there was a crow who was almost dying of thirst. She found a tall pitcher that was half full of water, but her beak was not long enough to reach the water down inside the pitcher. She tried with all her might to knock the pitcher over so she could drink the spilled water, but the big pitcher was too heavy for her to budge. What could she do?

Then the crow had an idea. She picked up a little rock in her beak and dropped it into the pitcher. The water rose a tiny bit in the pitcher. Then she dropped in another pebble. The water rose again a little. One by one she dropped hundreds of pebbles into the big pitcher until the water rose nearly to the top. As she took a nice long drink, she told herself, "Patience works where force fails."

In today's Bible lesson St. Paul tells his friends in Colossae in Turkey to clothe themselves with compassion, kindness, gentleness and patience, to be tolerant with one another and forgive each other the way Jesus forgives all of us. St. Paul knew, as Aesop did, that patience works with people even when trying to force them to do something doesn't work.

Sunday Between January 2 and 5 (ABC)

Second Sunday After Christmas

See page 28

January 6 or First Sunday in January (ABC)

Epiphany

See page 29

Sunday Between January 7 and 13 (C)

Baptism of the Lord/Baptism of Our Lord/
First Sunday After the Epiphany

Isaiah 61:1-4

Long ago the Hawaiian Islands were a separate nation led by their own kings and queens. Sailing ships from the United States of America, Great Britain, Russia, France and other powerful countries started visiting Hawaii, and the Hawaiians welcomed the sailors to their islands, giving them food and trying to be their friends.

Many nations wanted to conquer the Hawaiians, though, and rule the islands themselves. In February, 1843, a British fighting ship called a frigate sailed into Honolulu Harbor in Hawaii. Quickly the news traveled that the frigate's commander, Lord George Paulet, might attack Honolulu with the frigate's big cannons and his sailors and marines because he wanted to take over Hawaii and make it part of the British Empire.

Soon Commander Paulet made up an excuse to attack Honolulu, claiming the Hawaiians owed Great Britain some money and some land (which the British really had no right to have). Paulet also complained that the king of Hawaii was making British sailors and other British people obey the laws of Hawaii while they were there—which, of course, they *should* have done. Lord Paulet said he would attack Honolulu if the government of Hawaii did not surrender to him within eight hours.

The Hawaiians were very angry about this, as were many foreigners who were living in Hawaii, but the king and the Hawaiian government knew they could not win a battle with the frigate and its cannons. Sadly, the leaders of Hawaii surrendered to Commander Paulet.

Paulet sent his sailors and marines ashore with guns. They took over the fort which guarded Honolulu Harbor. They lowered the Hawaiian flag and they raised the British flag on the flagpole to show that Great Britain now ruled the Hawaiian Islands.

The Hawaiian people were peaceable and did not want to fight, but they also did not want to give up their independence. They wondered whether Paulet's bosses even knew what he was doing. So the Hawaiians sent a messenger to London, halfway around the world, to see Queen Victoria, ruler of the British Empire, and to tell her what Commander Paulet had done.

A few months later, another sailing ship of the British Navy, a huge man-o'-war commanded by Admiral Thomas, sailed into Honolulu Harbor. Admiral Thomas came with orders to Paulet from Queen Victoria herself: "I order you to lower the British flag in Honolulu," Queen Victoria said. "Raise high the Hawaiian flag. Restore the king of Hawaii to his throne. Let the Hawaiians have back their islands!"

There was great rejoicing throughout Hawaii. The Hawaiians thanked Admiral Thomas over and over again. They decided to name a park in Honolulu after him. And of all the leaders of other nations, the one they remembered most fondly was Queen Victoria, who gave them back their independence.

In today's Bible lesson we hear the prophet Isaiah promise that God will free people who are oppressed. I believe that God worked through Admiral Thomas and Queen Victoria to set the people of Hawaii free. And I believe that God keeps on setting people free today.

Sunday Between January 14 and 20 (C)

Second Sunday After the Epiphany/Second Sunday of the Year/ Second Sunday After the Epiphany

1 Corinthians 12:1-11

Once there was a terrible car crash on a freeway. People were thrown out of cars and onto the road. There were smoke and flames from burning cars, crying and screaming. Two children were lying on the road near each other, a little boy and an older girl.

"Help!" cried the little boy. "I can't walk! My leg hurts! Help!"

"Help!" cried the older girl. "My eyes sting! I can't see! I've got to get off the road. Help me, someone."

The girl was smart enough to know that she was in danger as long as she stayed on the freeway. The burning cars might explode. Another car coming down the road might crash into her. She had to get off the road, but she couldn't see. She couldn't tell which way to go.

Suddenly the girl had an idea. She called out to the boy, "Hey, you! I can't see, but I can walk. Tell me where we need to go and I will carry you."

"Oh, please do!" the little boy cried. "Come to me. I'm in front of you."

The girl got up and crawled toward him. "Here, I'm just a little to this side." The girl crawled some more, gently reached out to touch the boy, and then carefully lifted him up.

"I hope that doesn't hurt too much. Now tell me which way to go."

"Turn around," the little boy said. The girl turned around slowly, holding the boy carefully in her arms. "Now walk straight ahead. There's a grassy hillside. We'll be safe there."

The girl started to walk. "No, turn right!" the boy called. "The car in front of us is starting to burn." And with the boy's eyes and the girl's arms and legs, the two of them reached a safe spot. Together they saved each other's lives.

Today's Letter to the Corinthians tells us that people who follow Jesus should love each other. You see, we *need* each other's help to follow Christ together. You can find your own way to help the rest of us. Maybe you'll be like the boy in today's story and show other people which way to go. Maybe you'll be like the girl and be strong enough to help us get there. The Church needs you, and we all need each other.

This story could be used to explain the meaning of belonging in the Church, for worship services in which there will be a baptism, dedication of an infant, confirmation or reception of new members.

Sunday Between January 21 and 27 (C)

Third Sunday After the Epiphany/Third Sunday of the Year/ Third Sunday After the Epiphany

1 Corinthians 12:12-30

Once upon a time in a village in India there were six blind children—three boys and three girls who couldn't see anything at all. One day these six were walking through the forest together, holding hands so they wouldn't get lost. Suddenly they ran into something very large.

The first blind child felt its side with his hand and said, "I think we have come to a wall."

The second blind child reached out her hand and touched the leg. "No," she said, "it is a very large tree."

The third blind child touched its tail. "How can you say that?" he asked, "It is a rope!"

The fourth blind child felt its tusk. "It is not a rope," she insisted. "It is long and hard and sharp. It must be a spear."

The fifth blind child grabbed its trunk. "Stand back!" he shouted. "It's a snake!"

Just then the animal squirted water from her trunk all over the sixth child. "You're all wrong!" the blind girl sputtered. "It's a hose!"

A woman walking through the forest heard the children arguing. "Each of you has touched only one part of the animal," she said. "To find out what the animal is like, you must put together what each of you has discovered. What animal can you think of which has sides as big as a wall, legs as big as trees, another part like a rope, something long and sharp like spears, and can shoot water like a hose?"

"An elephant!" the children shouted, and that was exactly what they had found.

Often, it seems, we can only figure things out when we all share what we know. Today's Bible lesson reminds us that we need everyone's ability in the Church, because each of us has something special that we can do to help others in the Church. Each of you is like a part of a body, the Body of Christ, and every part of the Body is important.

This story was adapted from the poem "The Blind Men and the Elephant" by John Godfrey Saxe (1816-1887).

Sunday Between January 28 and February 3 (C)

Fourth Sunday After the Epiphany/Fourth Sunday of the Year/ Fourth Sunday After the Epiphany

Jeremiah 1:4-10

When you look at a little child, it is sometimes hard to believe that he or she might someday do something really important. In today's reading we hear the prophet Jeremiah tell God, "Why do you want me to speak for you? I'm too young!" But God can sometimes use even the youngest child to do important things. Look at what God asked a girl named Joan to do:

Joan of Arc grew up in an ordinary family in a little village in France long ago. She helped her family by growing vegetables, guarding their sheep and spinning wool. Joan's mother took her to church often, where she learned that God wants us to help others and make things fair.

Not far from Joan's village a war was going on and people were starving because of the fighting. Soldiers from another country, England, had invaded France and captured half of the nation. One summer day while Joan was working in her garden she saw a bright light and heard a voice. Who could be talking to her? What was this light? Was she imagining things? she wondered.

The voice said that Joan was supposed to rescue the king of France and free her country! Can you believe that? A thirteen-year-old girl rescue her king? And free her country? Would *you* believe a voice that told you to do something like that?

Joan didn't, at least not at first. She tried to ignore this voice and forget that she had ever heard it. She just could not believe that a girl like her could save her country and rescue her king. Then she heard more voices. She tried once again to forget about what the voices were telling her. Over and over again, for *four* years, the voices returned and told her the same thing. Finally, she was convinced that the voices must be sent by God and that she had better do what she was told.

English soldiers had already begun to surround the city of Orleans and were trying to starve the people into giving up. If Orleans surrendered, the English soldiers could take over all of France. The voices told her to march to Orleans.

Filled with courage and faith in God, this teenage girl marched to Orleans. She called others to join her and, seeing that she was not afraid, they followed her. They had only pitchforks and clubs, not the powerful weapons of an army, but soon there were thousands of them marching to Orleans. They bravely marched past all the English forts along the Loire River as the English soldiers watched helplessly from their towers. The English were prepared to fight a few French soldiers, not thousands of people who were not afraid of them. Joan and her followers marched right into the city of Orleans, bringing food to the starving people there, and there was nothing the English soldiers could do to stop the thousands of people she led.

Joan went on to lead the people of France in a revolt against the foreign soldiers who had come to steal their land. Guided by the voices Joan heard, she and her followers eventually drove the invaders out of most of France.

Who could have imagined that God would use a girl like Joan to do what grown-ups had not been able to do? Joan of Arc helped her people get back their country and end a long war that soldiers and diplomats could not end.

Sometimes God chooses a girl like Joan of Arc or a boy like Jeremiah, no matter how young he or she is, to do something very important.

Sunday Between February 4 and 10 (C)

*Fifth Sunday After the Epiphany/Fifth Sunday of the Year/
Fifth Sunday After the Epiphany*

Isaiah 6:1-8 (9-13); Luke 5:1-11

Easter can occur as early as March 22 and as late as April 25. When Easter is early, the number of Sundays after Epiphany is reduced as necessary, from as many as nine to as few as four. In addition, the Protestant lectionaries observe the Transfiguration of the Lord on the Last Sunday After Epiphany.

Have you ever wondered how God gets people to do something? How do you think God does it? Today's Scripture readings tell how Isaiah became a prophet and how some fishermen became disciples of Jesus. In both these Bible lessons people have to *decide* to do what God wants. God doesn't force them to do things; God *persuades* them.

Long ago in the land of Greece, more than six hundred years before the birth of Jesus, a slave named Aesop told this tale:

Once upon a time the North Wind and the Sun were arguing about which one of them was the strongest. The Sun looked down and saw a girl walking along a road. "Let's see who is strong enough to get her coat off," the Sun said.

"Oh, that will be easy for me," the North Wind said. "Watch me blow it right off her." The North Wind blew as hard as it could. A cold wind hit the girl and nearly did blow her coat away, but she grabbed it and wrapped it around her. The harder the North Wind blew, the tighter the girl pulled her coat around her to keep warm.

"I think I'll try a different way," the Sun said, smiling. The Sun beamed down gently, slowly, warming the earth. As the girl walked along and became warmer, she began to unbutton her coat. And when the Sun shone hotter still, she took it off, folded it over her arm and continued on her way. "You see," the Sun said to the North Wind, "persuasion works better than force."

And maybe that's why God doesn't force Isaiah to be a prophet or force the fishermen to become disciples or force you and me to follow Jesus. God would rather persuade us.

Sunday Between February 11 and 17 (C)

Proper 1/Sixth Sunday of the Year/Sixth Sunday After the Epiphany

Jeremiah 17:5-10

When I was a little boy, there was something wrong in this country—something called "segregation." Laws and rules in many parts of this nation said that black children couldn't use the same drinking fountains as white children or go to the same schools. Black families couldn't go to the park or the beach or the swimming pool with white families. Black people couldn't eat lunch or dinner in the same restaurants where white people ate. And the schools and parks and other places black children could go were much worse than the places white children could go.

Finally, after many years, people decided these laws and rules had to change. Many people, both black and white, decided they would go into restaurants together and sit down together and not move until the owners of the restaurants treated black people fairly and let them eat there.

The people who decided to do this were very brave, but also scared. They knew the owners of the restaurants would get mad at them; people almost always get angry when you show them how they are being unfair. They knew that the owners might attack them or call the police when they refused to leave the restaurant.

But then they remembered today's Bible passage. They knew that if they trusted God, they could be just as strong as a tree planted by a stream, with good strong roots in the ground. So when the restaurant owners yelled at them and told them to leave their restaurants, they sang (*sing*):

> We shall not, we shall not be moved.
> We shall not, we shall not be moved.
> Just like a tree that's planted by the water,
> We shall not, we shall not be moved.
> No more segregation, we shall not be moved.
> No more segregation, we shall not be moved.
> Just like a tree that's planted by the water,
> We shall not, we shall not be moved.
> We're black and white together; we shall not be moved.
> We're black and white together; we shall not be moved.
> Just like a tree that's planted by the water,
> We shall not, we shall not be moved.

And the song made them brave. Trusting in God, they were indeed as strong as a tree growing by a stream, and they got the laws of segregation changed.

Sunday Between February 18 and 24 (C)

Proper 2/Seventh Sunday of the Year/
Seventh Sunday After the Epiphany

Luke 6:27-38

Once there was a man who was in a class for teachers. He was learning how to help children begin to read. One of the projects he had to do was to make up a test to figure out how many words a child already knew how to read. He spent hours and hours making up this test, typing it up, finding photographs to go with it and putting it into a binder. When he turned it in to his professor, he was a little worried about whether or not he had done a good job.

His professor picked up the reading test, flipped through it quickly and said, "That's nice." The man felt disappointed and a little angry. After all the time he had spent on it, he wanted his professor to really *look* at what he had made. He wanted her to say more than just, "That's nice."

Then the man remembered how, earlier that same day, a girl in his kindergarten class had shown him her painting. She had worked on it a long time and all he had done was to glance at it quickly and say—guess what?—"That's nice." Suddenly he realized that every boy or girl in his class felt disappointed and angry whenever he did not take the time to really look at their work. And the next day at school he reminded himself over and over again to give the children he taught as much attention and praise as he wanted from his professor.

In today's Gospel Jesus asks us to learn what that teacher learned. He reminds us to treat other people the way we want them to treat us. No matter whether the other person is a friend or an enemy, we should do good to them, just the way we want people to do good things to us.

Sunday Between February 25 and 29 (C)

Proper 3/Eighth Sunday of the Year/Eighth Sunday After the Epiphany

Isaiah 55:10-13

Once, long ago, there was a young man in Germany whose name was Herr Ohnesorge, which means "Mister No-Worry." And he really was a happy person who trusted God and seldom worried very much about anything.

While he was in Berlin at a seminary, a school where he was studying to become a pastor, he had a chance to travel to Palestine, the land where Jesus lived. Herr Ohnesorge was delighted. How wonderful it would be, he thought, to walk where Jesus walked and to visit the great city Jerusalem.

So off Herr Ohnesorge went to Palestine and he had a grand time. While he was in Jerusalem he heard about a mountain near the city which had a beautiful view for miles and miles and he wanted to climb it at once.

"Oh, don't go there!" his friends warned him. "It's dangerous. There are lots of robbers near that mountain."

"Oh, I'm not afraid," he answered.

"Well, take a gun then!" his friends insisted.

"No, I don't need a gun," he replied cheerfully.

Herr Ohnesorge hiked alone to the mountain and climbed to the top. The view was certainly wonderful. He could see the Jordan River, where Jesus was baptized. He could see the Dead Sea. He could see for miles and miles!

Then, suddenly, he was surrounded by robbers! He could not understand the language they spoke, but he knew what they wanted. He took off his watch and handed it to one of them with a smile and gave his wallet to another.

There was very little money in his wallet, though, and his watch was not worth very much, so one of the thieves pointed to his coat and another to his vest. He took these off and handed them over. Then they took his shirt and his shoes and his socks. Perhaps they figured that he could not chase them very fast if he were barefoot. Finally they took his pants and his underwear and hurried away, leaving Herr Ohnesorge naked on top of the mountain.

He must have wondered how he would get back to town now, but he also remembered a hymn he knew. Stark naked, robbed of everything, Herr Ohnesorge stood and sang in a strong, clear voice (*sing*):

> A mighty fortress is our God,
> a bulwark never failing!

Down the hill, the fleeing robbers heard him singing. "What is this?" one of them asked in amazement, "We have just robbed him and yet he sings?"

"Whatever could he be singing about?" another thief wondered.

"I don't know," said a third robber, "but listen to how happy he sounds!"

Herr Ohnesorge went right on singing that hymn all the way through to the verse which reminded him to trust God even when he lost things:

> Let goods and kindred go;
> This mortal life, also!
> The body they may kill;
> God's truth abideth still!

All at once, he was surrounded by the robbers once more! Only this time they came with a look of awe and respect on their faces. "A holy man," they muttered. "He must be a holy man!" They knew they must not hurt a holy person, so, one by one, each came up to Herr Ohnesorge and gave him back what he had taken. Soon Mr. No-Worry had his underwear, his pants, his shirt, his socks, his shoes, his vest, his coat, his watch and even his wallet with all his money still in it. Nothing was missing. Then the robbers guided him down the mountain and all the way to the town of Bethlehem, so that no other thieves would bother him.

In today's Bible lesson Isaiah promises God's people that they will go in joy and be led in peace. That's what happened to Mr. No-Worry: He went in joy and God led him in peace—even in the midst of robbers.

Sunday Before Ash Wednesday (C)

Last Sunday After the Epiphany/Transfiguration of Our Lord

Psalm 99

Once, long ago, King George III ruled this country and treated people here unfairly. He lived extravagantly and taxed people in America heavily to pay for all his fancy clothes and luxurious houses and hundreds of servants. When people in America objected to the King's new taxes on any sugar or tea or paper or silk or linen cloth they bought, he began taking away their freedom to say what they thought. This angered many people in America, and some brave women organized groups called the Daughters of Liberty. These Daughters of Liberty refused to buy things from Britain which the King taxed, and many of these women later stopped buying anything at all which was made in Britain. Homespun cloth became popular, and women began using American wool instead of fancy British cloth. Many women also switched from drinking tea to drinking coffee, since the King did not tax coffee.

In Edenton, North Carolina, for example, fifty-one women passed a resolution saying they would not drink tea or wear English clothing, "until such time that all acts which tend to enslave our Native country are repealed."

At meetings of the Daughters of Liberty, which usually happened in the home of the parish pastor, young women—and sometimes girls—all wearing homemade clothes, would meet and spin wool together all day. Twenty to forty women and girls would crowd into each meeting, and sometimes there were as many as one hundred gathered together. When they took a break to eat lunch, they ate only food that was grown in America, not fancy imported foods that King George taxed, and they drank only herb teas made from local plants, not the English tea which the king taxed so heavily.

As evening came and it grew dark, the pastor would often preach to the women and girls. In Ipswich, Massachusetts, for example, the Rev. John Cleaveland once told the seventy-two women gathered in his home that if they bought only American products and made all their own clothes, "The women might recover to this country the full and free enjoyment of all our rights, properties, and privileges—which is more than the men have been able to do."

The hard work, courage and determination of the Daughters of Liberty inspired many Americans to seek freedom and fair treatment from England. These women and girls were brave enough to do this because they knew that what today's Psalm says is true: God is "a lover of justice."

This story could also be told on the Sunday before July 4. For more on the Daughters of Liberty, see

Sally Smith Booth, *The Women of '76* (New York: Hastings), 1973; Mary Beth Norton, *Liberty's Daughters,* (Boston: Little, Brown), 1980; and Linda Kerber, *Women of the Republic,* (Chapel Hill, N.C.: University of North Carolina Press), 1980.

Ash Wednesday (ABC)

See page 47

First Sunday in Lent (C)

Deuteronomy 26:1-11

Today's Bible lesson tells the story of how the people of Israel escaped from slavery. There is a song that helps to tell the story that's easy to learn. Maybe you would like to sing it with me. It goes like this (*sing*):

When Israel was in Egypt's land;
Let my people go!
Oppressed so hard, they could not stand;
Let my people go!
Go down, Moses,
Way down in Egypt's land.
Tell old Pharaoh,
Let my people go.

Long, long ago, the people of Israel were slaves in Egypt. The Book of Deuteronomy tells us like this: "When the Egyptians treated us harshly and afflicted us, by imposing hard labor on us, we cried to the LORD, the God of our ancestors; the LORD heard our voice and saw our affliction, our toil, and our oppression. The LORD brought us out of Egypt with a mighty hand and an outstretched arm..." (26:6-8a). Or, as the first part of the song says (*sing*):

When Israel was in Egypt's land;
Let my people go!
Oppressed so hard, they could not stand;
Let my people go!

But how do you think God got the people of Israel out of slavery? God told Moses and Miriam and Aaron to tell Pharaoh, the king of Egypt, to let the slaves go free, and to lead them to freedom whether or not the Pharaoh wanted to let them go. God told Moses what the second part of our song says (*sing*):

Go down, Moses,
Way down in Egypt's land.
Tell old Pharaoh,
Let my people go.

And that is what Moses and Miriam and Aaron did. That is how God set the slaves free.

Second Sunday in Lent (C)

Genesis 15:1-12, 17-18

Once I had a little kitten I called Tigger, since he had stripes like a tiger. He was a good kitten except for one thing: He ran too close to cars. One night as I drove into our driveway, Tigger jumped out of the bushes right in front of my car. I slammed on the brakes, but I still heard a horrible "Yeow!"

I leapt out of the car, afraid I had killed Tigger, just in time to see him run away. I was relieved to see he was alive but still worried that he might be hurt very badly. And in the driveway I found fur: One of the wheels of my car had ripped out a bunch of his fur!

I felt awful. I called and called to Tigger, but he wouldn't come. I looked for him all around the house, but I couldn't find him. I knew that Tigger was hurt and scared. Maybe he was afraid of me. Maybe he was mad at me. I wondered if my kitten would ever come back.

Then I realized that it must be hard for Tigger to trust me if he was hurt and that when I went looking for him I was probably just scaring him all the more. It would take Tigger a while to trust me again, so I sat outside the door and waited for him. Every once in a while, I called to him, but I made sure my voice was soft and gentle. I waited and waited.

After the longest time, I thought I saw something in the bushes. It was hard to sit still—I wanted to run and see if it was Tigger and if he was OK—but I just started talking to him softly.

Slowly, the animal in the bushes started to move toward me. It was Tigger! He was still scared, but was missing only a little fur. I reached out my hand slowly, to let him know I wanted to pet him. I could tell how hard it was for Tigger to trust me, but finally he came near and let me pet him, and then he trotted into the house.

Today's Bible lesson tells us about an old man and his wife, Abraham and Sarah, who have wanted for a long time to have a baby but have not been able to. It is not easy for them to trust God, but they do it. Like them, and like Tigger, you and I can be brave enough to trust God, even when we are hurt and scared.

Third Sunday in Lent (C)

Exodus 3:1-15

Today's Bible story tells how God got Moses to lead the Israelites out of slavery. Do you remember the song about Moses we sang two weeks ago? Maybe you can sing it with me.

Read Exodus 3:1-9, then sing:

Go down, Moses,
Way down in Egypt's land.
Tell old Pharaoh
Let my people go.

But Moses doesn't want to go. He says to God, "Who am I that I should talk to Pharaoh like that?"

God answers, "I will be with you."

Sing, a little more sternly:

Go down, Moses,
Way down in Egypt's land.
Tell old Pharaoh
Let my people go.

Then Moses objects, "I don't even know your name. How can I tell the Israelites who sent me?"

And God answers, "I am who I am. Tell them I AM sent you." *Sing, with some anger, shaking your finger:*

Go down, Moses,
Way down in Egypt's land.
Tell old Pharaoh
Let my people go.

"But they'll never believe me!" Moses says. "I've never even seen you!"

Read Exodus 4:2-9, then sing fiercely:

Go down, Moses,
Way down in Egypt's land.
Tell old Pharaoh
Let my people go.

"But I'm lousy at making speeches," Moses wails. "Please, send someone else."

By now God is pretty fed up. So he sends Aaron and Miriam along to help and tells Moses one last time (*sing, nearly shouting while you shake your finger*):

Go down, Moses,
Way down in Egypt's land.
Tell old Pharaoh
Let my people go.

And that's how God finally got Moses to lead the Israelites out of slavery.

Fourth Sunday in Lent (C)

Luke 15:1-3, 11-32

Long ago, in the year 800, Charlemagne ruled the Holy Roman Empire. He was the Emperor of France, Germany, Belgium, Switzerland, Italy, Hungary, Spain and the Netherlands. One day Emperor Charlemagne was riding on horseback in the forest in the Netherlands, hunting with his friends. He became separated from his friends and kept on going further and further into the woods. He didn't pay much attention to where his horse was taking him, because he was thinking sadly about his sister Emma. The emperor's sister had fallen in love with a poor man named Egenhart. The emperor had been so angry that he had thrown them both out of the castle.

Suddenly the emperor realized that he had wandered much too far and was hopelessly lost. It was growing very dark and it was very late. Then he saw a cabin ahead in the woods and an old woman outside. Charlemagne rode up to the cabin and asked the woman if he was far from the capital.

"The capital?" she asked. "Oh, you are very far indeed—much too far to go on tonight."

Charlemagne was already very sad and this news made him even more sad.

"You must be an important gentleman," she said, for she could tell this from his clothes and the fine horse he rode. "Sir," she said meekly, "I am only a poor woman and I have only stale bread and milk to offer you, but I would be glad to share it with you."

The emperor entered the little cabin and sat beside the blazing fire. He did not say much while he ate. He just stared into the fire.

The old woman watched him carefully. "Sir," she said, "we poor people think that the rich, important people must be happy. But you do not look happy."

"Do you think that Emperor Charlemagne is happy?" he asked.

"No," she answered. "*He* certainly is not."

The emperor was startled by her answer. "Why do you say that?" he asked.

"Sir, would you throw a young girl out of her home? Would you throw out your very own sister?"

"If she had done wrong," he said.

"But you would forgive her, wouldn't you?"

The emperor said nothing. For a long time he stared into the fire and neither of them said anything. Then the emperor asked, "Do you know about the emperor's sister, Emma?"

"I saw her once," said the old woman. "She and Egenhart live a few miles from here in the forest. They are very poor, but they have each other, and they love each other very much. I know you must go back to the capital tomorrow, sir. If you ever meet the emperor, tell him from a poor woman in the forest that one thing mars his glory."

"And what is that?" he asked.

"He does not forgive," she said.

Charlemagne said nothing more. All night long he sat by the fire thinking. The next morning, just before he returned home, he told the woman, "Thank you for how you helped a stranger and for what you taught the emperor."

"The emperor!" the old woman exclaimed. "But I had no idea! Why I—I—"

"Today," he said, "nothing shall mar his glory."

And Emperor Charlemagne got on his horse and rode home. He sent a message to Emma and Egenhart and called them home to the castle.

It is often that hard for us to forgive others and welcome them home. In today's Gospel Jesus tells a story about God. God, Jesus says, is like a father who is so eager to forgive us that God runs to us, hugs us and celebrates our return with a party.

Fifth Sunday in Lent (C)

John 12:1-8

Which do you like better, cats or dogs?

I used to like dogs much more than cats. I could make friends with nearly any dog I met, even dogs that frightened other people, but I just didn't feel the same way about cats. When my wife and I got married, I wanted to get a dog, but the place where we lived had only a tiny yard. Karen talked me into getting a cat instead, since they don't need as much room.

I noticed that my wife did something that seemed really strange to me: She talked to our cat. I don't just mean she said, "Come here!" or "Hello!" She loved cats so much that she talked to them the way you might talk to your best friend.

I didn't understand at all why she did this. In fact, I thought it was pretty weird. I would come home and hear her talking and our cat, Leah, meowing. Karen might be saying, "Well, Leah, what do you think we should have for dinner?...Is that right?...But that's a lot of work, you know....But you're right, it would be good....OK, that's what we'll have!"

But do you know what happened? *I* started listening to the cat and to Karen and before long, I was talking to the cat, too! I always talk to my cats now, and sometimes I think they understand me and that I understand them. The more I have learned to love cats, the more I have talked to them. Love sometimes makes you do silly things.

In today's Bible story Mary, a woman who was a friend of Jesus, does something that seems really weird to other people: She pours expensive perfume over his feet and wipes them with her hair. It seems that no one but Jesus understands why she did this. He knows that she did this silly thing because she loves him so much. And ever since then, Christians have never forgotten what she did for her friend Jesus.

Passion Sunday or Palm Sunday (C)

Luke 22:14—23:56

Long ago on the island of Puerto Rico there was an Indian woman named Iviahoca. Soldiers came from across the ocean, from Spain, and tried to make the Indians their slaves. There were terrible battles and Iviahoca's husband, a chief, was killed.

In another battle, Iviahoca's son, Ocoro, was taken prisoner by the Spaniards. When Iviahoca heard that her son had been captured, she marched bravely into the camp of the Spanish soldiers.

"I demand to see my son Ocoro," Iviahoca said.

"No," the soldiers said.

"Kill me and let him go," Iviahoca said.

"No," the soldiers said. So Iviahoca sat outside the tent of the Spanish captain and cried all night long.

Now the Spanish captain, a man named Don Diego de Salazar, had a problem. He needed to send a message to Ponce de Leon, the leader of all the Spanish soldiers in Puerto Rico. Don Diego knew that the Indians were very angry and he was afraid that there might be a big battle between the Indians and the Spanish soldiers. Don Diego needed Ponce de Leon's help to prevent this battle. Quickly he wrote a letter to Ponce de Leon and told his soldiers to send Iviahoca to him.

Don Diego said, "If you carry this letter all the way to Ponce de Leon, I will accept your offer. I will take you prisoner and let your son go." Iviahoca grabbed the letter and hurried. Even though she was old, she ran as fast as a deer.

Three greedy Spanish soldiers saw her leave, though. They wanted to steal the letter. They knew that if they took such an important letter to Ponce de Leon themselves, they would be rewarded. The three soldiers chased after Iviahoca with Becerrillo, a huge dog that had been trained for war.

But Iviahoca went through the thick brush even faster than the soldiers. The soldiers ran faster, Iviahoca ran faster still. Unable to catch her, the soldiers shouted at Becerrillo, "Go get her!"

The fierce dog bounded after Iviahoca. He tore through the bushes. He ran faster and faster, getting closer and closer to Iviahoca. The soldiers heard Becerrillo yelp as he caught up with the old woman, ready to tear her apart.

Iviahoca turned around and said, "Señor Dog, do not hurt me. I am carrying an important letter. Please do not hurt me."

The soldiers could not believe what they saw. There was the fierce dog listening quietly to the old woman! And then the dog let her go without following her.

Iviahoca darted away, faster than ever and soon was too far away for the soldiers to see her. Iviahoca escaped and got all the way to Ponce de Leon. Ponce de Leon gave Iviahoca a message to take back to Don Diego, and soon Ponce de Leon and his soldiers marched to Don Diego's camp. Don Diego told Ponce de Leon about the promise he had made to Iviahoca.

"Bring out Ocoro and untie him," Don Diego told his soldiers. The soldiers untied Ocoro and tied up Iviahoca instead.

"Thank you for keeping your promise," the old woman said to Don Diego. But Ocoro refused to go.

"I cannot leave my mother enslaved," Ocoro said. "I would rather die, or be a slave myself, rather than have my mother be a prisoner."

Don Diego and Ponce de Leon looked at each other. Without saying a word to each other, both captains knew what they should do.

"Let them both go!" Ponce de Leon ordered.

Iviahoca and Ocoro hugged each other and then ran together up to the mountains. The Spanish never forgot this mother and her son.

Can you imagine doing what Ocoro did? Can you imagine loving your mother so much that you would stay a prisoner until she was free? Can you imagine doing what Iviahoca did—giving yourself up so your son could be free? Today's Bible lesson tells us that Jesus loved you and me enough to give himself up so we can be free.

Passion Sunday or Palm Sunday (C)

Isaiah 50:4-9a

Once, back in the year 1775, the Quakers who lived in the the colony of New York were worried. Some white settlers had once again broken the promises they made to the natives in the area and many natives were at war with the settlers.

Many people fled for safety, but the Quakers stayed. They wanted to be friends with the natives, and they believed God would guide and protect them. Still, it was only natural that they were afraid. Many people were being killed in the fighting between settlers and natives. What would happen to the Quakers?

As they worried, the Quakers went about their work, farming and caring for their animals. One Sunday they gathered as usual in their meetinghouse to worship God and found that a Quaker leader from a faraway town had come to talk to them. Norbert Nisbet had walked for two days just to tell them, "God cares about you and will protect you."

Then Norbert Nisbet sat down and there was a time of silence, as there always is in Quaker worship. I imagine that the grown-ups thought about what Norbert Nisbet had told them, while the babies fell asleep in the arms of their mothers and fathers and the older children quietly looked around the meetinghouse and peeked outside through the cracks between the logs.

What they saw almost made their hearts stop! Blue, red and yellow feathers flashed through the trees of the forest and then disappeared. Branches moved, even though there was no breeze at all! Someone or something was surrounding them!

Then, suddenly, a band of natives burst into the meetinghouse wearing full war paint, with arrows in their bows. The sachem, or chief, looked quickly around the meetinghouse and was surprised to see that all were silent. He was even more surprised to notice that not a single one of the Quakers had a gun. What was this—white settlers without guns? The sachem made a silent signal to his warriors, with a wave of his hand, and they took the arrows out of their bows.

Who, he wondered, was the sachem of these settlers? He looked at Grandfather Hoxie, the oldest of the Quakers, and the two men stared at each other for a long time. I am sure that the sachem looked at the old Quaker with suspicion: Too many times the settlers had tricked and cheated the natives, killing them and stealing their land.

He saw that Grandfather Hoxie was worried—but also that he was looking back with love, not with hatred or suspicion. These settlers, he realized, must be different from the others. The sachem signaled to the warriors once more. They laid down their weapons and sat next to the Quakers. The Quakers and the warriors were quiet together for a long time, and the natives felt at home in this silent circle of people worshiping God. When it was time for worship to end, Grandfather Hoxie stood up and shook hands with Norbert Nisbet. Then he walked over to the sachem, shook hands with him, and invited him and his warriors to come to the Hoxie home for lunch.

After lunch the sachem said, "We came here to kill you. But when we saw you sitting quietly with no weapons, we no longer wanted to hurt you. Now we shall protect you, for we know you worship the Great Spirit that is in us, too."

Then the sachem tied a white feather to the door of the Hoxie home. "When any tribe sees this feather, they will not attack you," the sachem said. "From now on, we are your friends."

In today's Bible lesson the Servant of God talks about being hurt but not giving up. He says, "I trust in God's help." And that is exactly what Grandfather Hoxie and those Quakers did.

Monday in Holy Week (ABC)

See page 55

Tuesday in Holy Week (ABC)

See page 56

Wednesday in Holy Week (ABC)

See page 57

Maundy Thursday or Holy Thursday (C)

Luke 22:7-20

Once there was a leader in the British Navy called Admiral Horatio Nelson. When Admiral Nelson died, he was buried at a cathedral in London. Some sailors who had worked for Nelson and who loved him very much carried his body in a big fancy coffin covered with a British flag. The sailors brought the coffin in slowly and quietly set it down at the front of the sanctuary. Then, all at once, they grabbed the flag off his coffin and tore it to pieces.

Can you imagine why they did that? They loved their admiral so much that they wanted to save a piece of his flag to help them remember him.

Today's Bible reading tells us that just before Jesus was killed, he had dinner with his friends one last time. And during supper he lifted up some bread—or matzoh cracker—and said a prayer of thanksgiving for it and then broke it and gave the pieces to his friends. "Eat this," he told his friends, "so that you will remember me."

When we have Communion—the Eucharist—we share pieces of bread because we want to remember Jesus and to remember that he loved us enough to die for us.

Good Friday (ABC)

See page 59

Easter Vigil (ABC)

See page 61

Easter Day (C)

Acts 10:34-43 and John 20:1-18

Once upon a time there was an old couple who lived in a small village in Japan. The man and his wife loved each other very much and had lived together for forty years.

One day the old man went into the woods to look for some firewood. While he was gathering wood he saw the most beautiful bird he had ever seen. He followed it up into a high valley where he had never been before. He was tired and very thirsty from climbing, when he came to a spring of bubbling water. He scooped some up with his hands and drank it. The water was so cool and clear and fresh that he drank some more. Feeling sleepy, he stretched out on the grass for a nap.

When he woke up, the sun was low in the sky. Knowing that it was late in the day, he loaded his firewood on his back and hurried home, surprised at how straight he could stand up and how strong he felt. "Why, I feel just like a young man again!" he said to himself.

When he got home, his wife did not even recognize him. "Who is this person?" she wondered. "He is wearing the same clothes my husband had on when he left the house earlier, but this is not my husband." The old woman stared at his face and then shrieked, "You've changed!"—for his face looked just as it had when she had married him forty years ago!

"Why are you upset?" her husband asked. "What do you mean I have changed?"

The old woman ran and got a mirror and held it up before him. "How could I have become so young?" he muttered. "I know! That spring I drank from must have been a *magic* spring!"

"Oh!" his wife cried out. "Tell me where it is! I want to be young again too!"

Her husband told her where it was. Early the next morning, before her husband was even awake, the old woman set out alone to find the magic spring.

When he finally got up, her husband wondered where his wife was—but soon guessed that she had gone looking for the high valley. Time passed and she did not come back. Her husband grew worried and set out looking for her.

He climbed as fast as he could. When he reached the valley, he called out to her but heard no answer. He called out her name once more, but still there was no reply. As he came near the spring he shouted again, and this time he heard a noise nearby: the sound of a baby crying. There, in the bushes, was a little baby girl in the clothes his wife had been wearing.

"No!" he wailed. "No! You drank too much!" The magic water had turned her from an old woman into a tiny baby. There was nothing he could do but pick her up in his arms and carry her home.

Many stories like this are told around the world about magic springs whose water is supposed to keep people from growing old and dying, but the magic never seems to work quite right. Today's Scriptures tell us something wonderful. After Jesus was killed, Mary Magdalene went to the tomb where his body was buried. And do you know what she found? The tomb was empty! The body of Jesus was gone! God raised Jesus to life. There may not really be any magic spring that can keep people from ever dying, but the power of God is greater than death. And God can raise you and me to new life.

Easter Evening (ABC)

See page 64

Second Sunday of Easter (C)

John 20:19-31

Today's Gospel tells us about a time when a disciple named Thomas had a hard time believing what Jesus told him. Thomas did not believe at first that Jesus really has been raised from the dead. Then Jesus *showed* Thomas that he really was killed but is alive again, and Thomas finally believed that it is true.

In a way, the fact that a disciple such as Thomas could doubt and then believe makes it easier for you and me to follow Jesus, because sometimes it is hard for us to believe what God is trying to tell us. There is an old story from Ethiopia, in East Africa, about how this same Thomas helped others know that Jesus is alive:

After Jesus showed Thomas that he had been raised from the dead, he sent Thomas all the way to India. The king there wanted a new palace. King Vecius gave Thomas money to buy the materials for the palace and to hire workers to build it.

But do you know what Thomas did with the money? He gave it to people who were poor and spent all his time telling everyone about the life and death and resurrection of Jesus. Many people who heard him became Christians, even King Vecius' wife, Arsenia.

"How is the building of my new palace coming?" the king asked Thomas one day.

"Oh, fine," Thomas answered. "It is being built more and more every day!" So Vecius gave Thomas more money and Thomas gave it to the poor.

"How is the building of my new palace coming?" the king asked Thomas a few weeks later.

"Oh, fine," Thomas answered. "It is being built more and more every day!" So Vecius gave Thomas still more money. Thomas used it to help the poor, and went on telling people about Jesus. Soon nearly everyone in town was a Christian.

After a while the king became quite eager to see his new palace. He asked Thomas, "When can I see my new palace? Isn't it almost finished by now?"

"It is coming along very well, your Majesty!" Thomas told him. "I think you will be able to see your palace very soon."

"Why can't I see it today?" Vecius asked, becoming suspicious. "Take me to it right now!"

So Thomas took King Vecius on a walk through the town, pointing to various people and explaining to the king how their lives had changed for the better. "What is this all about?" Vecius complained impatiently. "Where is my palace?"

"Ah," said Thomas, "it is all around you, and it is a beautiful palace indeed. How sad it is that you cannot see it! I hope you will be able to see it later."

"What do you mean, you scoundrel! What have you done with my money?" Vecius demanded angrily.

"The new palace I have built with your money," replied Thomas, "is made of the lives of your people. They are no longer poor and they now believe in Jesus. They are the towers of your palace! God lives in them. Yours is indeed a magnificent new palace!"

When the king heard this, he was so mad that he had Thomas thrown in prison. He was even thinking of having Thomas put to death. But then the king began to notice how the people in the town had changed, how differently they lived now that they were Christians. His wife Arsenia began to tell him what she had learned from Thomas about Jesus.

King Vecius released Thomas from prison and became a Christian himself. Thomas had shown him the real power of the Resurrection, that Jesus was living in the lives of his people. Vecius learned from Thomas that it is better for a rich ruler to share his wealth with the poor and to live simply than it is to live in the fanciest palace on earth.

Third Sunday of Easter (C)

John 21:1-19 or John 21:15-19

In today's Bible lesson Jesus visits his friends after he has been raised from death. He helps his friends get food, just as he often gave food to people who had nothing to eat, and then he tells his friend Peter that if Peter loves him, Peter will feed other people, too. Ever since then, Christians have enjoyed feeding the hungry. This is the story of one brave woman who loved Jesus enough to feed a hungry man who had tried to rob her.

Elizabeth Fry was a preacher in the Quaker Church, which is also called the Society of Friends, more than two hundred years ago. She became angry when she discovered how badly prisoners were being treated in the prisons in England and she began telling other people that prisons and jails should help criminals learn how to stop doing bad things. She went to the House of Commons and told the men who made the laws how the prison laws should be changed. She worked to change prisons in England, Scotland, Australia, France, Germany and the Netherlands.

Once, while Elizabeth Fry was working at the prison in Bristol, England, she stayed at an inn—sort of like a small hotel. One night she left the cold, dark, damp prison and returned to the cozy, warm inn. She ran happily up the stairs and into her room, but she knew at once that something was wrong. The dresser drawer was open a little bit—and she had closed it when she left that morning. A shawl she hadn't worn for several days was flung over a chair. A candle from the night stand was lying broken on the floor.

And she could see a man's boot under her bed! There was a robber hiding under her bed.

Now, what would you do if you found a thief hiding under your bed? Do you know what Elizabeth Fry did? She slowly put the shawl back in the dresser drawer and closed it. She knelt beside the bed and prayed in a calm voice, "Dear God, please forgive this man for what he has done."

The frightened man stirred a little. "Dear God," she continued, "this man is confused. He needs thy guidance so he will steal no more." (In those days, Quakers said *thee*, *thou* and *thy* instead of *you* or *your*.)

The man suddenly crawled out from under the bed. He was dirty and skinny. "Why are you praying for me?" he demanded. "Why don't you just call the innkeeper? Why don't you just go ahead and call the police?"

"But thee must have a good reason for coming into my room to steal," Elizabeth said. He said nothing, but she waited patiently.

Finally the man replied, "I'm hungry, ma'am. I haven't had a thing to eat for days. I was hoping to find some money for food and a coat to keep me warm."

"I am glad thee came to my room," Elizabeth said, taking one of her husband's warm sweaters out of a drawer and handing it to him. "Now come downstairs and I will buy dinner for thee."

"And then you'll have me arrested and sent to prison?" he asked, his eyes darting toward the window.

"No," she replied, "I know what prisons are like. I couldn't send thee there."

"*You've* been in prison?" the man said, amazed.

"Yes," she chuckled, "I have been in many of them."

"So have I," the man protested, "but they're nothing to laugh about! Whatever could a fine lady such as yourself have done to be thrown in prison?"

"Come. Let us have dinner," Elizabeth answered, "and I will tell thee all about it."

So Elizabeth Fry took the robber to dinner and told him about her work. He told her he had been in prison three times: the first time just because he owed someone some money, the second time for stealing and the third time just because someone *thought* he had stolen something. Now he could not find a job: His clothes were so ragged and dirty that no one trusted him enough to hire him.

Elizabeth listened and gave the man money for new clothes and some soap. They talked about what kind of work he could do so that he could stop stealing.

The man had entered the inn hungry and cold and desperate. By the time he left, Elizabeth Fry had given him not only food but also the courage to change.

Fourth Sunday of Easter (C)

Revelation 7:9-17

In today's Bible lesson a man named John has a vision. He sees a special welcome in heaven for people who have come through persecution. "God will wipe away every tear from their eyes," he says (Revelation 7:17c). Do you know what persecution is? It is when you get in trouble for trying to do the things you think God wants you to do. Sometimes people get into trouble even though they have done nothing wrong. Let me tell you how this happened to one man—and how his wife helped him.

Long ago, in the land of Holland—which is now called the Netherlands—there was a terrible war between Christians who belonged to one Church and Christians who belonged to another. People fighting on both sides wanted to force everyone in Holland to belong to their particular Church, and they were willing to kill others to see that their own Church won.

Finally, some people said that it was stupid to try to change others' beliefs by force. One of these people, Hugo Grotius (or Huig de Groot, if you say his name the way the Dutch do), said that no law should make everyone in the nation belong to this Church or to that Church—which made sense to many in Holland. More and more people listened to Hugo Grotius and wanted the fighting between the Churches to stop.

You might not think that a good man could get in trouble for trying to do something good, but there was a governor named Maurice, the Prince of Orange, who was certain that his Church could win the war. Prince Maurice was very angry that people who listened to Hugo wanted to stop fighting, so he sent his soldiers to get Hugo. The soldiers arrested Hugo and hauled him off to a prison on a tiny island, and Prince Maurice said that Hugo would never leave that prison alive.

Hugo Grotius was lucky, though, to have a brave and smart woman named Maria von Reygersberg as his wife. Her friends told her, "You should throw yourself at the feet of Prince Maurice and beg him to let Hugo out of prison," but Maria replied, "I will not beg *anything* from that prince. My husband has done nothing wrong!"

Maria did not beg, but she did use her wits. She went to the prison several times to visit her husband. She noticed that every few weeks Hugo loaded a huge trunk full of laundry to be cleaned and books to be sent back to the friends he had borrowed them from and sent the trunk back to town. Hugo Grotius loved to read, so the trunk was always very heavy.

Maria also noticed that, while at first the guards carefully searched the trunk every time it was sent into town, they barely looked in it anymore, since all they ever found was books and dirty clothes. So do you know what Maria von Reygersberg did? She cut tiny holes in the bottom of the trunk so air could come in. She took most of the dirty laundry and stuffed it under the covers of Hugo's bed to make it look as if he were sleeping there. Then she put her husband in the trunk, covered him with a few clothes and a few books, and called for the guards to take the trunk away. Maria stayed in the prison cell, as if she wanted to visit with her husband after he woke up.

"This is heavy enough to have a man inside!" complained the guards as they carried the trunk out of Hugo's prison cell. Inside the trunk, Hugo feared that the guards would find him.

"Well, books are heavy things," Maria calmly told the guards.

The guards nodded and said, "They certainly are!" They locked the door to the cell, lifted the heavy trunk once more, carried it to the boat and sent it on its way to one of Hugo's friends. When Prince Maurice found out that Hugo had escaped, he wanted to keep Maria in prison for the rest of her life. The people of Holland were so impressed with her courage, though, that they forced him to set her free.

The people of the Netherlands rejoiced when both Hugo and Maria were free and no longer persecuted by Prince Maurice, and they still honor Hugo and Maurice as people who helped bring peace to their nation.

And, as John tells us in today's Bible lesson, there will be a special welcome in heaven for all who have been persecuted.

Fifth Sunday of Easter (C)

John 13:31-35

Once there was a boy named Johann Drake. He grew up in Germany, but he did not want to serve in the German army. So when the German government tried to draft him, he fled east, far away to Turkestan. There he lived with some Christians called Mennonites because he knew that the Mennonites would not fight in armies or carry guns, either.

It was hard for Johann to be so far from home. When his mother died back in Germany, Johann started stealing things and acting strange. When a girl he loved said she would not marry him, Johann completely lost his mind. A Mennonite family took him into their home and cared for him.

Then one day in 1883 a terrible thing happened. A gang of robbers broke into the home of a Mennonite family. Elizabeth Abrahams got away, but the robber shot and killed her young husband Heinrich. The men of the village set out on horseback to find the murderers. As they rode around a little hill, the Mennonites found the robbers dividing up the things they had stolen from the Abrahams. One of the Mennonites, Peter Unruh, was so enraged that he yelled at them, "You thieves and murderers!"—and was instantly surrounded by fifty robbers with guns.

"Kneel!" they ordered Peter. "Pray to your God, because we are going to kill you for calling us thieves and murderers!"—though that, of course, is exactly what they were. They pointed their rifles at Unruh, and he and all the Mennonites started begging them not to kill him.

Suddenly, Johann Drake, the mentally disturbed boy, ran up to Unruh, hugged him and shouted, "Brother, I will die for you." Then Johann told the robbers, "Kill me instead of this man. I am alone, but he has a wife and small children."

"This we cannot do," replied the leader of the thieves. "We do not want to shoot someone who has not harmed us. Go away and let us kill this man who insulted us."

But Johann Drake would not move. He just stood there with his arms around Peter Unruh. If the robbers were going to shoot Peter, they would have to kill Johann, also. The gang of thieves talked a moment and then lowered their guns. "We grant you both your freedom," they said, "and your lives." With that the robbers mounted their horses and rode away.

The courage of a troubled boy had saved another's life. In today's Bible lesson Jesus tells us to love one another the way he has loved us. That is exactly what Johann Drake did: He risked his life to save someone else.

For more information, see Fred Belk, *The Great Trek of the Russian Mennonites to Central Asia, 1880-1884* (Scottdale, Pa.: Herald Press, 1976), pp. 152-166.

Sixth Sunday of Easter (C)

Acts 15:1-2, 22-29

In Europe there is a country by the sea called the Netherlands or the Low Lands or, sometimes, Holland. Along the North Sea the Dutch who live there have built dikes, huge walls that hold back the North Sea so the Dutch can have more land for farms. Once upon a time, though, it is said, a terrible storm smashed down the great dikes, and the North Sea came rolling across the flat, green pastures of the Netherlands. When the storm finally stopped and the sea rolled back, a group of little girls went to carry some fresh water to the cows out in the pastures.

The Dutch girls were carrying their pails of water, happily splashing through puddles of water in their wooden shoes, when one of them shouted, "Look! Over there in that pool of water! I see a huge fish!" They raced toward the big fish tail they saw sticking out of the water, and what should they discover but a mermaid, a beautiful woman with the tail of a fish!

The girls ran home and told everyone what they had found. Soon people came and carried the mermaid back to town. She struggled and struggled, for she wanted to return to the sea, but they insisted on taking her into town. What were they going to do now with this mermaid?

The mayor said that she should not be permitted to remain a mermaid. "After all," he said, "mermaids are wild, fantastic creatures from the world of make-believe."

"But maybe she *wants* to be a mermaid," one of the girls objected.

"No," insisted the mayor, "we must turn her into a proper Dutch housewife."

The town leaders agreed this was the best thing for her to be. They covered up her long green tail with a long, long skirt. They gave her a big house in town and sent a strong young woman to show her how to be a housewife—how to sew and cook and clean, to work and work and work, and to have great pride in how clean her house was.

Bursting with pride himself, the mayor went to see this new housewife. The strong young woman who worked there opened the door and let him in. The mermaid had just finished mopping the floor and the mayor walked right across it in his muddy boots. Well, what do you think the mermaid did? She waved angrily to the strong young woman, who picked up that mayor like a little baby and carried him, kicking and screaming, to the front door, where she threw him and his muddy boots right into the street! That is what happened to the mayor who tried to make a mermaid into something she was not.

It is almost always foolish to try to force someone to be just like you. In today's Bible lesson lots of new people are joining the Church, and some of the old-timers think that the newcomers must become just like the old-timers. But the early Church discovers that God loves us without our having to act like somebody else.

Ascension Day (ABC)

See page 73

Seventh Sunday of Easter (C)

Acts 16:16-34

In today's Bible reading St. Paul uses God's power to set a slave girl in Greece free. I believe God is still doing things like that. This is the story of how God set a girl in our own nation free by helping her learn how to read.

Mary McLeod Bethune was born in Mayesville, South Carolina, not long after slavery was ended in the United States. Like other black children back then, Mary had to work hard as a little girl, picking cotton with her parents and pulling a plow. Black children were not allowed to go to school. One day when she was ten years old, Mary went to the home of the white family where her mother washed clothes. She was invited into the room of a white girl in the family and Mary picked up a book there. "Put that book down!" the other girl yelled at Mary.

"I wasn't going to hurt it," Mary apologized.

"Put it down!" the girl told Mary. "You know you can't read!" It was true: No one in Mary's whole family had ever had a chance to learn to read.

"I only wanted to look at it," Mary said sadly.

"Well, I suppose I could show it to you," the other girl said, taking the book and opening it to pictures of elephants in Africa. Mary knew that her great-grandfather had been a prince in Africa and that black people had been kidnapped in Africa and brought to the New World to be sold like animals.

"Oh," Mary sighed. "I wish I could read what your book says about Africa."

"Don't be silly," the other girl said. "You'll never learn how to read. Black people don't read."

As Mary walked home that day she told herself, "I will learn to read! Please, God," she prayed, "send someone to help me learn how to read."

A year later, when Mary was eleven, she finally got her chance. The Presbyterian Church sent a teacher to Mayesville to start a school for black children. Mary walked five miles every day just to be able to go to school. She learned how to read, and then the Church gave her a Bible of her own.

Now Mary could read Bible stories to her family after supper. And when the people who bought cotton from her mother and father tried to cheat her parents, Mary could read what the scales really said. No one could cheat her parents anymore. When Mary was a teenager, the Church gave money for her to go away to college and become a teacher.

When she graduated, Mary began to do wonderful things. She started her own school for black children. When a little girl from her school became sick and the hospital would not help her, Mary started her own hospital. When colleges would not let in the students from her school, Mary started her own college,

Bethune-Cookman College. She became a friend of presidents of the United States and even helped to write the charter of the United Nations.

Mary McLeod Bethune lived until she was eighty years old and never stopped working to make things better for her people. God set Mary free by helping her learn to read and then she helped others. God's power is still setting people free.

Pentecost (C)

Romans 8:14-17

Nassar was the toughest kid in his kindergarten and the bravest, too. One day he climbed onto the playground swing and started swinging with all his might, higher than anyone had ever done before. Then suddenly, as he swung forward, Nassar lost his grip on the chains and went flying through the air. He came down so hard that he broke his leg.

Nassar started crying and crying. "Mommy! Mommy!" he cried out. His teacher came running and tried to comfort Nassar, but nothing she did seemed good enough. Hurt and scared, Nassar wanted his mother. He didn't stop crying for her until she came for him and held him.

In today's Bible lesson St. Paul tells us the Holy Spirit makes us call out to God the way we call out "Mommy!" or "Daddy!" God will care for us the way Nassar's mother comforted him. "For all who are led by the Spirit of God," St. Paul says, "are children of God" (Romans 8:14).

Abba is often translated "Father," but it is really a much more intimate term of address than this. The German New Testament scholar Joachim Jeremias suggests that it is better understood as "daddy" or "mommy"—a baby's cry for comfort.

Trinity Sunday (C)

Proverbs 8:22-31

Once, it is said in China, there was a wise old woman who lived in a cabin in the woods. She found a coin one day and put it in her rice jar for safekeeping. The next day when she took some rice out of the jar to cook for lunch, leaving only a few grains in the jar with the coin. By dinnertime, however, she found that the rice jar was full again!

"How wonderful!" she thought. "Now I will always have enough food to eat."

Before long, though, a greedy wolf heard about this coin. He went to her door and demanded, "Give me your magic coin!"

"No," said the old woman.

"Then I will return tonight and eat you up and grab your coin!" the wicked wolf said.

How could the old woman protect herself from the wolf? She put some dried peas on the floor near her door. She put her mousetrap inside the rice jar. She set her hammer on the shelf next to the rice jar. Then she took her broom with her to her bedroom, stretched out on her bed and went to sleep.

That night the greedy wolf crept quietly up to the old woman's cottage. He peered through the bedroom window and saw that she was asleep.

He broke in the door, hurting his shoulder as he did so, slipped on the peas and fell flat on his face. As he stuck his hand in the rice jar the mousetrap snapped on his finger. "Yeow!" he cried, as he knocked the hammer off the shelf—and onto his foot! The woman jumped up and swatted him with her broom. She hit him again and again until she had chased him right out the door! Never again did that wicked wolf bother *that* woman!

Today's reading tells us that the Wisdom of God is like a very wise woman, someone like the wise old woman in today's story. The Book of Proverbs says that she was the first thing God created and that God made everything through her. She rejoices in God, in the world and in you and me.

Sunday After Trinity Sunday (C)

The Body and Blood of Christ

1 Corinthians 11:23-26

When José Limón was a little boy in a small town in Mexico, he enjoyed watching the many folk dances of his country. When he was seven years old, his family moved to the United States and José grew up in Los Angeles, California. He liked art and music as a boy, and his mother and father encouraged him to learn everything he could. He also was interested in ballet, but he thought only girls could be ballet dancers, so he never thought of dancing in a ballet group himself.

When he was twenty years old, José moved to New York City to study painting and become an artist. He didn't paint very well, though, so José left art school and had no idea what to do next with his life.

Then José Limón saw someone dance, a man from Germany who danced in a ballet company. José could see the strength it took the man to leap through the air and lift other dancers up high. He saw right then that a man could be a ballet dancer and be proud of his work. "What I saw," he later said, "simply changed my life."

So José Limón worked hard and became a very famous dancer himself, one of the people who created a whole new way of moving to music called "modern dance." He spent the rest of his life performing all around the world. Twice he was even invited by the President of the United States to dance in the White House. All this happened because José Limón saw one man dance.

In today's Bible lesson St. Paul tells us that at the Last Supper Jesus took bread and wine and said, "Eat this and remember me; drink this and remember me." When people share the Eucharist today, they remember how Jesus changed the lives of people who only heard him once or touched him once or ate dinner with him once. He is still changing people for the better.

Sunday Between May 29 and June 4 (C)

Proper 4/Ninth Sunday of the Year/Second Sunday After Pentecost

Luke 7:1-10

Use this story only after Trinity Sunday. If the Sunday following Trinity Sunday falls between May 24 and May 28, use Proper 3 (the Eighth Sunday After Epiphany) that day. The date of Easter determines the number of Sunday Propers after Pentecost. In addition, Roman Catholics delay the return to Ordinary Time by celebrating the Feast of the Body and Blood of Christ on the Sunday after Trinity Sunday.

Today's Bible story is about a time Jesus healed someone who was far away without even seeing the sick person he healed. Grown-ups sometimes have a hard time believing that miracles like this can happen.

Once, though, there was a man who drank too much beer. He got drunk over and over again. He yelled at his wife and his little girl. He spent a lot of the money he earned on beer and did not have much left to buy food or clothes for his little girl or his wife. He was sick with a disease called alcoholism.

Then this man became a Christian and many things changed. He admitted that he was sick and that he needed God's help to stop drinking. He went to a special kind of hospital where people knew how to help him get well. He started loving his daughter and his wife better, because he finally knew that God really loved him. He began to recover from his sickness.

His friends at work could not believe how much he had changed. It scared them, so they started teasing him about following Jesus. "Surely," they said to him, "you don't believe Jesus did all those miracles? How could he heal those people it talks about in the Bible? How could Jesus do that?"

Do you know what that man said? "I don't know if Jesus healed those people back then," he answered. "But I know he heals people *now*. I was sick and asked him for help. He healed *me*, and that was certainly a miracle."

Sunday Between June 5 and 11 (C)

Proper 5/Tenth Sunday of the Year/Third Sunday After Pentecost

Galatians 1:11-24

Use this story only after Trinity Sunday.

Long ago in England, a famous writer named Rudyard Kipling wrote a poem called "Mulholland's Vow." It tells the story of a man named Mulholland who worked on a ship that carried cows and bulls. Mulholland was a tough sailor who never thought much about what God wanted—until one day a terrible storm swept across the ocean and tossed the cattle ship back and forth. The ropes that tied up the cattle broke, and suddenly there were terrified bulls and cows running all over the deck of the ship as it plunged up and down in the waves. Caught right in the middle of the stampeding hooves and horns was Mulholland.

"Please God," Mulholland prayed, "save my life! Save my life and I'll do anything you want!" Much to Mulholland's amazement, when the storm was over, not a single hoof or horn had touched him.

"Thank you, thank you!" Mulholland cried out to God. "What can I do for you now?" he prayed. "Do you want me to become a preacher? Should I find the biggest church I can and tell everyone how you saved me?"

"No," God answered.

"Don't you want me to preach?" Mulholland asked in disbelief. "Don't you want me to tell others what you have done for me?"

"Yes, I do," God answered. "But I am sending you back to cattle boats instead. Go back where people know you. Preach there."

In today's Bible lesson St. Paul tells how he once tried to hurt the people who followed Jesus and that once he became a Christian himself he went right back to Damascus—the city where he had been trying to destroy the Church.

It seems that often this is what God wants: God wants us to start telling others about God's love for us, about Jesus and about how God has changed us—right where we are.

Sunday Between June 12 and 18 (C)

Proper 6/Eleventh Sunday of the Year/Fourth Sunday After Pentecost

Luke 7:36—8:3

Use this story only after Trinity Sunday.

Once upon a time there was a dragon who lived in a cave in the mountains. He had a huge head with gigantic teeth, and when he was angry smoke poured out of his nose and fire shot out of his mouth. The people of the nearby village were terribly afraid of this dragon. "Something must be done about the dragon," they often grumbled to one another. "Yes, someone must kill him!" they agreed.

When the children of the village heard talk like this they were frightened. A few of them, of course, said they would slay the dragon when they grew up, but nearly all of them were worried that the dragon might kill them first.

There was one little girl in the village, though, who was not afraid. On the day before her birthday she told her father there was someone she had forgotten to invite to her party.

"Well, by all means, go ahead," her father said. "We have room for one more. You can invite anyone you want! Is it a friend from school?"

"No," she answered.

"Is it someone from our neighborhood?" he asked.

"No," she replied.

"Is it one of your cousins?" he asked.

"No," she said.

"Well, then, who is it?" her father wanted to know.

"The dragon," said the little girl.

"The d-d-dragon!" he stuttered.

"Yes, the dragon," she replied.

"B-b-but he'll kill us all! You must be joking!"

"No, I'm not," she said. "You promised! I want to invite the dragon."

So early the next morning the little girl crept out of her house and hiked to the dragon's cave. "Hello, there, Mr. Dragon!" she called into the cave.

"Why have you come here?" he roared.

"I want to invite you to my birthday party," she said.

"Oh, no," thought the dragon. "It must be a trick. I bet those people from the village have come to try to kill me. I had better stamp my feet and breathe fire and smoke to scare them away!" So the dragon roared some more and stamped his feet and blew fire and smoke out the entrance to the cave. But the little girl still wasn't frightened.

"Wow! That was great, Mr. Dragon!" she said, "Now will you come to my birthday party?"

Well, it took that dragon quite a while to stop roaring, but finally he decided that the girl must really mean what she was saying. "Oh," he sniffled, as he shuffled out his cave, "no one has ever invited me to a party before. No one has ever invited me anywhere!"

"Maybe they're afraid of you," she said, "but I want to be your friend."

The dragon cried and cried gigantic tears—but they were happy tears. He went to the party and carried all the children on his back as he swam down the river and flew through the air. He told stories from the olden times to the grown-ups. He laughed and rolled on the grass when the little girl tickled his tummy. And he and the girl and all the villagers became good friends.

Today's Gospel tells us about a woman that everyone thought was a bad person. The people of her village hated her and were afraid of her and stayed away from her just the way those villagers had treated the dragon. But Jesus became her friend, and she cried for joy that someone wanted to be her friend. And just like the dragon, she needed only one friend to change her life completely.

Sunday Between June 19 and 25 (C)

Proper 7/Twelfth Sunday of the Year/Fifth Sunday After Pentecost

1 Kings 19:9-14

Use this story only after Trinity Sunday.

Once there was a boy who lived in the hills of Haiti. His mother was a farmer and one morning she told him, "Take this food I have grown into town and sell it in the marketplace. Then bring the money home."

His little sister helped him load the fruit and vegetables onto the family's donkey. Then the boy climbed onto the donkey's back and set off on the long trip toward town. Soon though, the donkey stopped and started braying, "He-haw! He-haw!"

"What's wrong?" the boy asked, patting the donkey's neck. "Are you hungry? Well, I guess it would be OK to give you just one of the apples."

So the boy gave her one apple. The donkey gobbled it up and continued happily down the road. Half an hour later, though, the donkey stopped again and started braying, "He-haw! He-haw!"

"What is bothering you?" the boy asked her. "Do you need more to eat? Well, here's a carrot." The donkey ate the carrot and once again went on for half an hour, then stopped and started braying, "He-haw! He-haw!"

"Are you *still* hungry?" the boy said. This time he gave her some corn. It went on like this all the way to town. The boy got more and more upset by the braying of the donkey and was ready to do anything to keep her quiet.

Finally, late in the afternoon, they reached town and stopped at the marketplace. But when he opened the bag to take out the food to sell, there was almost nothing left in the bag. He had given nearly all of it to the donkey.

What was he going to do? Now his mother would be angry at him, and he would have little money to bring home from the market. He wanted to run and hide. He huddled in a corner of the marketplace and started to cry.

God saw the donkey, who looked happy and well-fed, and saw the boy, who looked scared and miserable. Then God whispered to the boy in a gentle voice, in a faint whisper, "Next time feed your donkey grass instead."

In today's Scripture reading the prophet Elijah is frightened and has run into a cave to hide. God finds Elijah and speaks to him in a gentle voice, in a faint whisper, telling him what he should do next. Just as God spoke to the boy in this story gently, not yelling at him for making a mistake, God whispers to Elijah: "Go back by the road you took here. Pick a new king for Syria and a new king for Israel. Pick a new prophet and get rid of the evil leaders of this land." Elijah hears this gentle voice of God and does exactly what God has told him to do.

Sunday Between June 26 and July 2 (C)

Proper 8/Thirteenth Sunday of the Year/Sixth Sunday After Pentecost

Galatians 5:1, 13-25

In today's Bible lesson St. Paul says when Christ set us free he wanted us to stay free and to use our freedom to help one another. In China people tell this story about a little horse who learned to use her freedom to think for herself and help others.

Once there was a mare (a mother horse) who had a foal (a baby horse), who stayed beside her all day as she pulled plows and carts. One day the mare asked her foal to carry a bag of wheat to the mill to be ground into flour. The little horse raced toward the mill, happy to be big enough to help, but soon she came to a swift stream. Not knowing how deep the water was, she asked a big bull that was eating grass near the stream, "Mr. Bull, can you please tell me if I can cross this stream?"

"Of course!" replied the bull. "The water is very shallow. I crossed it myself only yesterday."

"Thank you, Mr. Bull," the foal said, as she started into the water. But a little squirrel beside the stream started chattering away at her, "Don't go in! You'll drown! The water is too deep!"

"Well, thank you, Mr. Squirrel," the foal said, backing out of the stream. Now she was confused. Was the bull right or the squirrel? Was it safe for her to cross the stream or not?

The foal trotted back to her mother and asked, "Which one of them is right?"

"I'm not sure," the mare said, as she rested a moment from plowing a field. "I was not there with you to see the stream for myself. The bull is tall, so every stream will seem shallow to him. The squirrel is small, so every stream seems deep to him. You will have to use your own eyes and your own head. See if the water is too deep for you. I know you can figure that out for yourself."

The foal pranced back to the stream, proud that her mother thought she was so grown-up. She ignored the squirrel and the bull, who were busy arguing with each other about how deep the stream was. So she looked at the stream and saw some rocks sticking up out of the water. She saw that she was much bigger than the squirrel and nearly as tall as the bull. "I am big enough to do it!" she said and crossed the stream with no trouble at all. She hurried to the mill, glad to help her mother.

From then on, whenever the foal did not know what to do, she asked others for their ideas and then used her own head. In this way the little horse used her freedom to help others.

Sunday Between July 3 and 9 (C)

Proper 9/Fourteenth Sunday of the Year/
Seventh Sunday After Pentecost

1 Kings 21:1-3, 17-21

In today's Bible lesson God's prophet Elijah condemns a king who was so greedy that he did terrible things to get some land he wanted. Do you know what *greedy* means? Here is a story from Okinawa, in southern Japan, about someone who was greedy.

Once there was a kind old couple who were farmers in Okinawa. One day they were out working in their field when their dog Shiro started barking and pawing at the ground furiously. "What is it, Shiro?" the old woman asked. "Do you want us to dig here?" Hanasaka-jiji asked the dog.

They dug where Shiro had been pawing and pawing. Soon they found a box filled with diamonds. "How did you know this was here?" the old man asked Shiro. "Maybe Shiro is a magic dog," his wife suggested. "We will never be poor again, and we will have money to share with other people."

There was a greedy, selfish neighbor who lived next to them, though, a man who wanted everything for himself and never shared anything. When he looked over the fence and saw what they had found, the man came over to their house and asked if he could borrow Shiro for a while. "Certainly," they said.

The greedy neighbor took Shiro back to his fields. "Now show *me* where to dig!" he shouted at the dog.

Shiro sniffed around and then pawed at the ground. The man eagerly dug where Shiro had pawed, but what do you think he found? Diamonds? No, only smelly garbage! The greedy man was so angry that he hit Shiro on the head with his shovel so hard he killed him.

The old man and his wife were heartbroken. They carried their dead dog back home. Hanasaka-jiji dug a grave for Shiro in their field and planted a little pine tree by it. Every day he stood at Shiro's grave and cried, his tears watering the little tree. In no time at all, the little seedling grew into a huge tree. "Why don't you make the wood from that tree into a bowl for pounding rice into flour?" his wife suggested. "Do you remember how Shiro loved the mochi rice cakes we made? That way we can remember him every time we pound rice."

"That's a wonderful idea," the old man said. So they cut down the tree beside Shiro's grave, carved the wood into a big bowl, filled it with rice and started to pound it. And do you know what happened? As soon as he started to pound the rice, it turned into gold coins! "It's magic!" his wife shouted.

Their greedy neighbor had been watching them, though, peering in through their window. Soon he knocked on their door and asked if he could borrow their bowl to make mochi himself. "Certainly," they agreed.

He took the wooden bowl back to his house, filled it with rice and started to pound it. "Now make *me* some gold coins!" he shouted. But do you think he got gold coins? No, all he got was garbage! Smelly, yucky garbage. He was so angry that he chopped up the wooden bowl with his ax and threw the pieces in the fire.

When the old man went to his neighbor's house for the bowl, all that was left were ashes. He cried and cried that there was nothing left to remind him of Shiro. Sadly, the old man cupped the ashes in his hands and carried them home. Along the way, though, the wind blew some of the ashes out of his hands and onto a dead tree. Suddenly the tree blossomed with beautiful flowers!

The news that a man made dead trees blossom soon spread far and wide. Before long the emperor heard about it and asked the old couple to come to the palace. He showed them an old tree that was dead, a cherry tree that the emperor had liked very much. "Can you make this tree bloom again?" he asked. Sure enough, as soon as some of the ashes touched the tree, lovely cherry blossoms appeared all over its branches. The emperor was so grateful that he invited the old couple to live with him in the palace.

When the greedy neighbor heard about this, he went to see them, asking if he could borrow some of the ashes. "Look," he told the emperor, "I can make trees blossom, too!" The greedy man took the emperor into a grove of dead trees and sprinkled ashes over them. Do you think he got any flowers? No, the branches were soon covered with smelly garbage!

"Throw him in prison!" the emperor told his guards, who hauled the man away.

That is the way it is: If you are greedy, nothing works right, not even magic.

Sunday Between July 10 and 16 (C)

Proper 10/Fifteenth Sunday of the Year/Eighth Sunday After Pentecost

Luke 10:25-37

How long can you stand on one foot? Would one of you like to show us how long you can balance on one foot? *(Give a child or two a chance to demonstrate.)* Grown-ups usually cannot stand on one foot for very long. Let's see how long I can do it. *(Demonstrate.)*

In the time of Jesus teachers tried to figure out what was the most important thing that God wanted us to do. A good teacher, they thought, should be able to take the whole Bible *(flip through a Bible)* and tell you everything you were supposed to do while standing on one foot!

That's why one day another teacher asked Jesus, "Rabbi,"—that means "teacher"—"what do I have to do to live forever?" Jesus asked the other teacher how *he* would sum up the Scriptures, and the man replied, "They say to love God with all your heart, your soul, your mind and your strength. They also say to love your neighbors as much as you love yourself."

Jesus told him, "You have given the right answer. If you do this, you will live forever."

But the other teacher really wasn't satisfied with such a short answer. He said to Jesus, "But who are my neighbors?"

And Jesus answered this question by telling the teacher this story.

Read Luke 10:30-37, preferably using a translation for children, such as the American Bible Society's *Contemporary English Version*, also called *The Bible for Today's Young Reader*, which is even easier for children to understand than their earlier *Today's English Version* or *Good News Bible*.

Sunday Between July 17 and 23 (C)

Proper 11/Sixteenth Sunday of the Year/Ninth Sunday After Pentecost

Luke 10:38-42

Once there was a girl who loved to walk by the sea. If you had been in England long ago, on a morning early in the nineteenth century, you could have seen her strolling along the beach at Lyme Regis and then scrambling up a cliff. A man climbed near her. He carried with him a basket, a hammer and a chisel as he crawled up the crumbling, chalky cliffs. Every once in a while he would stop, pound his chisel into the side of the cliff, pry something loose and put it in his basket.

The little girl hammered away at the rock, too, and dug something out of the cliff. "Look at this one!" she said with a big smile, holding up something for him to see. What were this man and this girl doing?

Mary Anning and her father Richard were hunting for fossils. Nobody in those days knew exactly what these funny-looking stones were. Some had patterns that looked like flowers. Others looked like seashells or bones. Mary and her father called these stones "curiosities." He set them on a little table in his carpentry shop and sold them to tourists who visited Lyme Regis every summer.

Many people in those days thought that girls—and women—should stay indoors and not take risks. Mary Anning was lucky to have a father who thought differently. He was proud of how brave and strong his little girl was. He loved to watch her chiseling away in places where most people feared to go. It made Richard Anning very happy to share his unusual hobby with his daughter, teaching her everything he knew about finding "curiosities."

Her brother James sometimes looked for fossils, too, but it was Mary who really took a liking to the hard, risky work of digging up ancient bones. Before long, Mary would need more courage than ever before. When she was only ten years old, her father got sick with tuberculosis, a disease in his lungs, and died suddenly. His family was shocked—and without the money Richard had earned building cabinets, they were now quite poor. Soon Mary had to drop out of school, never to return.

Not only was Mary unable to be with friends at school, she had lost her favorite climbing partner. She missed him so badly that she could not stand to walk by the sea where the two of them had searched for fossils. And with her father gone, she worried about how she might help earn money to feed her family.

Then, in 1810, someone in Lyme bought an ammonite Mary had found—a flat, coiled, ancient seashell. "I decided at that moment," Mary said later, "to go back to the beach again."

Soon the money she earned selling "curiosities" was helping to support her family. It was certainly an unusual job. In fact, Mary may have been the first person in the world to take up fossil-collecting as a full-time job. She would get up early in the morning and search the beaches, scaling cliffs all alone, to dig up creatures from the past. The next year, in 1811, her brother James found a very odd-looking rock and gave it to her. It was shaped like a lizard's long skull, with room for two hundred sharp teeth. By now Mary suspected that her "curiosities" were really parts of ancient plants and animals that had somehow turned to stone. "I *have* to find the rest of that creature!" she told herself. She grabbed her hammer, her chisel, and her collecting basket and raced to the beach.

What Mary found shocked the whole world. There, in the chalky cliffs near Lyme Regis in the year 1811, this eleven-year-old girl made one of the greatest fossil discoveries of all time. She found an entire skeleton—all the bones—of a huge prehistoric beast!

This sea monster was almost seven feet long (over two meters) and it was the strangest creature anyone had ever seen. The skull and chest were like those of a lizard with big eyes, but its teeth were like a crocodile's. It had a nose, jaws and flippers like a dolphin (or porpoise), but its backbone was like the spine of a fish, and its tail and fin were like a shark's!

This fossil was so big that Mary knew at once that it was much too important to sell to tourists. She hired men from town to help her dig the heavy skeleton out of the cliff. Then the family who owned the land where Mary discovered the skeleton paid Mary twenty-three pounds of silver and gave the skeleton to a museum (now part of the British Museum of Natural History in London) so that everyone could see it.

Mary's discovery set off a fossil hunt around the world, as thousands of people tried to find one themselves. Scientists from near and far came to the museum to see what Mary had found. Because her beast looked half like a fish and half like a lizard, scientists put together the Greek words for fish and lizard and called it *ichthyosaurus*: "the fish-lizard." Scientists eventually decided that ichthyosaurus swam the seas 180 million years ago, when brontosaurus, allosaurus and stegosaurus walked the land— but this was before anyone had ever heard of a brontosaurus or had seen the bones of any dinosaur at all. (Not until eleven years later did another woman, Mary Ann Mantell, find the first dinosaur fossil: a huge tooth from a giant iguanodon that she spotted in some rocks along a road near Lewes in England.)

In 1821, when she was still only a young woman, before anyone had ever seen a single dinosaur bone, Mary made a second discovery that startled the world: She found an ancient sea serpent! This big reptile had a small head, a long neck, a body shaped like a turtle's, a short tail and four paddle-shaped flippers. This creature is now called *plesiosaurus*—which means "almost like a lizard." Plesiosaurs swam the seas from the time of dinosaurs until the time when flowers and mammals—warm and furry animals—first appeared on earth.

And Mary kept digging. Three years later, in 1824, she found almost a whole skeleton of another plesiosaur, which the Duke of Buckingham bought from her for one hundred pounds of silver, and two ichthyosaurs that were some of the largest ones ever found, almost thirty feet (nine meters) long.

Then, in 1828, Mary made her third great discovery: the first skeleton of a flying reptile ever found anywhere in England. And what a creature it was! *Pterosaurus*—also called *pterodactyl* or "wing-finger"—had wings made of skin stretched tight between its back legs and the long fingers of its arms. Pterosaurs glided through the air when Mary's ichthyosaurs and plesiosaurs were swimming the seas, while fierce allosaurus battled armor-plated stegosaurs on land.

Mary was so good at her work that she was able to buy a house on Broad Street in Lyme Regis. She and her mother Molly lived in the back of the house and Mary turned the front of it into a shop where she sold fossils.

Her shop became a favorite place for tourists, fossil-collectors and scientists to visit. One day in 1844 she even had a king in her store! The king of Saxony (which is now a part of Germany) visited Lyme Regis in 1844; he came in and bought a six-foot (two-meter) skeleton of a baby ichthyosaur in a large slab of black clay. He paid Mary fifteen pounds of silver for it—and asked for her autograph.

Even as she grew older, Mary kept climbing cliffs with her dog Tray and digging for bones of prehistoric monsters. She particularly liked to walk on the beach early in the morning right after a big storm. She would stroll along the sea, looking for places where the wind and the rain had pounded away at the cliffs, sending rocks crashing down to the beach below, for this was the best place to find fossils that had been buried in the chalky cliffs. It was a cold and dangerous time to scramble up slippery, crumbling hillsides, but it was also the best time to find new beasts from the past.

The fossils Mary Anning found in Lyme Regis were sent to museums around the world, where they have been seen by millions of people. But she was particularly happy to show her fossils to the children who visited her little shop on Broad Street in Lyme Regis. She was delighted that they wanted to learn about prehistoric life and hoped that someday they would make discoveries of their own.

Mary Anning chose to learn everything she could about prehistoric creatures instead of doing what people expected women to do in those days. Today's Bible passage tells us about a time when a friend of Jesus named Mary wanted to learn everything she could from Jesus instead of doing the things people expected women to do. What do you think Jesus says about women who do such unexpected things, who are so eager to learn? Jesus says that Mary has chosen what is best and it will not be taken away from her.

Sunday Between July 24 and 30 (C)

Proper 12/Seventeenth Sunday of the Year/ Tenth Sunday After Pentecost

2 Kings 5:1-15b

This is what I saw one year at Halloween: A little girl slowly made her way down the city street holding onto her mother with one hand and clutching a plastic jack-o-lantern with the other hand. (It was sort of early in the day to see trick-or-treaters, but mothers and fathers were worried this Halloween. They were afraid of poisoned candy and were carefully checking every gift their children received. It was not a very happy Halloween for either children or grown-ups.)

As they came around the corner, the little girl's mother led her away from a homeless man who was lying against a wall with his hat laid on the sidewalk in front of him, begging for money. As the girl and her mother walked by, the man looked up and mumbled something to them. I wondered what he wanted, and for a minute the mother seemed not to know whether to stop or to hurry away.

Then the poor man held up a finger and motioned to the little girl. He reached into his hat, pulled out some coins and dropped them into the little girl's jack-o-lantern. And I had been sure that the homeless man was begging for money! It never occurred to me that he might want to give something to the little girl.

In today's Bible lesson someone named Naaman almost misses a chance to be healed of his sickness because he is sure he knows who can help him. Naaman won't listen at first to a little girl who tells him that a prophet in a foreign land, Elisha, can make him well. When he finds out that Elisha is not a king or a rich man but just a simple prophet, and that all Elisha wants him to do is to wash himself in the Jordan River, Naaman storms away in a rage. Only when Naaman gets over his prejudice about who can help is God able to heal him. We never can tell who God may use to help us!

Sunday Between July 31 and August 6 (C)

Proper 13/Eighteenth Sunday of the Year/
Eleventh Sunday After Pentecost

Luke 12:13-21

Once there was a young man who was going to school to learn how to be a pastor. He had time to work a few days every week and he thought it would be good to work in a church that was helping poor people. But he heard about another job in a wealthy parish about forty miles from his school.

The young man went out to visit the wealthy parish and the people there offered him the job. It was a long way to travel every weekend and he did not get to see his friends on Saturdays anymore, but he took the job anyway. He told himself that there were good reasons to choose this job, but the real reason was this: They were paying a lot more money than anyone else.

Boy, was he ever dumb! He didn't like the long trip on the train every weekend. He missed seeing his friends. He didn't like the people he worked with very much and before long he hated the work he was doing. He was just like the rich fool in today's Bible lesson: He got a lot of money, but he lost things that are more important than money.

Do you know why I am certain that he made a mistake? I was that foolish young man!

Sunday Between August 7 and 13 (C)

Proper 14/Nineteenth Sunday of the Year/ Twelfth Sunday After Pentecost

Luke 12:32-40

Do you know what greedy means? People in Norway tell this story about what happened to a troll—an evil monster—who was greedy.

Once three goats lived on the side of a hill near a swift river. They wanted to eat some berries that grew on the other side of the river, but to get there they had to cross a high, narrow bridge. Under the bridge lived a big, mean troll.

"Trip-trap, trip-trap," went the feet of the littlest goat as she started across the bridge.

"Who's that trip-trapping over *my* bridge?" growled the troll from underneath the bridge.

"It is I, the littlest goat," she answered.

"How dare you walk on *my* bridge!" roared the troll. "I'm going to eat you up!"

"Oh, don't bother with me," the clever goat said. "My big brother is coming along soon, and you'll have much more to eat then." So the greedy troll let her ccross the bridge.

Soon the second goat came to the bridge. "Trip-trap! Trip-trap!" went his feet as he started across the bridge.

"Who's that trip-trapping over *my* bridge?" growled the troll.

"It is I, the middle-sized goat," he answered.

"How dare you walk on *my* bridge!" roared the troll. "I'm going to eat you up!"

"Oh, don't bother with me," the clever goat said. "My big sister is coming along soon, and you'll have much more to eat if you wait for her."

So the greedy troll let the second goat cross the bridge. Soon the third goat came to the bridge. "TRIP-TRAP! TRIP-TRAP!" went her feet as she started across the bridge.

"Who's that trip-trapping over *my* bridge?" growled the troll.

"It is I, the third goat," she answered.

"How dare you walk on *my* bridge!" roared the troll. "Let me at you! I'm going to eat you up!"

And with that he leapt onto the bridge and ran toward her. But she lowered her head and butted that troll off the bridge and into the river below. And that was the last anyone saw of him. Because he was greedy, he got nothing at all.

In today's Bible lesson Jesus tells us that rather than being greedy and worrying about getting more and more for ourselves, we should share what we have with those who have less.

Sunday Between August 14 and 20 (C)

Proper 15/Twentieth Sunday of the Year/
Thirteenth Sunday After Pentecost

Psalm 10:12-18
Jeremiah 20:7-13

Once there was a Methodist preacher in Hawaii named Nick Dizon. Like many people who worked on the great big farms called plantations, Nick Dizon had come to Hawaii from the Philippines.

The people who owned the plantations where pineapples and sugar cane were grown gave the workers a little house to live in on the plantation, but gave them very little money for all the hard work they did. Not only did the workers' homes belong to the plantation owners, but so did the only stores where the workers could buy food and clothing and other things they needed. The plantation stores charged the workers much more money than the stores in town did, but the plantations were so far away from town that there was no place else where the workers could shop.

The workers knew they were not being treated fairly, but no one would help them. The plantation owners also owned all the church buildings on the plantations, paid the pastors and owned the homes where the pastors lived, so naturally most pastors were afraid to preach anything that the owners did not want the workers to hear.

God needed a prophet, someone brave enough to say the things God wanted to be said, even if this got the person who said these things in trouble. God needed a prophet brave enough to say that the workers must be paid more money and must be treated fairly. I believe that God raised up Nick Dizon as a prophet.

Nick Dizon began preaching about fairness for workers. The plantation owners were angry and told him to stop, but he went on preaching powerful sermons about how God loved everyone and wanted justice for everyone. The owners fired Nick and stopped paying him, but he went right on preaching. They threw him out of his home, but he kept preaching. They told him he could not even set foot on the plantation anymore, but he found a building near a plantation and invited the workers to worship with him there. When the workers went on strike—when they told the owners they would not work anymore until they were paid more money and were treated fairly—Nick Dizon helped them with their strike.

Nick had to be very brave to keep doing these things, but finally the workers won their strike and life began to get better for everyone who worked in Hawaii. The workers remembered how his sermons had given them courage to struggle to make things fair, how this prophet had helped them to bring justice to Hawaii.

In today's Scripture reading the prophet Jeremiah tells how hard it can be to be a prophet, but today's Psalm reminds us that God listens to the cries of the poor and gives them courage. The people of Hawaii saw how God heard the cries of poor people and used prophets such as Nick Dizon to help them and to give them courage.

Sunday Between August 21 and 27 (C)

Proper 16/Twenty-First Sunday of the Year/
Fourteenth Sunday After Pentecost

Psalm 84

Over three hundred years ago, people came to the colony of Massachusetts, in what is now the United States, from their homes in England across the Atlantic Ocean. They had been treated badly in England for wanting to worship God in their own Churches instead of in the king's Church, the Church of England, and they were happy to build new homes in Massachusetts. They thought it would be easy now to worship God their own way, without interference from the king, but they soon learned that their freedom would not be gained easily.

Some of these people, who were called Puritans, lived for a while in the town of Ipswich and then moved to a place nearby where they started the town of Essex. Going to Ipswich was a long trip on a horse in those days, especially in the winter, so the people of Essex wanted to build a new church in their own town.

In those days, though, the king's judge had to give permission for a church to be built! And the judge told the people of Essex that they could not build a sanctuary in their town but must keep going all the way to Ipswich to worship God. What the royal judge said was this: "No man in Essex may build a church building or hire a pastor to start a new church."

The *women* of Essex, though, were brave and smart. They noticed that the judge had said, "No *man* of Essex may build a church building or hire a pastor...." The judge had not said a thing about what the *women* could do. Secretly, without telling their husbands what they had decided, Hannah Goodhue (this author's grandfather's grandfather's grandfather's grandmother) and her friends, Mrs. Varney and Mrs. Martin, got the women of Essex together and made their own plans.

Early one spring morning in the year 1679, Mrs. Martin got on a horse and rode all the way to the town of Gloucester while Hannah Goodhue and Mrs. Varney rode all the way to Manchester. The three women hired workers in these towns and brought them back to Essex. Meanwhile, the other women in Essex had begun cutting down trees to clear some land. Together the women of Essex and the men they hired in the other towns built a church building—all in one day.

When the judge heard what the women had done, he was so angry that he sent his sheriff to arrest Mrs. Varney and Mrs. Martin and Hannah Goodhue and throw them in jail in Salem—even though they had not broken any law. The three women were very frightened to be put in jail, but when they finally got out, their town had its own church.

In today's Psalm we say how much we love God's temple, and how happy are those whose strength comes from God, who trust in God. Mrs. Varney, Mrs. Martin and Hannah Goodhue trusted God and God gave them the strength to build a new church for their town. And how happy they and the people of Essex were to have a place in their own town where they could worship God!

This story might also be used near Independence Day to celebrate some of the unsung heroines who helped bring religious liberty to our land.

Sunday Between August 28 and September 3 (C)

Proper 17/Twenty-Second Sunday of the Year/
Fifteenth Sunday After Pentecost

Luke 14:1, 7-14
Hebrews 13:1-8

Once, long ago, there was a girl named Theodora who grew up in a poor family in Byzantium, the city that today is called Istanbul in Turkey. Theodora's father took care of the bears at the circus in Byzantium, but he died when Theodora was just a little girl about four or five years old. This left Theodora's family even worse off than they had been before. It was hard for her to find a job, so while she was still just a girl, Theodora became a dancer and an actress—and in those days people thought that dancers and actresses were very bad and the owners of the theaters treated them terribly.

Then Theodora became a Christian, and her life began to change. She stopped working as an actress and a dancer. She lived very simply and spun thread to make money. A wealthy man named Justinian met Theodora and fell in love with her. Justinian asked her to marry him, even though his family was embarrassed that their rich son loved a poor girl like Theodora, particularly one who had worked in a theater. Later, Justinian became the emperor of the mighty Byzantine Empire and Theodora became the empress.

Theodora was now rich and powerful, but she was also a devout Christian. She loved good food and fancy clothes, but she also loved helping other people. Nothing pleased her more than to help build new churches, new hospitals for people who were sick, new orphanages for children who had no mother or father and new homes for people who were poor. She remembered what it was like to be poor and found joy in helping the poor.

Theodora also remembered what it was like to be ridiculed for being a woman who worked as an actress and a dancer. She got the laws changed to protect widows and the children of slaves. She also got the laws changed that forced women and girls to work for theater owners even if the owners mistreated them. She took one of her palaces and turned it into a convent called Metanoia, which means "change of heart," where hundreds of women and girls who had been mistreated began new lives.

Theodora did what today's Bible lessons tell us to do: She welcomed the poor, she opened her home to strangers and she cared for those who had been treated badly.

Sunday Between September 4 and 10 (C)

Proper 18/Twenty-Third Sunday of the Year/
Sixteenth Sunday After Pentecost

Ezekiel 33:1-11

In today's Bible reading the prophet Ezekiel warns people that God wants them to stop doing the bad things they are doing. Usually, though, people do not want to hear a prophet tell them things like this. When I was a boy there was someone many people thought was God's prophet. People certainly got upset by the things this person said. His name was Rev. Dr. Martin Luther King, Jr.

The first thing Dr. King said had to change was the way black people were treated in this country. Back then there were terrible rules and laws in many places in the United States that said black children could not go to school with white children, that they could not swim at the same beach or swimming pool, that they could not even drink out of the same water fountain—and black boys and girls almost always got lousy schools and playgrounds and homes and everything else. There were rules that said black families could not eat in the same restaurant as white families or go to the same church or go to the movies together. In some cities there were even laws that said that when white people got on a public bus, black people had to get up, give the white people their seats and then ride all the way standing up in the back of the bus.

Dr. King said that these rules and laws were unfair and that they were wrong, and that God wanted things to change. In Montgomery, Alabama, a brave woman named Rosa Parks refused to give up her place on a bus one day and was arrested. Dr. King asked all the black people of Montgomery to not ride the city buses until black people were treated fairly, and black people stopped riding the buses. This angered and scared many white people. Someone even threw a bomb at Dr. King's house, but he kept preaching that God wanted everyone to be treated fairly and with dignity and respect. Finally, after a year, the rules were changed on all the buses in Montgomery.

Across America, people joined together in what is called the civil rights movement, demanding that other laws and rules be changed so that black people would be treated fairly. Dr. King preached and led marches and demonstrations. He was shouted at and spat upon, beaten up and arrested, but he did not fight back or try to hurt anyone. He just kept preaching and showing that God loves everyone and wants justice for all people. Because of Dr. King and the civil rights movement, the laws that kept black people and white people apart were changed all across the United States.

The second thing that Dr. King said had to change was war. Back then the government of the United States was fighting a war in a little country far away called Vietnam. Dr. King said that it was wrong for our government to fight this war because God wanted peace, not war, and that the government should spend money to help people here in America, not to kill people in Vietnam. When Dr. King started saying this, many people were very angry because they thought our nation had to fight this war and that no one should question whether or not God wanted us to fight. Slowly but steadily, though, the people of America came to see that Dr. King was right about the war, that it was wrong and that it was a mistake, and that it would hurt our nation badly if we did not stop fighting the people of Vietnam.

The third thing that Dr. Martin Luther King, Jr., said had to change in this country was the way poor people were treated. He knew that it would not do much good to change a law that kept black people out of a restaurant if they still had no money to buy any food there. Dr. King said that poor people needed jobs—jobs that earned them enough money for them to take care of their families. Just before he died, Dr. King went to Memphis, Tennessee. The garbage collectors in Memphis were on strike: They said they would not work anymore until they were treated fairly and paid more money for their work. Dr. King felt that God wanted him to go to Memphis to help the garbage collectors with their strike, but he also knew that many people were angry at him for helping poor people. "Don't go!" his friends told him. "You may be killed!"

"But I have to go," Dr. King answered. "That is where God needs me. I have to tell people that God wants justice for those workers." So Dr. King bravely went to Memphis and helped the strikers. And someone did shoot him and kill him, someone who did not want to hear what God wanted Dr. King to say.

People often try to kill God's prophets, but killing Dr. King did not make people around the world forget what he had said. After he was dead, even more people around the world realized that he was right about the things that needed to change. They said that Dr. King was a prophet like Ezekiel, someone who showed us how God wants us to live.

This story could also be told to celebrate King's birthday, January 15.

Sunday Between September 11 and 17 (C)

Proper 19/Twenty-Fourth Sunday of the Year/
Seventeenth Sunday After Pentecost

Luke 15:1-10

How many of you have heard about a shepherd boy named David who became the king of Israel? How many of you have heard how David fought a giant named Goliath? David certainly was brave, wasn't he? David often rushed into things without thinking, though, and sometimes he did very bad things.

When David was a young man, he became the leader of a band of robbers—in fact, in those days many shepherds were thieves. David and his band of robbers were on their way to the wilderness of Paran. David sent a message to a grouchy man named Nabal demanding that Nabal give them some food. Nabal replied by insulting David and refusing to give David and his gang of thieves anything to eat. David was so angry that he decided to kill Nabal. He and his men buckled on their swords and headed toward Nabal.

When Nabal's wife Abigail heard about this, she knew that her whole family was in danger. Abigail quickly packed up two hundred loaves of bread, some wine, meat, raisins and figs and all kinds of other food. Without telling her husband, she sent this food to David and his men as a gift, and then got on her donkey and went looking for David and his gang.

When Abigail found the band of robbers, she told David that her husband Nabal was a fool and asked David not to kill him. She said to David, "It is God who has kept you from murder and from killing people in order to get even. You are going to be the king of Israel someday. If you murder Nabal and my family, you will feel terrible inside."

"Praise God for sending you to me today!" David said. "Thank God for what you have done today. You have kept me from murdering. Go back home and don't worry. I will do what you have asked."

Abigail went looking for this outlaw when he was about to do something wrong. The parable Jesus tells today tells us that God is just like that. God is like a woman who searches and searches for a lost coin until she finds it and then rejoices that she has found it. Like that woman, like Abigail, God comes looking for us when we are doing wrong.

Sunday Between September 18 and 24 (C)

Proper 20/Twenty-Fifth Sunday of the Year/
Eighteenth Sunday After Pentecost

Luke 16:1-13

Long ago there was a man named Lakish. He was a gladiator in the Roman circus, where he fought wild animals like lions and tigers, but then decided to use his strength to rob people instead. He joined a band of robbers and soon became the leader of their gang.

One day, legend has it, Lakish was hiding near a river, waiting for someone to come along whom he could rob. Along came Rabbi Jochanan, a great Jewish teacher. Lakish jumped down on top of Rabbi Jochanan from his hiding place with a mighty leap. "Give me your money!" he shouted.

"What a wonderful leap! How strong you are!" Rabbi Jochanan said. "Your strength is certainly a gift from God. What a pity you waste it on such foolishness as robbing people."

"What do you mean, *waste* it?" Lakish demanded.

"If you used your strength to study the Scriptures," Rabbi Jochanan told him, "you could be a genius."

Lakish did not know what to say. He had never thought of himself as being very smart, let alone a genius!

Then Rabbi Jochanan told him, "If you give up your evil ways and become my student, I promise you that you will have a great future and real happiness."

And that is exactly what he did. Mighty Lakish was strong enough inside to change. He stopped being a robber and became Rabbi Jochanan's student and eventually a rabbi himself, a great teacher and the most famous of Rabbi Jochanan's disciples. He is known today as Rabbi Simeon Ben Lakish or "Resh Lakish"—which means "Captain Lakish."

Resh Lakish was known for his honesty and courage. When he learned that Rabbi Jochanan was depressed because he had been robbed, Lakish chased the thieves until he got back everything they had stolen from his teacher. When Lakish heard that Rabbi Isi had been captured by bandits, Lakish rushed to save him, risking his own life.

Once people had feared the strong arms of Lakish; now they admired how strong he was inside. Just as Rabbi Jochanan had promised, Resh Lakish had a great life and real happiness. Today's Bible lesson tells us that God often does something very much like what Rabbi Jochanan did. When God finds someone smart who is using his or her brains to cheat other people, God tells them this: If you're really smart, you'll do what God wants.

Sunday Between September 25 and October 1 (C)

Proper 21/Twenty-Sixth Sunday of the Year/
Nineteenth Sunday After Pentecost

Luke 16:19-31

Once there was a man who lived in a nice house on top of a hill. When he looked out the window each morning, he saw his fields, his barn, his sheep and his cows. "All mine!" he said each day with a smile.

Then one day he went for a walk through the village below his house. As he walked down a narrow street he heard a terrible racket around the corner: "Ruff-ruff-ruff!" and "Fft-fft-fft!" He peeked around the corner and saw a tiny orange kitten trapped by two huge barking dogs. The dogs were about to pounce on the little kitten when the man swung his walking stick at them and chased them away. "Here, kitty," he said to the frightened kitten, who was gasping for breath. "Now, now, you're OK. You're safe now. What's your name, kitty?" he asked, picking her up in his arms and petting her to calm her.

"I don't—I don't—want to tell you," she said, still gasping for breath.

"What's this?" the man said. "You can talk?"

"Thank you for saving me," the orange kitten said, "but I must be going now."

"I don't believe it!" he shouted. "You can really talk! Hey," he said, "if you are magic, you can use your magic for me. I want to be rich! I want to live in a mansion!"

"Very well," said the kitten, who turned and walked away.

"Hey, wait!" he called. "Where are you going!" But when he got home he saw that his house had been changed into a huge mansion. "All mine!" he said with a smile.

The man was very happy in his new mansion—for a week or so. Then he wanted more. He strolled back into the village and looked for the kitten. "Magic kitten!" he whispered. "Where are you?"

"Yes?" said the orange kitten as it came around a corner.

"I want something more," said the man.

"What do you want?" asked the kitten unhappily.

"I want... I want...," the man said, stopping to think a moment, but he never thought to ask for anything for someone else. "I want to be an earl," he said. "I want to be lord of this village and this mountain and the whole valley down below."

"You may have your wish," the kitten said and turned away. Suddenly the man was wearing a nobleman's clothes. He hurried home and found that his mansion had been turned into a manor house. "All mine!" he said with a smile.

The man was happy being an earl—for about a week. Then he went back to the village and called to the kitten.

"What do you want now?" the kitten said.

"I want more!" he said. "I want...I want to be king!"

"King!" howled the kitten.

"Yes, king!" the man shouted. "Remember, I saved your life!"

"Have it your way," the orange kitten said as it stalked away.

In the twinkling of an eye, the man was wearing a king's robes and standing before a royal coach. "Your majesty," servants said as they bowed before him. As he rode up the hill to his castle, he gloated, "All mine!"

To be king was great—for about a week. Then he went looking for the kitten once more. "Magic kitten!" he shouted.

"*Now* what?" snarled the orange kitten.

"Make me emperor of the whole world!"

"What!" yowled the cat. "Have you lost your mind!"

"King is not enough!" he shouted. "I want to rule everyone on earth!"

"No!" the kitten replied. "You want too much and you want it all just for you! Now you shall lose everything." And after saying that, the kitten disappeared.

"Kitten!" the man called from his carriage. "Don't go! Don't—" but just then the carriage disappeared and the man fell on the ground. His royal robes were gone, too, and he had only the rags of a poor beggar. He heard shouts coming toward him and turned to see his castle in flames. The people of the village had burned it and were hunting for the king. That greedy man got up and ran for his life. He ran and ran and did not stop until he was far, far away.

Everything that man got ended up doing him no good at all, because he wanted everything just for himself. Today's readings from the First Letter to Timothy and from the Gospel of Luke tell us that being rich will not help us if we are not willing to share what we have with others.

Sunday Between October 2 and 8 (C)

Proper 22/Twenty-Seventh Sunday of the Year/
Twentieth Sunday After Pentecost

Amos 5:6-7, 10-15

In today's Old Testament reading the prophet Amos warns the people that they hate those who challenge injustice and have oppressed the poor. "Do what is right!" he tells them. I believe that God is still sending us people to tell us things such as this and that God is still looking out for the prophets. One of my teachers, a man named Walter Wink, is one of those people God has looked out for and protected.

A few years ago Walter went on a trip to Africa. He visited the country of Botswana, and he wanted to go to South Africa to help the people in that nation who were working to stop the unfair things their government was doing. But the government of South Africa knew that he had spoken out against the way it oppressed blacks, so they would not give him a visa—a piece of paper that would allow him to enter their country.

Walter decided to risk sneaking into South Africa without their permission, without a visa, even though he knew he might be arrested and thrown in jail. Some friends of his, a group of nuns in Botswana, stayed up all night long, praying with him for his safety and asking God to help Walter to do something to make things right in South Africa. As the sun came up they sang a hymn together.

Walter was nervous and a little scared as he went to the border between Botswana and South Africa. He came to a bridge between the two nations and started to walk across it. On the other side were South African soldiers who were supposed to stop all the people who came across the bridge and ask to see their visas before letting them into the country. Walter, of course, had no visa, no permission from the government to enter the country. Walter couldn't imagine how God could ever help him sneak into South Africa, but he kept on walking.

Then something amazing happened. The soldier who stopped Walter just forgot to ask for his visa. The soldier seemed to be thinking about something else as he hummed a tune. And do you know what song he was humming? The very same hymn that the nuns had sung with Walter that morning as they prayed with him. Do you think maybe God made sure that soldier forgot to look for a visa?

So Walter managed to sneak into South Africa and had a chance to encourage the people there who were working to make things fair, and he had a chance to tell the government what Amos told his people in today's Bible lesson: "Do what is right."

Sunday Between October 9 and 15 (C)

Proper 23/Twenty-Eighth Sunday of the Year/
Twenty-First Sunday After Pentecost

Psalm 26

In today's Psalm someone speaks of singing a hymn of thanksgiving and telling about all the wonderful things God has done. Did any of you sing this morning? Did you sing a hymn of thanksgiving? Is it usually easier to sing a refrain, the part of the words that we sang over and over again?

Once, over a hundred years ago, a woman named Annie Hawks wrote a poem and showed it to her pastor in Brooklyn in New York City. Her pastor, Robert Lowry, told Annie, "This would make wonderful words for a hymn!" He offered to write music to go with her poem, but he insisted on adding a few words to her poem: a chorus or refrain that would be sung over and over again.

"I'm glad you like my poem," Annie Hawks told him, "and it is very kind of you to offer to write music for it, but why do you want to add anything to it? Isn't it good enough the way I wrote it?"

"It's a fine poem," Robert Lowry assured her, "but I want everyone to be able to sing it, even people who cannot read. If we repeat a part of the hymn again and again, even the little boys and girls will be able to sing along. I want to include the children—everyone—in singing the hymn."

This seemed like a good idea to Annie Hawks. So Robert Lowry wrote a tune and added a chorus that said (*sing*):

> I need thee, O I need thee!
> Every hour I need thee!
> Every hour I need thee!
> O bless me now, my Savior,
> I come to thee.

Sure enough, the very first time they sang the new hymn in Annie's parish in Brooklyn, the boys and girls were able to learn the words in the chorus right away and join in the singing. Would you sing it with me? (*Sing the chorus again.*) Because Robert Lowry and Annie Hawks added the chorus, children in Brooklyn—and everywhere else the hymn has been sung—have been able to sing along with the adults and "I Need Thee Every Hour" became a favorite hymn of millions of people. And when you and I do what today's Psalm says, when we sing a hymn of thanksgiving to God, we can do the same thing Annie Hawks and Robert Lowry did: We can include everyone.

Sunday Between October 16 and 22 (C)

Proper 24/Twenty-Ninth Sunday of the Year/ Twenty-Second Sunday After Pentecost

Luke 18:1-8

Once there was an old woman named May Lemke who lived in the state of Wisconsin. She and her husband had raised five children who had all grown up and had moved out of the house. They thought they were all finished raising babies, but then they learned about a baby who really needed them. This baby was very sick. He could not move his arms or legs and he had no eyes, so he would never be able to see. May and her husband adopted this baby as their own son and named him Leslie Lemke.

The Lemkes gave Leslie all the love they could. Day after day, for years and years, May prayed that her son would someday be able to walk. Her husband took the boy into the lake near her home and held him up in the water. Here, for the first time in his life, the boy moved his arms and legs a little, so they took Leslie back to the lake over and over again.

The Lemkes tried to get a wheelchair for their boy from a nearby hospital, but the people at the hospital wouldn't give them one, saying, "It's no use trying to help him. Leslie will never be able to do anything."

But May Lemke would not give up. Do you know what she did next? She had her husband tie Leslie, who was now a big boy, onto her back so that his feet were just touching the ground. Every day she walked through the woods with Leslie tied to her back, and every day she asked God in her prayers to help her son walk. Little by little, Leslie started to move his feet and then his legs. Finally, when he was twelve years old, he stood up by himself for the first time.

May believed that there was at least one thing that every person could do especially well, so she kept praying, day after day, asking God to show them what Leslie's talent was. And the Lemkes kept caring for their son and loving him, even though he still could not say a single word to them.

Then one night when Leslie was about twenty years old, long after his mother and father had gone to sleep, Leslie crawled out of his bed and sat down in front of the piano that his parents kept in his room. He put his fingers on its keys and started to play. He didn't just bang on the keys the way little children do sometimes. All at once, he was playing beautiful music.

His parents could not believe what they heard coming from Leslie's room. They rushed in and saw him playing a complicated piece of music by a composer named Rachmaninoff which he had heard on the radio—a piece that most people have to practice for years before they can play it. It seemed like a miracle!

May Lemke thanked God for showing them what Leslie's talent was, and Leslie showed the whole world what he could do. Because Leslie was blind, he could not read the marks on the page that most musicians use to show them what to play, and he could not see the keys on the piano, but somehow he was able to hear music and figure out which keys to play. When he was twenty-eight years old, Leslie began to talk and discovered that he could do the same thing with the words of songs. As soon as Leslie heard a song just once he could sing the words himself, and he could do this even if the song was in Spanish or Greek or almost any other language.

In today's Bible lesson Jesus tells us that we should pray to God like a woman who keeps coming back to a judge over and over again until the judge makes things fair. That is how May Lemke prayed, day after day, for twenty years, asking God to help her son and never giving up on him herself. And May Lemke found more than she ever asked for.

Sunday Between October 23 and 29 (C)

Proper 25/Thirtieth Sunday of the Year/
Twenty-Third Sunday After Pentecost

Luke 18:9-14

Once two little girls went to church with their fathers. One girl was named Amy and the other was named Lisa. Amy was always putting other people down, and when it was time to pray, Amy silently prayed, "I am glad you didn't make me a bad girl, God. I'm glad I don't do naughty things or get in fights or get scolded by my teachers. I'm so glad you didn't make me like that bad little girl over there—that Lisa!"

But while Amy was saying this prayer, Lisa prayed, "God, I don't always do the right thing. Please forgive me, God."

Now which one of these girls do you think God could help? The one who knew she *needed* God's help, of course! Today's Gospel is a story like this. Jesus told it once to people who thought they were perfect already and a lot better than other people.

Read the story, preferably using a translation for children, such as the *Contemporary English Version*

Sunday Between October 30 and November 5 (C)

Proper 26/Thirty-First Sunday of the Year/
Twenty-Fourth Sunday After Pentecost

Luke 19:1-10

Once upon a time there was a businessman who sold food in a poor neighborhood. He charged much, much more for the food than he paid for it himself. The people in the neighborhood didn't like this, but they couldn't do much about it, because he owned the only food store in the area and they had no way to get to other stores. The grocer was not breaking the law, but he was being very greedy. He became richer and richer while the people in the neighborhood became poorer and poorer. Everyone was jealous of how much money the businessman had, but they hated him, too.

Then one day everybody heard that a famous priest was coming to town. They all wanted to see the priest as he passed by and the man who owned the store wanted to see him, too. He was very short, though, and couldn't see over other people's shoulders and heads, so he climbed up on a fire escape to get a better view.

You can imagine how surprised the businessman was when the priest called out to him, "Hurry down. I want to go to your house." And you can imagine how shocked everyone else was when they heard the priest tell him, "I want to stay at your house tonight."

"What!" they grumbled. "That crumb! Why should the priest go see that lousy guy who charges us so much for food?"

But do you know what the businessman said when the priest got to his home? "I am going to give half of the food in my store away for free to people who don't have enough to eat. Then I'm going to give half of my clothes away and half of my money away and half of everything else I own to poor people. Then I'm going to start giving back money to all the people in this neighborhood who have had to pay me too much money for food. For every extra dollar I charged them, I am going to give them back four dollars!"

In today's Bible lesson there is a man like this named Zacchaeus, who has charged people too much money in taxes, and there is a famous rabbi—Jesus. Listen to what Zacchaeus does:

Read the story, preferably using a translation for children, such as the *Contemporary English Version.*

Sunday Between November 6 and 12 (C)

Proper 27/Thirty-Second Sunday of the Year/
Twenty-Fifth Sunday After Pentecost

2 Thessalonians 2:13—3:5

Long ago there was an evil king named Antiochus who told the Jewish people in his kingdom that they could no longer worship God the way they wanted. He ordered them to worship his gods, not the God of Israel, and he told them they could not go to their temple in Jerusalem to worship anymore. He said they could no longer pray to God in their own language, Hebrew, or even learn how to read Hebrew, and that his soldiers would kill anyone who disobeyed his cruel orders.

The Jewish people were terribly worried. If they could not teach their Hebrew traditions to their children, their children might soon forget about the Jewish religion. But do you know what the Jewish boys and girls made to help save their religion? They made little clay spinning tops called *dreidels*!

How could little clay tops help save their religion? This is what the children did: While the children studied Hebrew or read the Scriptures or learned the Jewish prayers, one child would keep a sharp lookout. If that boy or girl warned that the troops were walking down the street, the rest quickly hid their books and papers under their clothes and started spinning their dreidels.

"Well, there doesn't seem to be anything wrong here," the soldiers would tell each other, "—just some kids playing with tops." Then, as soon as the soldiers had passed, the children started studying again.

And the trick worked. For three years Jewish children managed to learn about their religion secretly. When the Jewish people finally drove out Antiochus and his army and got back their temple, their children still knew about their Scriptures and their language, and still knew how to pray.

Today's Bible lesson tells us to stand firm and hold to the traditions we were taught—just as those Jewish boys and girls held to their traditions.

Sunday Between November 13 and 19 (C)

Proper 28/Thirty-Third Sunday of the Year/ Twenty-Sixth Sunday After Pentecost

2 Thessalonians 3:6-13

Felisa Rincón de Gautier grew up in the town of Fejardo on the eastern tip of the island of Puerto Rico. Her family was well-off and, like many people, she imagined that others must live the way her family lived: in a big house with beautiful gardens on a clean street.

Then one day when Felisa was still just a little girl, she walked from her nice home in her pretty neighborhood to the slum where her family's maid lived. There, for the first time, she saw unpaved streets of dirt and mud, the rickety shacks where poor people had to live, rats running through the slum and hungry children who did not have enough food to eat. Felisa ran home sobbing, and she never forgot what she had seen that day. When she was older, she promised, she would do something to make things better for people who are poor.

Felisa grew up and moved to the big city of San Juan where she opened her own business, a store where she sold clothes she designed herself and made lots of money. She used some of this money to start a new political party, one that worked to build better schools, houses and hospitals for the poor. Soon the party wanted Felisa to run in an election for mayor of San Juan, but both her father and her husband were against this. There were hardly any women mayors anywhere back then, and they thought it was wrong for a woman to be the leader of a city. Together, her father and her husband talked Felisa out of trying to become elected.

Then, in 1945, a terrible storm hit Puerto Rico and destroyed the homes of thousands of people in the slums of San Juan. Felisa did what she could to help these homeless people, but she realized that she could do much more if she were mayor. She decided that she would run for mayor in the next year's election, no matter what her father or her husband thought. In 1946 Felisa Rincón de Gautier became the first woman ever elected mayor of San Juan.

As the new mayor, Felisa set out immediately to make some changes. She had streetlights put up in the slums; she had the roads paved and she had fresh water piped in. Every Wednesday she opened the door to her office at City Hall and invited the poor to come in. She listened to their problems and did everything she could to help, finding jobs and good homes for thousands of people.

Today St. Paul tells us never to get tired of doing good things. Felisa Rincón de Gautier never tired of doing good things, and the people of San Juan loved her so much that they reelected her mayor over and over again for twenty-two years.

Sunday Between November 20 and 26 (C)

Proper 29/Christ the King/Christ the King

Psalm 95
Colossians 1:11-20

When I was a boy, many people thought that the very worst enemies of our nation were the communist countries. Most people, of course, knew that the people who lived in other countries were not our enemies, even if our governments hated each other, but some folks hated all of our enemies so much that they even hated little boys and girls who were born in any nation that had a communist government.

Every year at Halloween, the youth group in my parish went from house to house asking people to give money to UNICEF, the United Nations Children's Fund. Lots of churches in my hometown had been doing this for years and years, and it made us feel good to help children in other nations who were poor. We learned how giving just a few pennies could pay for medicine that would keep a child from getting a terrible disease. We looked forward to collecting the money and to the party we had when we finished trick-or-treating for UNICEF.

Then, when I was in the seventh grade, a few people in the town went to a meeting of the city council and said that UNICEF was a terrible organization. They had found out that some of the food and medicine and blankets that UNICEF gave to poor children was going to little boys and girls in Poland and Yugoslavia. "These are communist countries!" they objected.

"But the money does not go to the government of Poland or Yugoslavia," someone pointed out. "It goes to help children."

"It is better for a child to die," the protesters claimed, "than to grow up in a communist country!" Hearing that, the city council of my hometown made it against the law for anyone to collect money for UNICEF.

What were we going to do? We did not want to break the law and we certainly did not want to go to jail, but this new law was very wrong. We knew in our hearts that God loves children no matter what kind of government their nation has, and we knew that God wanted us to do everything we could to help those who were sick or starving.

The grown-ups who helped with our youth group had a meeting for all the kids and their parents. They told us that the pastors of all the churches had gotten together and had decided not to cancel the trick-or-treating for UNICEF. They said that a lawyer from one of the parishes had volunteered to help anyone who got arrested. "Still," the grown-ups told us, "each family will have to decide for themselves whether or not to collect money. And whether you go trick-or-treating or not, we hope you will come to the Halloween party afterwards."

In the end, nearly everyone in our group went collecting on the Sunday night before Halloween, as did hundreds of kids from other churches. We felt very brave—but also very scared. No one knew whether or not the city council would arrest us or whether people would give us any money. At some houses, people slammed the door in our faces. At a few places, people screamed at us and shouted, "Go away, you communists!" Two girls from our group were so upset when a man yelled at them that they started crying and crying. The woman who lived next door came over to see what the fuss was about and ended up comforting the girls, giving them hot cocoa and going with them to every other home on the block.

Mostly, though, people were nice to us. Maybe they felt sorry for us because we looked a little frightened. Or maybe they admired our courage. Maybe they wanted to show us that they, too, knew that God wanted love and not hate.

Whatever the reason, when we got together for the Halloween party that night, we found that we had collected more money for UNICEF that year than we had ever collected before. Furthermore, not a single kid was arrested. And what a party we had! Just like the person who wrote today's Psalm, we wanted to sing for joy to the God who protects us. We also learned that night what St. Paul says: that God will give us the strength to bear anything joyfully.

Special Days

January 1 (ABC)

Holy Name of Jesus/Mary, Mother of God/Holy Name of Jesus

Numbers 6:22-27

Today's Bible lesson has a blessing in it, a prayer that asks something like this: "May God take care of you. May God be kind to you. And may God give you peace."

Peace is a blessing from God. Sometimes it even seems like a miracle.

A few years ago there was an old man named Ferdinand Marcos who had ruled the Philippines ruthlessly for twenty-one years. Many people were fed up with this dictator. When he cheated Cory Aquino out of the election for president of the Philippines which she had already won, it was more than they could take. The Minister of Defense, the highest ranking general in the army, and many Filipino soldiers rebelled against Ferdinand Marcos and barricaded themselves in two military bases in Manila, the capital of the Philippines. Many Filipinos feared that there would be war right in the middle of their biggest city.

Cardinal Jamie Sin went to the Catholic radio station and said to the whole nation, "We want to prevent bloodshed. I ask you to go out tonight with food and candles to surround the bases, give the rebel soldiers something to eat and stop the war."

And do you know what happened? By noon the next day more than a million people filled the streets around the forts. As the soldiers of Ferdinand Marcos arrived in tanks to crush the rebellion, they found a million people praying and singing hymns. Women began throwing flowers, saying "Don't shoot! We are your brothers and sisters in Christ!"

And *then* do you know what happened? The soldiers of Ferdinand Marcos turned their tanks around and left without firing a shot. Within two days, Marcos fled the country and Cory Aquino became the new president of the Philippines. Because of the courage of one million Christians, God gave their land peace.

January 1 (A)

New Year's Day

Deuteronomy 8:1-10

Once, more than a thousand years ago, a boy named Willigis grew up in Germany. His mother and father were quite poor. His father made plows and wooden wheels for carts, with Willigis and his mother helping him, and they were very poor.

Willigis studied hard in school, though, and became a priest. Before long he was chosen to be a bishop, the leader of many Christians. This surprised people, because usually only the sons of rich people became bishops. And it angered the nobles who thought that their sons should have been chosen instead of Willigis.

Before long, people were even more surprised: Willigis was chosen to be the archbishop of Mainz, the boss of several bishops and the leader of all the Christians in a huge area around the city of Mainz.

Some rich people, jealous that Willigis had become more important than their own sons, started spreading rumors about Willigis. "How can a poor man rise so high in the Church?" they asked. "He must have done something pretty tricky," they whispered. "Maybe he used black magic," they suggested.

Soon there was all sorts of evil gossip about Willigis using black magic and making bargains with the devil. "What about that secret room of his?" people asked. "Why does he go in there alone every day? Could that be where he gets his secret power? Could that be where he meets with the devil?"

Eventually these rumors reached Otto the Great, king of Germany and ruler of the Holy Roman Empire. Otto worried. Could the archbishop really be using black magic? Could the man whom he trusted for advice really be meeting with the devil? "If he is," the emperor roared, "I'll kill him!"

Determined to find out the truth, the emperor led some soldiers to Willigis's home and stormed right in the door. "Show me the room!" Otto demanded.

"What room do you mean, Your Majesty?" the archbishop asked. "And what has you so upset?"

"I want to see your secret room!" Otto insisted.

"Whatever do you mean by *secret*, your Highness?" the archbishop replied.

"I demand to see the room where you go all alone!" Otto shouted, becoming even more suspicious. "They say that every time you go there, you come out with new strength. You are going to show me that secret room right now!"

"Oh, I see," Willigis muttered. "You know about *that* room, do you? Very well, I will show it to you if you insist."

Otto and his soldiers followed the archbishop to a door with three locks on it!

"Ah-ha!" the emperor thought. "With three locks, he must surely have something in here to hide."

The archbishop unlocked the first big lock, then the second and finally the third lock. Slowly he swung open the heavy door.

And what do you think Otto found? Much to the emperor's astonishment, the room was nearly empty. Why, there was hardly anything at all in this secret room! There was only a simple plow with two wooden wheels, the sort of wheels Willigis had made as a boy with his poor parents. On the wall was a picture the archbishop had painted, a picture of two wooden wheels with these words:

> Willigis, Willigis,
> Always remember from where you came.

Then the emperor realized how the archbishop had become an important leader of the Church and how he renewed his strength: He remembered the poor people from whom he had come. Never again would Otto the Great mistrust Willigis, the archbishop of Mainz.

Today's Scripture lesson from the Book of Deuteronomy tells us to remember how God led the Hebrews through the wilderness. Just as Willigis drew strength from remembering the people from whom he had come, God wants us to remember where we have come from.

January 1 (B)

New Year's Day

Sirach (Ecclesiastes) 3:1-13

Once, long ago, the United States of America was a new nation, sort of like a baby nation. Like most babies, it was very impatient and had a hard time waiting for anything. The people of the United States had won their independence—the right to be their own nation with their own government—from Great Britain, the mightiest empire on earth. But Great Britain still ruled the land of Canada, north of the United States, and the Americans wanted Canada to be part of their new nation, too.

The young government of the United States sent messages to the people of Canada, saying, "Why don't you break away from Great Britain and become part of our country?"

The Canadians answered, "Thanks, but no thanks. At least not now. We want to be your friends but not part of your nation." Some Canadians, I guess, liked Great Britain and were still angry about the way the American army had invaded their land and their biggest city, Montreal, during the American Revolution. Some Canadians wanted to unite with another country, France. Some wanted Canadians to have their own government and their own nation. Others liked the United States but weren't sure if it was worth joining the Americans because that might mean fighting a long war with Great Britain. And many people in Canada did not want to be rushed into deciding one way or another.

Many people think that if Americans could have waited a while, the Canadians would have decided to join us. It might have been nice if the Americans could have told their neighbors to the north, "OK. Let's be friends now and talk later about uniting," but our baby nation was not that patient. Instead of waiting for their neighbors to decide what they wanted to do, the government of the United States sent its army north into Canada in the year 1812 to take Canada away from Great Britain and make it part of the United States.

Well, the Canadians fought back, and once again a terrible war broke out between the United States and Great Britain. It went on for three years and many people were killed. So many Americans thought it was wrong to invade Canada again that the New England states nearly broke away from the rest of the United States. And when it was all over, Canada was still not a part of the United States.

Finally the Americans admitted that the Canadians really did not want to unite with their nation. When Americans learned to relax and wait, Americans and Canadians became friends. In more than a century and a half, there has never been another war between Canada and the United States, and the long border between our two countries has no soldiers stationed along either side of it.

Today's Bible lesson says that there is a time for everything. So we should relax and enjoy life. When Americans finally learned how to relax and wait, we found peace with our neighbors and became friends.

January 1 (C)

New Year's Day

Isaiah 49:1-10

In today's reading from the Book of Isaiah the Servant of God tells how God needs someone to speak out, to tell the truth—even though people may not want to hear the truth. Did it ever seem hard to you to tell the truth? I never knew how hard this could be until I heard this story.

Once there was a college teacher named Solomon Ashe. He asked grown-ups to come into a big room and look at a lot of pairs of lines and tell him which ones looked longer. The people thought that Mr. Ashe wanted to test how well they could see, but what Mr. Ashe really wanted to test was whether or not they would tell the truth. They didn't know it, but all the other people in the room were actors and actresses who were helping Mr. Ashe with the test.

Well, they looked at lots of lines and eventually got to the real test. They were shown two lines like this: *(Hold up a large card with two lines made with a felt-tip pen, the longer one labeled "A" and the shorter line labeled "B".)* They were asked, "Which line is longer, line A or line B?" They could see that A was longer, of course, but Mr. Ashe had all the actors and actresses in the room say, "B is longer."

Do you know what Mr. Ashe discovered? A whole lot of people were afraid to say "A is longer," which they knew was true, when everyone else in the room said "B is longer." He discovered that you have to be very brave to tell the truth if nobody else will.

Then Solomon Ashe did his test all over again with a new group of people. This time he had just one of the actors or actresses in each group say, "Line A is longer." And do you know what Mr. Ashe learned? People are much more likely to tell the truth if even just one other person in the room tells the truth, too.

I guess that is why God needs servants who are willing to suffer, because if even just one person is brave enough to be honest, that makes it easier for other people to be honest, too. And that is why God needs you and me to tell the truth.

February 2 (ABC)

The Presentation of Our Lord

Luke 2:22-40

If you were going to draw a picture of God, what would it look like? Long ago, a famous painter in Italy named Leonardo da Vinci painted a picture of God which still surprises many people the first time they see it.

In this painting, called "The Virgin, Baby Jesus and Saint Anne," Jesus—who Christians believe is God in human life—is a baby. He is tugging on the ears of a little lamb. His mother Mary is smiling at Jesus with love you can see all over her face, but she is also reaching down to keep Jesus from hurting the lamb.

Did you ever think of God as being a baby like you were once? Did you ever think of Jesus' mother needing to keep him out of mischief?

Today's Bible lesson tells us something that I think Leonardo da Vinci tried to show in his painting: "The child Jesus grew and became strong, filled with wisdom; and the favor of God was upon him." God became a real human being like you and me. Jesus grew up—just like we do.

March 25 (ABC)

Annunciation

Luke 1:26-38

When Barbara Troxell was a little girl she sometimes wondered what she would do when she grew up. People told her she should learn how to cook and clean and wash dishes. She learned how to do these things—but she wanted to learn other things, too. She felt God wanted her to go to a special school called a seminary, where she could learn more about Jesus and the Bible.

People told her, "Girls can't go to a school like that," but she decided to try anyway. She studied very hard in high school and she got into Union Theological Seminary in New York, one of the very best Protestant seminaries in the whole nation.

It must have been a little lonely and scary for her to go there, since there were hundreds of men at the seminary but hardly any women at all. But she was brave and she studied hard and graduated a few years later.

She knew now that God wanted her to work in the Church, but people told her, "Women can't work in the Church." And it was true that hardly any women in her denomination, the Methodist Church, had any jobs but secretaries' in the Church. The Protestant Churches did not have any nuns and there was almost no way a woman could get hired by a Protestant Church in the 1950's to do any ministry. But Barbara Troxell knew what God wanted her to do and she was brave enough to try.

Eventually she found a job working for an organization called the Young Women's Christian Association (YWCA). By the 1960's she was working as a campus minister at Stanford University in California—where I was going to school at the time—helping college students. Later she became the pastor of a Presbyterian parish where I worshiped and a teacher at the seminary where I studied. In all these jobs, she helped me when I needed help.

Barbara Troxell let God lead her—and she learned that God can make possible things that seem impossible. In today's Bible story a young woman lets God lead her into an even bigger miracle. A teenage girl named Mary is told that she will become the mother of a holy child, and that this will happen because *nothing* is impossible with God.

Like Barbara Troxell, Mary agrees to let God lead her into things that seem impossible. Mary agrees to become the mother of Jesus, saying she is God's maidservant, ready to do whatever God wants.

May 31 (ABC)

Visitation

Romans 12:9-16b
Luke 1:39-57

Four hundred years ago in France, there was a girl named Louise de Marillac. Louise grew up in a noble family. Her mother and father both died while she was young, but their money made it possible for her to get a good education, something few people—and even fewer girls—had a chance to receive in those days.

Louise loved to learn, and when she married a doctor she learned medicine and surgery from her husband. After he died in 1625, when Louise was thirty-four-years old, she dedicated her life to carrying for the sick and the poor. Working with St. Vincent de Paul, she established the society of visiting nurses called the Daughters of Charity in 1633.

Hospitals were terrible places to be in those days, particularly if you were poor, and peasant girls had little chance to learn how to do important work. So Louise began her group of sisters with girls from poor peasant families. Louise prepared medicines for her helpers and taught them how to care for sick people better than anyone had cared for them before. Her nurses dressed very simply when they worked in hospitals, since St. Vincent urged them to show sympathy for poor patients every way they could.

Not only did Louise and her sisters reform the hospitals of France to make them better, they went on to care for sick convicts in prison, for orphans, for poor elderly people and for the mentally ill. Later, Louise sent her sisters to Poland, and they eventually traveled around the world to help people.

Today is called the Visitation in memory of Mary's visit to Elizabeth and of how Elizabeth blessed this poor, scared girl through her hospitality by welcoming Mary into her home when Mary really needed a friend. Today's lesson from St. Paul's letter to the Church in Rome urges us to practice hospitality and make friends with the poor. St. Louise de Marillac found great joy in doing just that.

This saint is also known by her married name, Louise Le Gras, but she resumed her maiden name after her husband's death. It was under this name that she did the work that made her famous.

August 15 (ABC)

Assumption

Luke 1:39-56

Long ago, during the time called the Middle Ages, there was a scholar named Muretus who wandered from town to town. He was a very smart man who had studied many things, but he was also very poor. He became sick while he was traveling through Italy and was taken to a hospital for homeless people.

Several doctors looked at him and were discussing his illness. The doctors spoke to each other in Latin, which all educated people knew in those days, never dreaming that poor Muretus could understand a single word.

"Well, since he is obviously only a worthless wanderer," one doctor suggested to the others in Latin, "perhaps we should use him for medical experiments."

At which point Muretus shocked them all by looking up and answering in perfect Latin, "Call no one worthless for whom Christ died!"

Those startled doctors never forgot what their poor patient taught them about how Christians should treat everyone with respect, even those who may seem worthless or lowly to other people.

In today's Gospel lesson Mary sings her song of praise, the Magnificat, praising God for the child she is going to have, Jesus. In this song Mary says something that poor Muretus knew: Jesus came "to lift up the lowly."

September 14 (ABC)

Holy Cross/Triumph of the Cross/Holy Cross

1 Corinthians 1:18-24

Once there was a young man who loved telling stories to children at worship but who couldn't sing worth beans. His voice was very deep and he did not know how to read music, so he was never sure if he was singing the tune right. He would sing in the shower or sing in his car or sing in church if there were so many other people singing around him that no one could hear his voice, but he would never let other people hear him singing all by himself.

One week this young man wanted to tell the children of the parish how the Hebrews escaped from slavery. There was a wonderful song about this story, one that slaves in America had sung to help them be brave enough to escape to freedom. When they had to cross a big river and were afraid, they would sing "Wade in the Water" to remind themselves how God had helped the Hebrews cross the water to freedom.

This young man knew that if he used this song as he told the story, it would make the story much better. Maybe the children would even sing along as he sang it. But how could he start singing it in front of all those children and all those grown-ups? He was sure he would feel very foolish when other people heard him sing.

Then this young man remembered the words from today's Bible lesson. St. Paul wrote to his friends in Corinth that "God's foolishness is wiser than human wisdom." So the young man mustered his courage, told the boys and girls how Moses led the Hebrews to the edge of the water, and then he sang what Moses told them:

> (sing)
> Wade in the water,
> wade in the water, children.

And the children of the parish listened to that story better than they had listened to any story in a long time. Soon they were singing with him,

> Wade in the water:
> God's gonna trouble the water.

As St. Paul reminds us today, sometimes we have to risk looking silly in order to share the Good News of how much God loves us.

November 1 or the First Sunday in November (ABC)

All Saints Day

Matthew 5:1-12

Once, long ago, there were two children who lived in Germany in the city of Wismar, along the coast of the North Sea. It was Christmastime in the year 1553. The two children were having a great time walking along the harbor of Wismar and rolling in the snow and throwing snowballs. As they skated across the frozen harbor the little girl shouted out, "Look—ships!"

"You're right!" her brother said. "What would sailing ships be doing in the harbor at this time of year? Why would they come here and get stuck in the ice?"

By the time the children got home, they found nearly everyone in town talking about the ships stuck in the ice. They learned that the ships were carrying refugees from England, members of the Reformed Church who had left England to escape persecution by the government.

"But why don't they just walk across the ice into town?" the boy asked his father.

"Because our town government is run by Lutherans who persecute the Reformed Church, too!" his father answered in disgust.

"It isn't fair!" the little girl protested. "They shouldn't have to stay out there. They must be cold and hungry!"

"No, it isn't fair," her mother agreed. "Let's ask the priest what we should do."

This family belonged to a group called "Anabaptists" and their priest was a man named Menno Simons—who had argued bitterly with the leader of these refugees, John à Lasso. Menno Simons must not have been very happy to see his rival Lasso and these refugees in Wismar, but he said, "We must remember what Jesus taught us: Happy are those who show mercy to others, because they will receive mercy themselves. The government of our town may not be willing to help these people, but we must show mercy to them."

So Menno Simons and his parishioners gathered up food and blankets for the refugees and carried them across the ice to ships that were stuck in the middle of the harbor. You can imagine how happy this made these refugees—and how embarrassed it made the leaders of Wismar! Soon the government gave Menno Simons and his parishioners permission to invite the refugees into their homes for Christmas.

On Christmas Day Menno Simons led a worship service in the home of one of the Anabaptists—it had to be secret because the government of Wismar said people could worship only in Lutheran churches—and Simons invited the Reformed refugees to come, too.

Menno Simons read the story about how Jesus was born from St. Luke's Gospel. When he got to the part of the story where Mary and Joseph were sent away from the inn in Bethlehem because there was no room for them, Herman Bakereel, one of the refugees, sighed, "Ah, there was no place for our Lord, but you have found a place for us, the homeless, on the night of his birth!"

The Anabaptists of Wismar showed mercy on these refugees from England and helped them until they could continue on their way to the city of Luebeck and then on to Poland. And one hundred years later the Anabaptists became refugees themselves, fleeing from Germany. And do you know what happened? Someone from England named William Penn showed mercy to them, giving them land for new homes in America.

And so it was that Mennonites showed mercy and received mercy themselves. As Jesus said, "Blessed are the merciful, for they will receive mercy" (Matthew 5:7).

November 1 or the First Sunday in November (B)

All Saints Day

Revelation 21:1-6a

When Japan began to lose the Second World War, its government became so desperate that it asked its airplane pilots to crash into enemy ships and planes to blow them up, even though the pilots would almost certainly be killed. On August 14, 1945, Sakai Kobayashi, just twenty-one years old, sat in his airplane waiting to take off. He was supposed to crash his plane into an American bomber to keep it from bombing Tokyo. As he waited, thinking he had only a few minutes to live, the news came that Japan had surrendered and the war was over.

Sakai went home and found that his house had been destroyed by American bombs, killing his grandmother, and that his brother had been killed while fighting as a soldier. Everyone in Japan was poor, and there was little food to eat. Day after day, Sakai looked for a job so he could buy food for his family, but he could not find a job because many factories and other businesses had been ruined by the war.

After a whole year of looking for work, Sakai found a job as a guard, a night watchman. He was glad to have a job, but it was lonely work. One night at work, though, he met a girl named Michiko Toyama, and they soon became friends.

Sakai noticed that Michiko often carried the same book with her and asked her what it was. She told him that it was the Bible. "Why don't you come to my church to learn more about it," she suggested. When Sakai went with her to worship the next Sunday, he heard these words of Jesus: "Love your enemies."

Sakai Kobayashi told Michiko that this was the craziest thing he had ever heard. How could he love his enemies? How could he love the Americans, for example, after they defeated his nation and took it over? How could he forgive those who killed his brother and his grandmother? "How can we love our enemies?" he asked Michiko.

Michiko only smiled and said, "You'll see."

She gave Sakai a Bible of his own to read and invited him to worship with her again. Then one day he read some words from the Book of Revelation, where God says, "The old things are gone....Look, I am making all things new." Sakai read these words over and over again. He knew he wanted God to make him new and that he himself wanted to help make the world new so that everyone could really love their enemies.

The next morning, Sakai Kobayashi told his father that he was becoming a Christian and had decided to go to a Christian seminary to become a pastor. The young man who was ready to die in order to kill others now wanted to live in order to love others. God was truly "making everything new."

November 1 or the First Sunday in November (C)

All Saints Day

Luke 6:20-36

In the country of Greece over 2,500 years ago a slave named Aesop told this story:

"Once upon a time a little ant was walking along on a hot sunny day. "I'm thirsty," she sighed.

Overhearing her from a nearby tree, a bird told her, "Why don't you go over to that stream and get a drink of water? Be careful you don't fall in, though."

"Thanks for the idea," the ant said. She walked over to the stream and leaned over the water carefully to get a drink. Just then, however, a gust of wind blew her right into the stream.

Quickly the bird broke off a tiny twig from the tree where he was sitting. He swooped down to the stream and dropped it in the water right beside her. She climbed onto the twig and floated to shore. Walking safely to shore, she thanked the bird over and over again for saving her life. "I'll help you anytime I can!" she promised.

"Little you? Help me?" chuckled the bird.

Not many days later, though, the ant saw a hunter creep up through the woods, right beside her. And the hunter was getting ready to shoot the very same bird who had saved her life. The ant knew she had to do something quickly, so she scrambled up his foot and bit the hunter as hard as she could right in the ankle.

"Ouch!" cried the hunter. The bird heard this and flew away to safety.

The bird had saved the ant's life and now the bird, who never imagined a tiny ant could help him, was saved by that little ant. In today's Bible lesson Jesus tells us to have pity on others the way God has pity on us. That's what this bird and this ant did: They had pity on each other the way God has pity on all of us.

Thanksgiving Day (A)

2 Corinthians 9:6-15

The readings for Thanksgiving Day in the Common Lectionary are not strictly tied to Year A, B or C.

It is said in the land of Latvia that once upon a time there were an old man and woman who longed to have a child. On their farm they had pigs that squealed and chickens that clucked and roosters that crowed "cock-a-doodle-doo!" But they had no children to fill the air with the sound of their laughter and their games.

One day the old man took his pigs into the woods to hunt acorns and they went a little deeper into the forest than ever before. Much to his surprise, he found a little cottage and there, in front of the cottage, sat the Forest Mother, wearing a crown of white clover.

"This is a gift for you," she said, handing him a basket. "But you must not open it for three days." And before he could even say thank you, both the Forest Mother and her cottage disappeared!

Bewildered, the old man gathered up his pigs and carried the basket home. "What have you got there?" his wife asked.

"A gift from the Forest Mother," he answered, "but we must not take a peek for three days."

The next morning the basket trembled. The following day it rocked and jiggled. And on the third day the old couple awoke to the sound of cooing. Lifting off the lid of the basket they found a baby inside! This, however, was the strangest baby they had ever seen: a tiny baby boy all covered with stiff, bristly fur like a hedgehog!

The old man and his wife were so happy to have a child that they didn't care how he looked. They loved him and raised him, and found that he was a smart boy who was cheerful and a hard worker. Before long he took the pigs into the woods himself to hunt for acorns to eat.

Then one spring day, three princesses rode their horses into the forest. A rabbit darted in front of the youngest of them and scared her horse. He reared and plunged and galloped away. The princess screamed at her horse to stop, but he thundered on through the trees. The hedgehog boy heard her cries and ran beside her horse. He grabbed the reins and pulled the horse to a stop. Gasping for breath, the princess said, "You have saved my life." But then she saw his prickly fur and was frightened. "I must go," she blurted out.

"Please stay and rest a minute," the boy begged.

"No, I must return to the castle," she insisted. "Mother and father will be worried."

"The castle?" he said in amazement. "You live in a castle?"

"Yes," she replied, a little embarrassed. "My parents are the king and queen. I must go now." And she turned her horse around and rode quickly away.

Years passed. Then on a summer day when he was tending his pigs in the woods the boy heard the jingle of spurs and the thump of a horse's hooves. It was the king himself, lost in the forest. "Tell me how to find my way home, boy," the king called out, "and I will give you a penny."

"I will show you the way," the hedgehog boy answered, "only if you let me marry your daughter."

"What!" roared the king in anger. "Never!" And he charged away on his horse, headed in the wrong direction.

The next day the hedgehog boy found the king, tired and hungry—and still lost. "Come, show me the way home," the king said wearily, "and I will give you a whole barrel of fish."

"I will show you the way," he replied, "only if you let me marry your daughter." Once again, the king thundered away in a fury.

A day later the hedgehog boy came upon the king again, limping, covered with mud and exhausted. "Help me," he begged, "and I'll give you a fine farm with a sturdy cabin."

Again the boy replied, "I will show you the way only if you let me marry your daughter." Gloomily, the king agreed. The hedgehog boy led him safely home and promised. "I will come for my bride on Midsummer Eve."

When Midsummer Eve came, the hedgehog boy presented himself at the castle. The princess looked at him and shuddered, but remembered how he had saved her life also. Wedding bells rang from the cathedral, while the royal family grumbled about this horrible-looking groom but did nothing to stop the wedding. Finally the priest said, "You are now husband and wife."

The cathedral bells rang again. Bonfires were lit to begin the Midsummer Festival. And the hedgehog boy and the princess went to their new home in the castle. "I'm not sleepy yet," the princess told him, "you go ahead to bed."

So he took off his clothes and hung them in the closet. He took off his coat of bristly fur and hung it on the bedpost, and crawled under the covers.

As soon as he was asleep, the princess snatched his fur coat off the bedpost, tiptoed outside and tossed the fur coat onto a Midsummer bonfire. It burst into flames at once and soon was nothing but ashes.

By the time the princess got back to their bedroom, her husband was shivering and shaking under the covers. "I'm so cold," he groaned over and over again. For days he lay in bed near death. The king rather hoped he *would* die, but the princess filled their room with sweet-smelling flowers and fed her husband honey. She prayed that God would help him live; she told God how sorry she was that she had not loved him the way he was.

Slowly, day by day, he got better. Finally he was able to crawl out of bed. Much to her amazement, he no longer looked like a hedgehog boy, but like a handsome young man.

The king and the queen announced a big feast to celebrate his recovery. His father and mother were invited. And the princess and her bridegroom danced all night until the sun came up and the roosters crowed to greet the morning.

The love the princess gave to the poor hedgehog boy when he was sick helped her learn how to love him more. That's what today's Bible reading says: If we give to others who are poor or lonely, God will always make sure we have plenty more to give.

Thanksgiving Day (B)

1 Timothy 2:1-7

Today's Bible lesson tells us to pray for everyone. It also says that there is only one God and only one mediator between God and humanity, Jesus Christ, who sacrificed himself for everyone. Once there was a whole nation of people who remembered these words and lived them.

At the beginning of the seventeenth century, the government of England was persecuting everyone who did not belong to the Anglican Church, the Church of England. Roman Catholics were thrown out of their jobs and sometimes thrown in jail, as were Puritans, Presbyterians and other Protestants. Just reading a book written by Protestants could get you in trouble. Just being a priest of the Roman Catholic Church could get you killed.

One group of Protestants decided that they had better leave England before they were all sent to prison. But where could they go? Where could they be safe? They heard that in Holland, the nation now called the Netherlands where the Dutch people live, no one was forced by law to join one Church or another. In Holland, it was said, people were free to say or read or write whatever they wanted, which was certainly not true in Anglican England.

So these people sold their homes, packed up everything they owned and sailed across the North Sea to Holland. You can imagine how scary it must be to a little boy or girl to become a refugee like this—to flee the town you know and sail off to a new land where people speak a language you cannot understand. Would the Dutch people really let them be safe?

When these people from England got to Holland, they found a world that seemed very strange to them. Hardly anyone spoke English. None of the Dutch people belonged to the same Church as these refugees from England. But the Dutch welcomed the English refugees and helped them in every way they could. The Dutch gave them jobs and helped them find new homes. The Dutch invited the English people to their churches, but also let them build their own. They let the refugees think and say and read and write whatever they wanted.

After many years in Holland, these English people decided that they wanted to come to the New World to build new towns of their own in a new country, a place where they could welcome other refugees from England and offer them freedom. When they crossed the wide Atlantic Ocean in a sailing ship called the Mayflower and built homes in Massachusetts, they got a new name, the Pilgrims.

In the new world these Pilgrims started a new holiday, one we still celebrate today, Thanksgiving. They gave thanks at the first Thanksgiving for their new friends, the Native Americans who welcomed them to Massachusetts, and for their old friends the Dutch, who had helped them escape from England and had shown them how wonderful freedom can be. They never forgot how thankful they were that the Dutch knew what today's Bible lesson tells us, that there is only one God and one mediator between God and humanity, Christ Jesus, who sacrificed himself for everyone. Because God loves us all, the Pilgrims learned from the Dutch and the Native Americans, we should love everyone.

Thanksgiving Day (C)

Psalm 100

No one would have expected Martin Rinkart to thank God for anything. He was the pastor of a parish in Germany that had nothing but trouble. First, there was a plague, a terrible disease that killed many people in that town. Second, there was a famine: Many crops died and people did not have enough food to eat. Then there was a war, a very stupid war fought between different Christians about how people should worship God. And the war went on for thirty years. Just think: Little girls and boys who were only three years old when that war started were thirty-three-year-old women and men with children of their own before it ended!

Finally, though, the war was over. Martin Rinkart was so happy that the killing had stopped that he wrote a song that Christians around the world still sing today (*sing*):

> Now thank we all our God
> With heart and hands and voices,
> Who wondrous things has done,
> In whom the world rejoices;
> Who from our mothers' arms
> Has blessed us on our way
> With countless gifts of love,
> And still is ours today.

Today's Psalm tells us to worship God with joy, to come and give thanks. Like Martin Rinkart, even when we have been through hard times, we can still thank God for the good things God does in our lives.

December 8 (ABC)

Immaculate Conception

Luke 1:26-38

Once, long ago, there was a man named Sequoyah. He was born more than two hundred years ago in the Cherokee town of Tuskeegee, along the Tennessee River.

None of Sequoyah's Cherokee neighbors thought of him as lucky when he was a young man. Sequoyah's mother was the sister of a Cherokee chieftain, but his father was a soldier and trader from Virginia who abandoned his wife and child. Sequoyah was partially disabled as a youth, perhaps by disease or in a hunting accident. And during his lifetime his people were forced to move long distances on foot, first to Arkansas and later all the way to Oklahoma.

Despite these hardships, Sequoyah learned how to be a craftsman and make beautiful things out of silver. He also invented a written alphabet (a "syllabary") for the Cherokee language. It expressed so well the sounds that Cherokees spoke that they could learn the alphabet in a week or less. By 1822 Cherokees all the way from Arkansas to Georgia were learning Sequoyah's new alphabet. By 1828, the General Council of the Cherokee Nation had its own printing press and was using Sequoyah's alphabet to publish their own newspaper, the *Cherokee Phoenix.*

The Cherokees made Sequoyah "President of the Western Cherokees." He was welcomed by leaders in Washington, D.C., and by Cherokees as far away as Mexico. He was called upon often to make peace between the Cherokee government and the white government, as well as between different factions among the Cherokees.

Who would ever have called Sequoyah lucky as a child? Who would ever have dreamed that a disabled young man, abandoned by his father, would ever do these things?

And who would ever dream a poor peasant girl like Mary would be chosen to give birth to the Son of God? Today's Gospel lesson tells us, though, that choosing someone unlikely to be chosen is just what God did. And when Gabriel, God's messenger, greeted Mary and told this frightened teenage girl "You are truly blessed!" he was telling the truth.

For more on Sequoyah, see Grant Foreman's *Sequoyah* (Norman, Okla.: University of Oklahoma Press, 1938) and Grace Steele Woodward's *The Cherokees* (Norman, Okla.: University of Oklahoma Press, 1963).

Scripture Index

Scripture Index

Themes Index

Topical Index

Themes Index

Topical Index